Praise for
The Scent Trail

"A magical journey of the senses."   —*Yorkshire Evening Post*

"*The Scent Trail* is dense with fascinating facts, stories, literary references, and history."   —*The Times Literary Supplement*

"When Celia Lyttelton set out to have a scent created solely for her, she found herself propelled into an adventure that would take her across the world, investigating the origins, history, and culture of wonderfully exotic ingredients. . . . *The Scent Trail* tells her story."   —*Woman and Home Magazine*

"A fantastic book about perfume and our sense of smell."   —Times Online

"The intriguing relationship between scent, memory, and place is the underlying note in Lyttelton's journey through the history, creation, and business of perfume. We are whisked to traditional perfumers' workshops, with their vial-filled antique cases, to the spice souks of Marrakech, Ottoman houses in Turkey adorned with necklaces of peppers and chilies, iris farms in Italy, and the mossy-floored cedar forests of Azrou."   —*The Australian*

"Have you ever had that overwhelming surge of emotion when even a faint smell transports you back to another place and time? This is exactly the type of feeling Celia Lyttelton sets off to explain as she embarks on a journey of discovery. . . . This book offers an insight into the foreign origins of the perfumes lining chemist shelves, while taking us on a sensory adventure around the globe."   —RealTravel

continued . . .

CELIA LYTTELTON

THE
Scent Trail

HOW ONE WOMAN'S QUEST FOR THE PERFECT
PERFUME TOOK HER AROUND THE WORLD

New American Library
Published by New American Library, a division of
Penguin Group (USA) Inc., 375 Hudson Street,
New York, New York 10014, USA
Penguin Group (Canada), 90 Eglinton Avenue East, Suite 700, Toronto,
Ontario M4P 2Y3, Canada (a division of Pearson Penguin Canada Inc.)
Penguin Books Ltd., 80 Strand, London WC2R 0RL, England
Penguin Ireland, 25 St. Stephen's Green, Dublin 2,
Ireland (a division of Penguin Books Ltd.)
〈dc20〉Penguin Group (Australia), 250 Camberwell Road, Camberwell, Victoria 3124,〈dc0〉
Australia (a division of Pearson Australia Group Pty. Ltd.)
Penguin Books India Pvt. Ltd., 11 Community Centre, Panchsheel Park,
New Delhi - 110 017, India
Penguin Group (NZ), 67 Apollo Drive, Rosedale, North Shore 0632,
New Zealand (a division of Pearson New Zealand Ltd.)
Penguin Books (South Africa) (Pty.) Ltd., 24 Sturdee Avenue,
Rosebank, Johannesburg 2196, South Africa

Penguin Books Ltd., Registered Offices:
80 Strand, London WC2R 0RL, England

Published by New American Library, a division of Penguin Group (USA) Inc. Previously published
in a Transworld Publishers edition. For further information contact Transworld Publishers, a division
of Random House Ltd., 61–63 Uxbridge Road, London W5 5SA, England.

First New American Library Printing, February 2007
10 9 8 7 6 5 4 3 2 1

 REGISTERED TRADEMARK—MARCA REGISTRADA

Printed in the United States of America

In memory of my mother, Margaret Lyttelton

Contents

Acknowledgements

M Y AGENT, CLARE CONVILLE OF CONVILLE AND WALSH, my editor, Angela Mackworth Young, and my editor at Transworld, Brenda Kimber, for their patience and tact in guiding me through several drafts of this book. My father, Adrian Lyttelton, who read through the book, giving many helpful suggestions. Stephen for driving me all the way from London to the Sahara and back, and Tarquin for map reading "toddler style." Barry Flanagan for his advice and generosity. Brida McAlinden for looking after her grandson, Tarquin, during my many road trips abroad.

For the following chapters, I would like to thank:

One: Anastasia Brozler, who guided me (and my nose) to compose a formula scent.

Two: Roberto Henrichson, for putting up with us, and putting us up in Paris; Christof Kicherer, for giving me introductions to perfumers in Grasse; Pamela Roberts of L'Artisan Parfumeur; and to my brother Francis Lyttelton and Dee Grayling Montgomery, who had us to stay on the island of Ibiza, while we "regrouped" for our trip on to Morocco.

Three: Cécile and Cyril Commargue, my interpreters and companions for when I met Serge Lutens and Dr. Belkamil; Professor Martin, an ethnobotanist who guided me around the medina and its myriad plants, spices and scents in Marrakech.

Four: M. Roca of Robertet, who gave me an introduction to their Turkish Rose Factory; and to M. Allard and Mr. Timour for their hospitality at the Rose factory itself.

Five: Nicola Howard for introducing me to Valeria Rosselli of the Iris Garden in Florence; and to Matthew and Maro Spender and Charlotte Horton for their hospitality and Chianti-fueled suppers of roast porcupine.

Six: Mrs. Helga Perrera Blow for her kind hospitality at her hotel, the Folly in Kandy, and to Julian West for having me to stay at the Old Stone House and introducing me to the "movers" and "shakers" of nutmeg.

Seven: The late Jeremy Fry and his son Francis for having me to stay up in the Palani mountains, and to Francis, for being a hilarious traveling companion on some of my trips around India and Sri Lanka, and for being a superb dancing partner at the Madras Taj Disco.

Eight: I am indebted to Douglas Botting, who gave me so much encouragement and advice about Socotra, assuring me that there were no Al Qaeda cells on the island; Barnaby Rogerson, who introduced me to Botting and also gave me advice for Chapter 2; and Tim Mackintosh Smith for his advice and scholarly tips, characteristically laced with jokes.

Nine: I am grateful to my driver, Mohammed, and my interpreter, Jamil, and to the noble tribes of Socotra for their hospitality. Thanks too to Anthony Milnroy of the Socotra Conservation Fund for his advice.

Introduction

S CENT HAS GREAT POWER. ITS DEVELOPMENT CHARTS THE spread of civilizations, the beginnings of science and medicine, the movement of faiths and the links between the ancient, classical, medieval and modern worlds.

And because scent evokes memories—at one time or another we have all experienced those sudden unexpected moments when a trace of scent instantly reminds us of an incident from childhood, or a forgotten landscape, or the presence of a long-lost lover—we tirelessly search for the right one. The personal associations that are bound up with scents are wonderfully vivid for every one of us; there are certain scents and certain smells that lead to instant recall, often with hallucinatory clarity.

According to Proust, each hour of our lives is stored away in a smell and in a taste, and when those smells or tastes are reexperienced memories are triggered. The more prosaic reason that the connection between smell and memory is so strong is that the olfactory nerves transport information to the brain's limbic system *and* to its cortex. The limbic system is the primitive part of the brain where our memories are formed, our emotions and moods are regulated and our sense of smell is lodged. The cortex is the complex part of the brain that has to do with conscious thought.

The sense of smell also has the power to suppress the rational, critical left brain and to stimulate the creative, dreamy right brain, so it evokes memories with more emotional force than any other sense. I am convinced that we wear scent not just to make us feel more attractive, but because it unlocks the emotions associated with memories that come flooding back when we smell the scent of the lipstick our mother wore or the fragrance of the woodsmoke from the fire in the cottage where we spent an idyllic weekend.

Sight and sound are physical senses, but smell and taste are chemical: when you breathe in the smell of a pine forest, or your mother's skin, you are taking molecules right inside your body, and that makes smell a very intimate sense. Kipling wrote, "Scents are surer than sounds or sights to make your heartstrings crack."

From birth to death our eyesight and other senses deteriorate, but our sense of smell never weakens because the cells regenerate every twenty-four days. We don't use this sense enough; the nose is capable of recognizing some 500,000 different odors, and although, consciously, the brain might not register them all, once you've smelled something for the first time, the next time you encounter that particular smell you can immediately identify it.

In my case smells transport me, literally. The buttery smell of iris takes me straight to the hills of Tuscany where I spent most of my childhood. I used to watch the iris roots being harvested in the summer and I saw them laid out to dry on straw mats in the sun. Jasmine takes me to the plains of Rajasthan, and the smell of vetivert, an aromatic grass from India, reminds me of a green Tuscan lake where I used to swim. Lavender and heather, or oak moss, remind me of autumnal leaves and fungi and ground me in the Yorkshire moors, where I have a cottage, and when I smell basil I am instantly reminded of the warmth of the sun and the sparkling seas that surround the Aegean islands, where I have spent several summers and where I swam for hours in the sea, breathing in the ozone-and-seaweed-scented air.

It isn't surprising that scents so often take me to places: I have been lucky enough to travel a great deal. I traveled as a child with my archaeologist mother, Margaret Lyttelton, and I have not stopped traveling since. My earliest scent memories are of my grandparents' house, where I often went to stay. It was full of the smells of woodsmoke from the fires, cigars, leather, dark chocolate and my grandmother's rich peppery and rose scent (which she had made in Cairo during the war and the formula of which she kept so that she could have it copied in Paris).

In 1982, when my mother was researching a book on the spice trade routes, I traveled with her to Yemen, which, in the 1980s, was a wild and lawless place. We trekked deep into the interior, where the groves of frankincense and myrrh flourished, but we found that they were guarded by tribesmen armed with Kalashnikov rifles. We were ambushed and the Land Rover that the British embassy had lent us, and the maps we'd been using, were seized. We had to return, alone, across the deserted black lava fields until, eventually, we came across some friendly Bedouin who escorted us to safety.

Once we'd recovered from our ordeal we set about exploring the labyrinthine souks of Sana—the capital of Yemen—through which a blind man could have found his way simply by following his nose. The pungent atmosphere of the spice bazaar, the acrid smell of the qat market (a leaf narcotic which the Yemenis chew), the perfumers' balmy-smelling street and the fragrant smoke from the burning gum resins of frankincense and myrrh wafting down the alleyways—those memories remain with me to this day and are the driving force behind this book. I wanted to revisit those places and particularly those smells, and above all I wanted to unlock their secrets.

I wanted to discover what the fundamental ingredients of scent were and how they were grown and harvested. I wanted to know how a scent was made, from the first glimmer of an idea to the final product. And I decided that the best way to do that would be to ask a bespoke perfumer to make a scent for me from a recipe that combined my own favorite smells: things like nutmeg, Indian zambac—a heady and carnal Indian jasmine— vetivert and iris roots, and then to travel to the countries where those ingredients were indigenous.

I also wanted to meet the people who contributed to the making of the scents, from those who harvest the crops to the highly specialized perfumers who are known as "noses" in the trade. And so I began what I came to call my olfactory odyssey, or scent trail.

When I was in the thirteenth-century souk in Aleppo I found a scent made of unguents of lilies mixed with real musk; whenever I wore it people were rooted to the spot by its stunning smell. Shop assistants, bus conductors and children sniffed me and people at parties clustered around me. I have noticed that nowadays perfumers are returning to the use of natural essences and essential oils instead of synthetics; in other words they are adopting a more holistic approach to the making of perfumes. *Senteurs* recognize the need people now feel to identify with a smell, rather than being smothered in, say, a cloud of Poison or Opium.

Coming onto the market are new scents whose properties are restorative, calming and relaxing, and aromatherapy reiterates what the ancients believed about the mind-enhancing power of essential oils. For example, Tibetan monks burn sandalwood to help them empty their minds before meditation; lavender has a calming effect on the mind; and women going into labor often breathe in frankincense to lessen the pain.

People want a scent which is personal and not packaged; they want their own "bespoke" scent made to a secret formula just for them.

I felt exactly the same way. So I set off to meet Anastasia Brozler, a bespoke perfumer, in whose paneled drawing room I began my olfactory odyssey.

CHAPTER ONE

THE BESPOKE PERFUMER

A Recipe for a Scent

He saw that there was no mood of the mind that had not its counterpart in the sensuous life, and set himself to discover their true relation, wondering what was there in frankincense that made one mystical, and in ambergris that stirred one's passions, and in violets that woke the memory of dead romances, and in musk that troubled the brain, and in champak that strained the imagination; and seeking to elaborate a real psychology of perfumes.

OSCAR WILDE
The Picture of Dorian Gray

THERE ARE ONLY A HANDFUL OF BESPOKE PERFUMERS IN London, and Anastasia Brozler, the founder of Creative Perfumers, is one of them.

When I asked her to concoct a formula for my own bespoke perfume she immediately drew me into the world of scent and the magic that smells can conjure up. When I first met her, before she'd founded her own company, we sat down together in front of a cabinet modeled on a Chinese medicine chest which had about one hundred tiny little drawers. From these drawers she randomly took out lumps of balmy myrrh, earthy orris (iris) roots, vanilla pods—which smelled mouthwateringly like chocolate—exotic Iranian saffron, heady Indian sandalwood, spicy nutmeg oil, aromatic cloves and bergamot, basil and even tomato oil. The smell of those last three together reminded me of al fresco suppers on Greek islands.

Some of the ingredients Anastasia held under my nose I'd never imagined making up a perfume: tomato oil, for instance, and guaiac wood from the Holywood tree of Paraguay; and some smells, such as ambergris, musk and civet, I had never smelled before. In parts of the Middle East real musk and civet are still used and sold, but covertly, because the trade is illegal. Ambergris—which comes from the vomit of sperm whales—can still be bought, but it is exceedingly rare, as the whales are difficult to find. So most perfumers use synthetic substitutes.

The synthetic musk that Anastasia waved under my nose

smelled—to put it bluntly—like a condensed fart. The civet smelled similar to the musk, but was even more aggressive. But mixed with other scents in a perfume formula, musk provides a smooth, sensual, erotic base note. Anastasia told me that when you smell pure musk, you rarely catch the undertones because the overtones are so revolting.

The smell of pure ambergris was quite a different matter from the smells of musk and civet. Ambergris smelled like sensual, warm, suntanned skin, with a touch of ozone and seawater; it was very addictive and its subtlety left me wanting more. It also reminded me of truffles and oysters, and it began to affect me like a drug, inducing waves of euphoria. When Anastasia closed the vial we were both a little dizzy from the vapors.

Ambergris is still—occasionally—extracted naturally because, unlike civet and musk, its extraction does not harm the sperm whales that produce it. When the whale swallows, say, a squid, secretions from its stomach form a protective coating around the indigestible parts of the prey and, every so often, when the whale vomits up an undigested squid, the squid floats like a gelatinous honeycomb on the surface of the sea and is eventually washed ashore and collected. Ambergris is made from the secretion from the whale's stomach which has enveloped the undigested matter. It is aged in alcohol over several years before it can be used; like a vintage wine, it mellows with age, whereas musk can be used straightaway.

The musk trade was ruled illegal because, even though the process of removing musk pods from male deer doesn't harm the animal, the deer were often trapped in the process and so died before the trappers arrived to remove their musk pods. I have smelled real musk in the Middle East; compared with synthetic musk, the real thing is far more potent, but, apart from the fact that I didn't want anything that was the result of cruelty to an animal in my bespoke scent, I thought the synthetic musk quite strong enough!

We moved on to florals, and Anastasia produced three types of jasmine, one from Grasse, one from Morocco and finally Indian zambac, which was deliciously heady. She told me that jasmine gets stronger the farther east or south you go because the molecules of indole increase. Indole is a chemical which occurs naturally in many essential oils, including jasmine, neroli and orange blossom; it is a crystalline substance with an odor which is too pungent unless it is greatly diluted. Anastasia waved a sampler of aldehyde with another of zambac under my nose and the jasmine was instantly transformed. Jasmine turns vulgar on the skin, but aldehyde—which is an alcohol—dilutes it so that the scent floats and does not overpower.

Anastasia told me that she worked with over three thousand different oils and unguents. When we sat down in front of an ornate cabinet shaped like a fan and reminiscent of a musical instrument—which is called the perfumer's organ—in her drawing room in South Kensington, she told me that it contained seven hundred vials of pure perfume, extracts, absolutes, essences and attars. I realized then that it was going to be possible to return to all the places I have loved without having to leave her house in London.

Anastasia said that people who love warm, sultry nights veer toward a scent with patchouli and jasmine, with woody notes, whereas people who are low on energy often prefer a perfume with rosemary, eucalyptus oil and Sicilian limes. I realized that the ingredients you choose to make up your own perfume can match and reflect your character, as well as enhancing your charisma.

A really good scent is a palimpsest and the layers are made up of what, in the trade, they call "notes." The top notes, of citrus, "float"; the middle notes are floral and longer lasting; the base notes are usually woody and the most enduring. Anastasia said that in some ways the concoction of a scent resembled a greyhound race. As you breathe it in the citrus notes hit you first because they have very strong molecules, but they linger for the shortest time. Then you notice other notes, for instance the woody resins, and then the base notes, like musk and civet, make their impression on you. It is said that Napoleon was attracted to Josephine by her civet scent and he urged her not to wash so that he could just smell her.

Different scents react differently on different skin types and they change with a particular body's chemistry. Body temperature also affects the chemical balance and character of a perfume. Anastasia said that because my own skin is pale, a French jasmine would suit me because it is delicate, whereas the stronger Indian jasmines suit darker skins. However, I preferred the Indian zambac jasmine. My skin is also smooth, which means that it allows scent to escape more rapidly than rougher skin, or greasy skin, both of which hold perfume longer. So, for that reason and because my skin is also dry, Anastasia said I would need a fairly tenacious scent.

There are seven "families" of smells: fougère (fern), floral, citrus, chypre, woody, leather and oriental, and as I watched

Anastasia conjure up what perfumers call "my perfume profile," waving wands of perfume samplers under my nose, I thought that what she was doing was akin to what a medieval alchemist would have done.

Composing a Perfume

PERFUME COMPOSITION IS A VERY DELICATE ART, A MATTER OF personal taste and refined imagination: it is essentially an abstract art. To compose a perfume is to combine certain scents deliberately and create a perfect unity from them. Perfumers smell the raw materials, mix them and once in a while they get a good result. Most perfumes contain anything from thirty to several hundred ingredients.

It takes years to get to know and distinguish the hundreds of different smells, and a perfumer has to learn what effect one odor will have on another when they are mixed together. He must learn how to smooth or sharpen a scent, how to bring all the smells to a common ground so that one does not overpower another. Most important, he must learn how to achieve the top, middle and base notes, and finally how to fix a perfume so that it will last. Perfumers also have to be skilled chemists. Relying on a highly trained sense of smell, the "noses," as they are known in the trade, will test their compositions as they progress with blotters: small wands of blotting paper which are dipped into the mixtures and then allowed to dry. But the olfactory nerves tire quickly and so the process is a slow one. A perfume may take up to three years to perfect. François Coty took five years to come up with L'Aimant, while Guerlain's Chant d'Aromes took seven years and Caron's Infini was fifteen years in the making.

The first step in composing a perfume is almost always an idea inspired by nature. Then the perfumer must develop a scent that has high stability under evaporation and an unvarying aroma, together with a harmony of raw materials. A perfumer is like an armchair traveler: alone in his laboratory he is surrounded by hundreds of essences and absolutes from all over the world, but his intention is to transpose the memory of, say, the fragrance of a cedar or the scented shadow of a magnolia, the memory of a tropical forest or a garden in the rain, or something more abstract, like a piece of music, into a perfume.

Having come up with the idea of, say, a forest at dawn soaked in dew and a pair of lovers whose sweat mingles with the dew on the forest floor, he will begin to associate particular olfactory images with the visual images. He might think, for instance, that these would be well represented by a fougère, a fresh but erotic woodland scent with sensual undertones. He may include top notes of lavender and pine essence; middle notes of oak moss and patchouli, which he might blend with bergamot; then he might blend these with another equally pleasing odor of mossy base notes anchored with an amber, a spicy accord of musk and myrrh to represent the amorous embrace of the lovers.

In this way, using his olfactory judgement, the perfumer obtains the essence of the scent. Then he must impart "character" and perfect the composition. He knows that, for a flowery note, he has a whole range of natural plants, from the sweetness of jasmine to the velvety charm of tuberose. The initial impression of a scent should always be fresh and vigorous. It should suggest the presence of flowers, fruits and herbs, things that titillate our senses of smell and memory. Then the fragrance has to be "anchored" by a fixative such as orris root, benzoin (a resin) or oak moss. Finally the perfume is left alone for a while so that it can mature, like a wine, before the perfumer returns to his perfumer's organ.

When Serge Lutens—whom I met in Marrakech—makes a perfume, the process has less to do with practicalities and methodology than it has to do with his intuition and imagination. Serge never had any formal training—he simply discovered his own way. He said that he is merely the intermediary through whom the perfume is created, and that to make a perfume requires a state of permanent nervous tension that remains with him for a year. When a perfume is finally perfected it is, he said, not unlike an epiphany, or a short-lived ecstasy.

It can take years to perfect a perfume, but although the art of the perfumer is a refined one, some scents have come about through happy accident. Shalimar was born when Jacques Guerlain accidentally tipped some vanilla essence into an existing rather dandyish cologne called Jicky (Jicky was also the first scent to combine natural and synthetic materials). But the traditional process of extracting a flower's scent to make the top notes in a perfume is very elaborate and time-consuming: it takes 100 kilograms of petals to yield just 1 liter of essential oil.

Finally, synthetic imitations of animal secretions and real ambergris are used, sparingly, as fixatives. In the days when real musk and civet were used, scents lasted for decades and were sexier than they are today because the animals' secretions are so similar to our own. Real ambergris holds its scent for centuries.

While we smelled the scents, Anastasia plied me with hundreds of questions. It was a bit like concocting an entry for *Who's Who*. She wanted to know what my favorite foods and drinks were, how old I was and what my hobbies were. Some of her questions made me feel as if I were on the psychiatrist's couch: she wanted to know about my dreams and my childhood memories, what home meant to me, how I thought people saw me and how I saw myself. And then she asked me what scent meant to me.

I said that I knew I wanted an ancient smell rather than a modern one, and I wanted more than just a "pretty" scent. We began to match my memories from childhood with individual smells. My memories of aromatic plants and the smell of the green lake I used to swim in as a child; the scent of the Tuscan lemon trees, the pine forests and the blackberries and, of course, the buttery iris roots. Anastasia thought vetivert and iris would suit me, and then, as I told her about my grandparents' house, she immediately suggested that my scent should have some woody and smoky notes, with vanilla, perhaps, to remind me of the dark chocolate, and ambergris, to induce a euphoria reminiscent of those bracing salty sea breezes in the Aegean.

When I said that I loved creamy sauces with fish and vegetables flavored with nutmeg and garlic, we added nutmeg to the list of possible ingredients. Then we began to discuss the things that excite me. I said that traveling was one of my passions, partly because I always remember the olfactory details of different countries: the burnt musky, pungent and wild perfumes of Yemen and the souks; the spices of the Middle East, where the fountains are perfumed with rosewater and where the perfume itself is much more powerful and oily than Western perfumes.

I said that I would love to find the unguent of lilies mixed with real musk that I'd discovered in Aleppo, and that I loved frankincense and myrrh, which I'd first smelled in Yemen. I told her I loved Syria's damask rose and the jasmine that reminded me of the garlands hung over doorways and the little jasmine bracelets that girls sell in India. I said that I liked ancient and mysterious smells that were evocative of distant lands.

We sniffed tonka bean, a narcotic bean, which had a rich vanilla smell and reminded me of truffles and almonds. We were gradually building up a fan of samplers, and a scent was beginning to evolve, but we also needed to concentrate on shading or rounding off the predominant scents. Before I chose the final ingredients, Anastasia sent me off for a "color profile" because, as she told me, color is related to perfume and she wanted to see whether my favorite colors accorded with my favourite smells.

As Baudelaire wrote in his poem "Correspondences":

All scents and colours meet as one,
Perfumes are as sweet as the oboe's sound,
Green as the prairies,
Fresh as a child's caress.

And in Huysmans' *À Rebours*, the protagonist, Des Esseintes, transposed poems by Baudelaire into perfumes, creating aromatic stanzas.

Many of the famous scent formulas are color coded: spicy

and oriental odors are coded red and orange, floral and citrus ones tend to be coded yellow and green, while in the fougère group, which evokes an accord of lavender, oak moss, coumarin (a synthetic that imitates the scent of the tonka bean) and bergamot, notes are coded in greens and browns. Chypre, which was made by Coty in 1917 from oak moss, labdanum (cistus) and patchouli, is coded in the browns and yellows of those ingredients, and the ozonic scents—a new classification—which are watery and limpid with a whiff of sea air, are coded blue.

Anastasia sent me to Adam James, a color expert and colleague of hers. When I arrived for my appointment he immediately opened a cabinet containing shelves and shelves of little bottles filled with colored liquids. Some were bright, while others were pale and opalescent. He asked me to choose my favorite colours and instantly I went for the cool, pale, pastel colours, the light cerulean blues, the violets and the lemon yellows, the pale purples, pale greens and the blues of my favorite gems: sapphire and aquamarine. I was worried that these colours might define me as fey, ungrounded and indecisive, but I had chosen the ones I honestly preferred and I listened, fascinated, as Adam told me how the colors I had chosen related to the scents that Anastasia and I had thought likely to make up my bespoke perfume.

The light purple represented iris; the aqueous blue was ambergris. Adam told me that my color selection showed that I possessed intellectual clarity, inner joy and that I was self-aware. He told me that the colors I had chosen also represented beauty and refinement, but he suggested that I was about to face a period of change and new beginnings. The green I'd chosen represented my love of nature and suggested that I was intuitive and inspirational. He said there was something ethereal and otherworldly about me.

I felt a little as if I were having my palm read, but some of what he'd said rang true, so I suspended disbelief and felt more confident about his observations when he said that my color selection suggested that I was about to embark on a journey. When I told him about the book he said that my traveling would not only be for the book, but that it would be a journey for myself which would be cathartic.

Adam also thought that I needed a darker color, some base notes, to ground me. He said that there was a lot of water in the colors I had chosen, but that the earth's qualities shouldn't be neglected. So I chose a darker orange, and then Adam matched the colors I had picked almost exactly with the scents Anastasia and I were veering toward. He said that my colors represented bergamot, mimosa, green tea, cedar wood, root resins, vetivert bourbon, Mediterranean flowers, frankincense and myrrh, peaches and apricots, figs and cassis.

Adam sent me away with a bottle filled with Marrakech jasmine, honeysuckle and water lilies, telling me that even though jasmine, the scent, is white, on the color table it is red and that would also help to ground some of what he called my "wackiness" and wildness.

When I returned to Anastasia's house with Adam James's report, she suggested that my scent should include some citrus notes. She waved a vial of petitgrain under my nose. Petitgrain is distilled from the twigs and leaves of bitter orange trees, so it has a bittersweetness that I liked. Anastasia also recommended the powdery essence of mimosa and said that, because I'd said sensuality was important to me, I should add musk and jasmine, both of which have strong erotic properties.

Gradually we composed a synthesis and symphony of smells. It was aromatic and mood-enhancing, spicy and floral, breezy, euphoric and erotic. It included neroli, which is an uplifting citrus; jasmine, which recalled hot sultry nights in India; mimosa for its powdery, smoky aroma; iris, a reminder of my childhood; nutmeg for its flavor and narcotic properties (if taken in large quantities nutmeg makes people hallucinate); damask rose, redolent of the souks in the Levant; petitgrain for the aromatic landscapes of the south; and musk for its erotic properties. We also chose vetivert for the greenness in my nature; ambergris, which is evocative of the euphoric salty sea air; and frankincense and myrrh, those ancient, mysterious aromas.

At the end of my second session with Anastasia I tucked all the samplers of the scents I had chosen into the pages of my notebook. Many hours later when I unzipped my bag, a scent wafted up that was so delicious that I knew we'd chosen the right ingredients. Emotions and memories welled up in me as I breathed in and I felt confident about my olfactory odyssey, if a little anxious about Adam's prediction that it would be a personally cathartic journey.

This is the pyramid formula we came up with for my scent for a lifetime—the scent that no one but me would ever wear.

MY BESPOKE SCENT
The Pyramid Formula

THE TOP NOTES
Neroli citrus: *heavy but fresh*
Citron petitgrain: *aromatic, zingy and slightly bitter*
Zambac jasmine: *erotic, exotic, warm, fruity and rich*

MIDDLE (HEART) NOTES
Mimosa: *earthy, powdery and spicily floral*
Damask rose: *musky and floral*
Iris: *warm and richly rooty—as the air smells after a summer
shower—with aromatic fennel-like overtones*
Nutmeg: *spicy, musky and masculine*

BASE NOTES
Vetivert aromatic: *earthy, damp and cooling*
Frankincense: *pine and lemon notes at first, then heady,
spicy and sweet*
Myrrh: *redolent of the forest floor; honeyed with hints
of lemon and rosemary*
Ambergris: *breezy, euphoric, redolent of warm suntanned skin*

So I set out for the places where these ingredients grow,
to meet the people who harvest them and to discover at least
some of the secrets of perfume making from the perfumers who
"magic" the raw ingredients into scent. I was curious to find out
whether the formula that Anastasia and I had conjured up really
was the right magical formula for me.

CHAPTER TWO

MIMOSA

Grasse, the Cradle of Perfume

Then were not summer's distillation left,
A liquid prisoner pent in walls of glass,
Beauty's effect with beauty were bereft,
Nor it, nor no remembrance what it was:
But flowers distill'd, though they with
    winter meet,
Leese but their show; their substance
    still lives sweet

WILLIAM SHAKESPEARE
Sonnet V

THE POWDERY SCENT OF MIMOSA HAUNTS THE HILLS around Grasse, the cradle of perfume. Rose, jasmine, jonquil, lavender and herbs also perfume the hills in Provence: it is as if a perfumer has just opened several vials of essences and attars and held them out in front of you. Mimosa has been cultivated in the hills above Grasse since the eighteenth century and was once so much in demand that a special train left Menton every day to convey large quantities of cut branches to the florists in Paris.

Today mimosa is still valuable to the perfumer for its fougère (fernlike) woodland scent and it is still grown in the hills above Grasse, but in smaller quantities. As well as its fougère quality, it also has a spicy floral note, although it is not overtly floral; nor is it delicate, but rather it is warm and earthy and full of buttery pulverulence. Mimosa's heart note infuses many classic French scents, but it is not usually used as a single note in perfume because, on its own, some think it too sweet and almost sickly. A distinguished nose, Marcel Carles, who worked in the 1950s, regarded mimosa as a little nauseating: it made him quite queasy and he didn't think of it as being very clean-cut. He actually said that it made him think of a woman of doubtful reputation. On the other hand, Marcel Proust's favourite scent was Jean Patou's Vacances, which is a bouquet of lilac, hyacinth and mimosa. I liken mimosa to a dessert wine: I think of it as golden, honeyed, summery, dry and earthy, with an oleaginous sweetness that makes it a very rich perfume. To me, mimosa is to vetivert as Sauternes is to Sauvignon.

Thirty varieties of mimosa grow on the Côte d'Azur, but there are no records to show when it was introduced to Europe from Africa or Australia, where it is indigenous. All thirty varieties have compact globular heads of fragrant yellow blossoms, and the trees can grow up to 30 feet tall. Its essence is extracted by a volatile solvent and ends up in the form of a concrete, a solid viscous substance, or as an absolute, which is the purest of all scent commodities; it is the refined product of the concrete after the wax and alcohol have been removed.

I knew that I would be able to breathe in the rich, sweet scent of mimosa as Stephen and I and our eighteen-month-old son, Tarquin, drove down through the hills above Grasse, but first I'd planned to meet Les Hauts Parfumeurs in Paris. I hoped they would give me introductions to the Grassois noses who would, in turn, educate me about the Grasse perfume business in general and the extraction of mimosa essence in particular. We crossed the Channel without incident and, when we arrived, an Indian summer sun shed its golden light on Paris.

I decided to walk to my first appointment—with Pamela Roberts of L'Artisan Parfumeur—because I wanted to drink in the elegance of Paris in the astonishing October sunshine. I walked from the Marais to Montparnasse, pounding the boulevards from the Place de la République all the way along Boulevard Beaumarchais. I crossed the Ile Saint-Louis and caught tantalizing glimpses of Notre-Dame and the Louvre (but there was no time to sightsee). I walked along the Boulevard Saint-Germain, past Montparnasse cemetery and the ghosts of Man

Ray, Baudelaire, Sartre and de Beauvoir, and down the Boulevard Raspail. It was uplifting.

When I arrived, Pamela ushered me into a room full of classic scent bottles and wooden trays with sprinklings of raw ingredients. There were vanilla pods, cloves, ambrette seeds and much, much more, all arranged on podiums. I also smelled the single-note mimosa—L'Artisan Parfumeur makes the only single-note mimosa scent that I know of—and I became instantly addicted. Anastasia Brozler had been right: I knew instantly that I had to have this scent, with its warm earthy richness—which also reminded me of two of my favorite colours, green and yellow—as a heady heart note to my own scent. I also spotted crystalline granules of frankincense and myrrh, and we debated where the best frankincense and myrrh came from; Pamela insisted on Somalia, I on Yemen and Oman.

L'Artisan Parfumeur's best-selling perfume is Mur et Musc, blackberry and musk, and is redolent of late summers and mellow fruitfulness. It reminded me of picking blackberries as a child. Pamela said that good perfumes open the doors to our memories, and that although expensive ingredients are important, they are not enough. She believes that the accords and harmonies and the image or memory or atmosphere that the perfumer is trying to evoke are what is really important.

I told her that I was heading south to the souks of Morocco. She gave me a withering look and said that the world of perfume was deeply secretive and that the farther east you go the more deceptive it gets. She warned me to be careful when I went into the souks because everything there is bought from Grasse, although they pretend it is from their own country. I hoped I would prove her wrong and, before I left, she graciously gave me the names of several people to see in Grasse.

I took a taxi to the Rive Gauche to see Frédéric Malle at Éditions de Parfums, because I'd walked all the way to L'Artisan Parfumeur in my Emma Hope shoes, which, although quite beautiful, aren't very practical, and my feet needed a rest. Monsieur Malle is one of the most fashionable names in perfume circles; he has commissioned celebrated noses, including Edmond Roudnitska, to make signature perfumes for him. When I arrived I saw a minimalist gray slate-and-glass shop with four enclosures that looked like space capsules, each filled with a different intoxicating scent. I assumed that you got inside the capsule, so I tried to climb into the one marked "Iris Poudre." An assistant politely showed me that you are supposed to put only your face inside and immerse yourself in the scent by breathing it in.

While I was greedily drinking in the scents from the space capsules, Frédéric Malle appeared. He did not look like a perfumer at all. I was expecting someone rather dandified, but he was dressed in corduroys and a tweed jacket. He looked like an intellectual. We sat down on metal Castiglioni chairs with cowskin seats and he began by telling me how his grandfather had founded Christian Dior, while his mother created classic fragrances like Eau Sauvage. They were, literally, made on Frédéric when he was a boy.

Frédéric explained that the best way to make a fragrance is to have someone else wear it. Frédéric told me that he designed the smelling cabinets (the space capsules) because, as he said, his fragrances were made to be smelled from a distance. He also said that fragrance must create an illusion, a bit like theatrical decor. When you smell scents close up, you do not get a very good rendition, so the smelling cabinets reproduce the aura of the fragrance—something a blotter cannot do.

I asked Frédéric about pheromones, the new buzzword in the science of smell. I asked if it was really possible to make a pheromonal perfume with the excretions from flowers that attract pollinators. But he said, dismissively, that the pheromone business had gone bust. He said that the idea that you can make a fragrance that turns everyone on was hardly serious.

I left Editions de Parfums with a little box full of bottles, which I very nearly spilled on the bus on the way back to the Marais, such was my excitement as I tried each one. There was a rich Parfum de Thérèse, which was aromatic and almost prim, while Une Fleur de Cassis, which was made from blackcurrant, smelled mildly of aniseed. There were also En Passant, a blend of green notes; Iris Poudre, from orris roots; and a sweet, overpowering Angéliques Sous la Pluie. Lastly there was an even sweeter and more potent Lipstick Rose. I got some strange looks on the bus as the scented djinns were released from their bottles, and, as I smelled them, I thought that the concentration of mimosa in my own scent would be "up to the nose," by which I mean that it would create the right harmony within my own scent by providing a resonant, earthy heart note. Prompted by the delicious aromas wafting from the bottles Frédéric Malle had given me, I reflected on what he'd said about pheromones.

I knew that pheromones should not be confused with our sense of smell. And I knew that scientists had long known about the affinity between scent and the sex drive. They know that certain odors stimulate the sex drive and that scent is a refined and subtle instrument of seduction. But you can't smell pheromones. In 1956 the pheromone was first identified as a sexual attractant in the silkworm moth; Lyall Watson devoted several chapters to the subject in his book *Jacobson's Organ* (2000); and in her book *A Natural History of the Senses* (1990), Diane Ackerman wrote that pheromones were "the packhorses of desire." Pheromones are biologically active substances which supposedly affect biorhythms, but many scientists remain unconvinced that people harbor and react to pheromones, and their chemical structure is still unknown. The only pheromone system for which scientists have found evidence, so far, doesn't exist in humans, but in insects.

As I got off the bus holding my box full of bottles of scent, however, it occurred to me that even if pheromones could be captured in a scent, they aren't necessary, because even the faintest trace of a beautiful scent inspires our imaginations, stimulates our senses and, if the scent belongs to a loved one, fills us with longings and memories. I discussed this with Stephen as we packed our bags, and he agreed.

As we drove through Paris past the Luxembourg Gardens and headed for Grasse, the unseasonably hot October sunshine poured through flame-colored trees, burning the scene and its autumnal smells into my memory. We took an unintentionally circuitous route via the Alps. The late-afternoon sun threw the jagged mountainside into relief as great shafts of light fell into the valleys, creating an amphitheatre of light and shadow. We stayed in an Alpine town where the icy wind whipped around the steep narrow streets, and when we left, at dawn, the church bells rang. As we traveled down into the foothills of the Alps, the mountains gave way to hills that rippled like waves. The morning sun hid behind fortified towns built on sheer rock faces; towers and battlements were thrown into black-purple shadow like the background of a Giorgione painting. Olive and cypress trees grew beside fields of fruit trees neatly wrapped in nets shaped like fans. Cumulus clouds floated over valleys of chestnut woods and forests that were fired with the yellows, reds, oranges and purples of their autumnal leaves.

At last we saw the first of many billboards advertising scent. It was an old Molinard poster of a seventeenth-century courtesan behind whom perfume stalls mushroomed along the roadside selling clay jars of lavender oil, while hunters and dogs gathered by paths into the forests, waiting to sniff out truffles.

Scent Schools

THE WORLD'S MOST SPECIALIZED SCENT SCHOOLS ARE IN GRASSE. UNTIL recently trainee perfumers took up to ten years to learn their trade, but now the length of training has been reduced to three years and many of the schools have closed down. One of the most famous schools is still in Grasse, however. It is the Givaudan-Roure school.

The first stage for any trainee is to memorize a vast vocabulary of smells, a skill that perfumers continue to perfect throughout their lives by a process of association. So, for example, if they smell patchouli they think of damp leaves by a lake, or they might

> associate pine essence with holidays by the sea. Trainees keep personal association notebooks.
>
> In the perfume schools students learn the building blocks of scents and their chemistry. They are given formulae and, for practical training, they work in processing plants. In the final stages of their tuition, trainees work on charts and sketches of perfumes. The acid test is to make imitations of existing perfumes. In the final exam, the student is given a scent and told to copy it. The copy is then taken to the head perfumer, and if the two scents are indistinguishable to him, the trainee is ready to become a junior perfumer.

Grasse lies in the foothills of the Maritime Alps. It has a superb microclimate, clement, frost-free and sheltered from the winds, but as you approach the town you see the coastal plain littered with urban development: villas, blocks of flats and houses. Sadly, the days when gutters were awash with jasmine petals, and sprigs of jasmine were handed to you at petrol stations, are gone, but the names of the streets, such as Place des Erbes, testify that Grasse was, for centuries, a thriving perfume-production town. It is built on a vertiginous hill: steep alleyways and narrow streets cascade downward, echoing to the strains of North African Rai music. And Grasse itself has a peculiar smell: the residues of chemicals and solvents spew from the laboratories' chimneys in the foothills of the town, but, as we drove through the hills above Grasse, I breathed in the rich, sweet scent of mimosa that I'd been looking forward to. It haunts the hills.

Acacia farnesiana is the mimosa most commonly used by the perfumer because its flowering season is longer than that of the other mimosas. This, and the rose, jasmine, jonquil, lavender and herbs that have also grown in and perfumed these hills for centuries, ensured that Grasse became the cradle of the perfume industry—although it didn't begin quite as you might expect.

In the Middle Ages Grasse was famous for its tanneries, but the stink of urine, the tanning agent, was so overwhelming that the tanners—who by the sixteenth century had begun to make a name for themselves as fine glove makers—took to perfuming their leather (and themselves) with scent, and very soon their scented leather gloves had become a flirtatious, fashionable accessory. The Earl of Oxford gave a pair of soft leather perfumed gloves to Elizabeth I and, for many years, that particular scent was called the "Earl of Oxford's scent." But it was Catherine de Medici, Queen of France from 1519 until 1589, who began the process that saw Grasse evolve from a tanning town into a perfumer's paradise. In 1553 she set up a laboratory in Grasse. She wanted France to make perfumes to rival the then fashionable Arab perfumes, and *gantiers-parfumeurs* (gauntlet-perfumers), as they became known, and apothecaries sprang up everywhere. Local peasants strapped copper alembics (distilling apparatuses) to their donkeys and distilled wild herbs and flowers on the spot. Mountaineers in the Alps collected lavender and other wild aromatic plants and came down to sell their wares to the *gantiers-parfumeurs* of Grasse.

By 1745 the Guild of Gantiers-Parfumeurs—founded by Jean de Galimard—had some seventy members, but not long afterward production of the famous Grasse gauntlets ceased, partly because of the exorbitant taxes imposed on leather goods in the late seventeenth century. From then on the Grassois concentrated on the production of perfume for its own sake, and by the early 1900s Grasse, with its warehouses, distilleries and crops of flowers and herbs, led the way for worldwide production of perfume. It is still the place where many other perfumes and plant materials from around the world are brought to be brokered and turned into essential oils, concretes and absolutes. No other town in the world boasts such a concentration of technical know-how, researchers, scientists, chemists, botanists, technicians and, of course, the noses and perfumers themselves. And the Parfumerie Galimard still exists today, just outside Grasse.

The Language of Music is the Language of Perfume

PERFUMERY USES MUCH THE SAME TERMINOLOGY AS MUSIC. Making a scent is like composing a symphony of harmonies, cadenzas and stanzas. Even the ingredients are referred to as notes and accords, and the noses—those highly trained creators of the scents—work, just like composers, at keyboards or, as they are known in the trade, perfumer's organs.

The perfumer's organ has row upon row of flasks and vials arranged on shelves that fan out around the nose so that he has hundreds of fragrant ingredients at his fingertips, or, more to the point, at the ends of his nostrils. For the perfumer, his nose is the means of control: he will compose his scents from his olfactory memories. He will imagine the perfume and then try to make it; just as a musician does not have to have an instrument at hand to compose, but simply writes down the notes from his memory bank of sounds, so it is with the perfumer. The final triumph is to conceive a perfume, mentally, and then to make a literal translation into tangible liquid form.

There are hundreds of raw materials, and there are certain accords or harmonies that coexist between them. For example, an accord might consist of lemons, which contrast with and enhance sandalwood; sandalwood, which contrasts with clove; and clove, which contrasts with orange, bringing you back to the citrus note.

Scents, like sounds, appear to influence the olfactory nerve. There is, as it were, an octave of odors just like the octaves in music: certain odors coincide, just as certain notes of music harmonize. For instance, almond, heliotrope, vanilla and clematis blend well together, each producing different degrees of a similar scent. Citron, lemon, orange peel and verbena form a higher octave of smells, which blend in a similar way.

I had read about the way that the mimosa that grows in the hills around Grasse used to be transformed into perfume. Until the second half of the twentieth century, some 200 tons of mimosa flower heads were harvested in Grasse every year. In the traditional process, in specially built barns called mimoseries, hot water was piped down into shallow troughs into which sprays of mimosa were thrown. The resulting water was bottled and sold in the flower market in Nice. Now, sadly, the mimoseries no longer exist, but mimosa is still harvested in Grasse, and *Acacia farnesiana*, or cassie (not to be confused with the biblical scent of cassia) blooms from January to March, which makes it easy to harvest because its blossoms are successive. This means that some flowers are ready for picking while others are scarcely formed, so as one harvest is being gathered and passed through the laboratory, the next is growing.

The yellow blossoms are not petals but are made up of stamens which are so fragile that they must be treated within twenty-four hours of being picked. Mimosa used to be treated by maceration with suet. Spent globular stamens were replaced by fresh ones until a mimosa suet pudding, or cassie pomade, yielded a rich scent. *Huile de cassie* was prepared in the same way, but the suet was substituted with almond or olive oil, producing a fragrant olivaceous odor. In Grasse, these days, mimosa is treated by distillation, as I was about to find out from the Grassoise noses. Distillation is a much more efficient, but rather less culinary, process.

Until the 1960s the origin of every perfume molecule you could possibly want came from Grasse, but with the increased use of synthetics the flowers that grew so well in the region were no longer such an important commodity, and crops dwindled while labor costs soared. Naturals like jasmine and roses now mostly come from the Third World. However, the naturals that still grow in the hills and valleys around Grasse, or those which are treated here, are the most expensive in the world. There are crops of carnations, violets, jonquils, lavender, tuberose and the rare *Rose de Mai*, of which there are only a few fields left. Many of the established perfume houses, such as Chanel, have franchises on these fields and their crops.

As we drove down into the town the glorious scents of the hills faded, and later, as I walked to my first meeting with Monsieur Roca, the director of Robertet (one of the three great Grasse firms that produce naturals), I suddenly felt sick. I realized I was walking through—and breathing in—a mephitic cloud of noxious chemical fumes, and the more I breathed, the more nauseous and dizzy I felt. I made it into Robertet's air-conditioned front office gasping for clean air.

The receptionist handed me a glass of water and said that after a while you got used to the fumes, but as I read Robertet's company catalog, which told me that Robertet made perfumes from natural products and that, in the past year, they'd generated sales of €88.9 million, I couldn't help wondering how natural their perfumes really were; the malodorous nebula outside made me doubt what I was reading.

When I met Henri-Joseph Roca, I remarked on the overpowering smells, and he said that his wife often commented that he smelled of the factory when he got home from his day's work. He ushered me into his office, where we discussed natural and synthetic scents. Volatile chemicals are used to extract natural scents from raw materials *and* to manufacture synthetic scents, and some of these chemicals exude noxious fumes—the very fumes that had nearly overpowered me. We talked about how a century ago a perfumer had about one hundred ingredients to play with, while today there are about six hundred natural extracts and over three thousand synthetic ones. The rising cost of natural essential oils has led to the introduction of synthetics, although natural materials are still the backbone of the industry, particularly because perfume crops and flower cultivation have spread farther afield to the countries of South America, to India, China, Tunisia, Morocco and Egypt.

We also discussed the fact that modern perfumery owes much to chemistry. Nature's smells can be replicated in the laboratory with the aid of synthetics. Nitrobenzine, for example, has the crude smell of almonds, coumarin is an imitation of the tonka bean, while benzene (a synthetic) produces a powerful smell of musk and citronella echoes lily of the valley (a flower that cannot be extracted or distilled), while linalool is just like bergamot. But although the chemistry of synthetics has improved, perfumes are not really much more advanced than their counterparts two thousand years ago. The Egyptian kyphi (an ancient holy incense) had at least twenty ingredients, while the ancient Greeks understood the sophisticated idea of applying different scents to different parts of the body: mint for the arms, palm oil for the jaws and breasts, marjoram for the hair, myrtle for the neck and roses in wreaths around their heads. In spite of technical know-how and advances in science, perfume production is still rooted in nature and it is, of course, nature that inspires scents.

Monsieur Roca and I agreed that perfumery is and always will be a magical combination of alchemy, olfactory imagination and memory, and that smells are the guardians of the past. They evoke what Proust called "A night-light in the bedroom of memory." I asked how many fields are still devoted to flower cultivation in Grasse. He told me that, these days, cost is paramount and that the big flower crops, such as jasmine, tuberose and rose, are all smaller than they used to be because it takes several hours to pick enough flowers to fill one small bottle of perfume, and that makes the price of the local product quite unacceptable for a middle-class fragrance. It is, however, still commercially viable to grow and handpick roses because they are reasonably easy to gather: eight kilograms of rose petals can be picked in one hour by two rose pickers.

Enfleurage

THE ANCIENT EXTRACTION PROCESS KNOWN AS *ENFLEURAGE* WAS first used by the Egyptians. The method used grease, or fat, instead of water, to immerse the flower heads, which were then laid out on glass frames, a bit like flower pressing. Enfleurage enabled perfume makers to extract essential oils by steeping petals, and other fragrant parts of the plant, in cold-pressed fat treated with benzoin to prevent it becoming rancid.

The most fragile flowers, such as jasmine, tuberose and even daffodils—which can spoil if heated—were spread in drawers or on glass trays, known as *chassis en verre*, which were laid one on top of the other. Every twenty-four hours the flowers were replaced and the process was repeated several times with fresh flower heads, until the essential oil was totally absorbed in the fat. The resultant product was known as a pomade. The pomade was then scraped off the glass and the aromatic oil retrieved from the fat by dissolving it at low temperature in alcohol, and straining it. The process is very labor-intensive and as a result has by and large fallen out of use. However, in France jasmine is still extracted by *enfleurage*, and Robertet uses the method for the tuberose.

Monsieur Roca told me that Robertet is more than 150 years old and its perfumers have expert knowledge of natural raw materials and aromatic chemicals. The company works with over five hundred materials, employing about five hundred people. Today they mainly extract perfume using solvents or distillation by water (hydrodistillation), but they do still extract tuberose by the traditional process of *enfleurage*. Some local ingredients are still used—a delivery of lavender was expected to arrive from nearby later that day—but their cistus comes from Spain and their oak moss from Macedonia. Essential oils are delivered by boat or air, although those from countries like India are not always properly distilled, so Robertet rectifies and redistils them. Their mimosa, however, is from the hills around Grasse, and, as Monsieur Roca had heard that I was particularly partial to mimosa, he took me to see how it is distilled.

As we walked around the warehouse it was as if I were breathing all the smells of the earth. There were sacks of ingredients from the most exotic and far-flung corners of the world: ginger from the Indies, vanilla pods from Zanzibar, petitgrain from Paraguay, coriander and oak moss from Morocco, patchouli from Indonesia, rosewood from Brazil, ylang-ylang from the Comoros, tuberose from India, ambrette seeds from Peru, sandalwood from Indonesia, iris from Tuscany, jasmine from Morocco and, of course, mimosa from Grasse itself.

The warehouse was chilly: the harvested crops and volatile essential oils need to be kept cold for maximum freshness before they are distilled or extracted into essential oils, absolutes and concretes. In the sheds, bales of compressed oak moss from Macedonia had just arrived. Monsieur Roca explained that because the moss arrives in a very dry state it has no aroma, but that once they have dipped it through solvent it regains its natural softness and all the molecules and cells burst open.

We went into the distillation and extraction plants, which were filled with every kind of apparatus imaginable: vats, boilers, pipes and pipettes to draw off otto (attar) from water; maceration pans, flasks, alembics, bains-marie, extraction pressers, rolling machines, pulverizers, generators, thermometers, valves, cooling vats . . . it reminded me of a Heath Robinson cartoon. Men in white overalls were shoveling raw materials into the extractors, and beside the steaming vats were sacks of orris root, dried mint and more unusual ingredients like fenugreek, a Brazilian tea, seaweed, beeswax, tomato leaves and tobacco.

In the next unit raw materials were being distilled rather than extracted. The fragrance was heavenly—I stood rooted to the spot. I smelled freshly cut hay on a hot summer's day. I smelled ripening berries and something spicy floating on a warm breeze. They had just completed the distillation of pepper oil, Moroccan lichen and hay. Bubucchu oil from the Cape Town area was also steaming away, its scent fruity, like blackcurrants. I was ecstatic. I wanted a perfume made from everything I could smell, immediately. Monsieur Roca just laughed and reminded me that it wasn't that simple.

Then I saw the delicate yellow mimosa blooms bursting out of sacks, blooms which would soon be transformed into a tangible, cloying scent. I watched the stamens being shoveled into giant stainless-steel vats, colossal boilers, and I imagined the heady heart note they would eventually contribute to my own scent. In another towering 15-foot steaming vat, seaweed was being distilled. Ozonic vapors, redolent of sun, sea and salt, mingled with a cloying smell, like pine resin, from galbanum—a gum resin that grows in Syria and Afghanistan. The oceanic seaweedy smell immediately took me back to an Aegean island in the midday sun, sitting under the shade of a fig tree sipping retsina—the Greek wine that is aged in pinewood vats sealed with pine resin—its smell full of eucalyptus and the wind blowing through lemon trees.

As Monsieur Roca and I stood beside a simmering still, he held an ingredient under my nose for which I could find no corresponding memory. But then I have never been to Peru, and it turned out to be a Peruvian balsam called tolu. Monsieur Roca then showed me a tonka bean, telling me that when you approach tonka bean fields you feel like falling asleep, and if you do fall asleep you have vivid dreams. He made it sound just like a magic potion from a fairy tale. He said that the tonka bean, which contains natural coumarin, an anticoagulant, has a very sweet aroma, like vanilla, with a fougère note of hay. I had a fleeting childhood memory of eating rice pudding with a vanilla pod in it.

In the next section, in even bigger extractors which hold 6,000 liters and produce 900 kilograms a day, they were extracting cistus. Cistus, or labdanum, which oozes from the stems and leaves of the rock rose, is sometimes called amber because it resembles ambergris. In a smaller unit nutmeg and mint were being treated in the delicate process of *enfleurage*. Here I experienced the perfect symbiosis of taste and smell: mint juleps and a creamy rich nutmeg sauce over tortellini came to mind, but in this waxy odorous state it had an uplifting peppery perfume. I was relieved to find that nutmeg really is used in scent, and that I liked its smell, because it is one of the more unusual ingredients that I had chosen for my own scent.

Monsieur Roca then propelled me toward a cabinet of concretes: samples for visitors to smell. Among them were a thyme concrete, patchouli, iris roots, *Rose de Mai*, carnation, narcissus and one of violet, which is extracted from the leaves, not from the flowers. Diane Ackerman, in *A Natural History of the Senses*, describes violets as smelling "like burnt sugar cubes that have been dipped in lemon and velvet." The next two concretes, thyme and oakwood, immediately transported me to damp northern climes full of rotting vegetation, verdant chamomile lawns, thyme-scented breezes and forest floors.

Monsieur Roca held another concrete under my nose and asked if it reminded me of tea. I breathed in a refreshing green note of verbena, a smell that was so quintessentially English that I felt suddenly nostalgic. It was a daffodil scent; it symbolized spring and the hope that spring always brings. And finally he held out the mimosa concrete for me. As I breathed in its heady aroma I forgot all about the noxious fumes I'd inhaled as I'd walked toward the Robertet factory.

Outside at the end of my tour, Monsieur Roca showed me the finished products, in big blue company canisters, waiting to be shipped. Their destinations were many and varied and, in some cases, the products were going back to the places, such as Sumatra, from where the raw materials had originally come. Finally, Monsieur Roca recommended that I go to the Robertet factory in Turkey for the rose harvest in June. He showed me a photograph of Turks up to their waists in rose petals. I left the Robertet compound overwhelmed by the olfactory orgy I had experienced. My nose had had a real workout, for good and for bad.

Distillation and Extraction

BY THE NINTH CENTURY THE ARABS HAD DISCOVERED HOW TO distill rosewater. A physician called Salernus, who lived in Salerno in the eleventh century, records the process of distillation in his book *Antidotarium Magnum*, while Albert le Grand (1193–1280), a man of the church and a philosopher, wrote recipes for the distillation of alcohol in his book *De Secretis Mulierum*: one was for *L'Eau Ardente*, and was highly flammable; another was for *Eau de Vie*; and there were recipes for *Esprit de Vin* and *Eau Flagrante*. These fiery waters and volatile liquids replaced some of the oils in perfumes. The art of perfume distillation, however, was not perfected until the seventeenth century.

By the early fourteenth century most perfumes were a combination of alcohol and essential oils. For instance, rosemary and *Eau de Vie* were distilled in a bain-marie, an invention of a hermit who made one especially for Queen Elizabeth of Hungary in about 1370. In sixteenth-century Tuscany, distillation was the preoccupation of all scientists. The quality of the essences improved when the process of heating the perfume was slowed down. Essences were put into an alembic, which was placed in a bain-marie with a mirror of steel beside the alembic to capture the sun's heat and so warm the essence gently.

Toward the end of the sixteenth century two further important discoveries were made: how to siphon off the scented water and how to preserve the droplets of oil to make the essence. The Florentines invented the Florentine vase, which was serpentine and had

➤

two apertures, one for oil and one for water. At the same time a kind of *enfleurage* was discovered, in which orange flowers, jasmine, rose and violet leaves were immersed in layers of almond oil so that the odor of the flowers was absorbed by the oil. And Leonardo da Vinci invented the process of maceration—softening the ingredient by steeping it in a liquid—and then used solvents to extract essences.

These days raw ingredients, such as rose heads, oak moss or mimosa stamens, are distilled in vats, where they are boiled with water or a solvent so that the essential oils are released as a vapor with the steam. The scented steam then passes up and along a pipe, where it cools back down into a mixture of water and essential oil, which, in turn, drips down into a vat. As most oils float on the surface of water, they can then easily be siphoned off. Most flowers have to be distilled when they are fresh, just after they have been picked.

With natural components, the top notes often disturb the terpenes (volatile aromatic hydrocarbons which occur naturally in essential oils), so, to obtain a cleaner odor, the terpenes have to be taken out. In an essential oil there are hundreds of natural components, and sometimes some of those disturb the dominant odor, so, to produce a finer product, a second distillation is required. This is called molecular distillation.

Products are often decolored, too, because these days people prefer colorless and transparent perfumes. An absolute of rose, for example, which is naturally dark orange, can be made transparent. Each time a product is altered, all the machinery, every boiler, valve and pipe, has to be steamed to prevent "odor pollution" which, once it has set in, cannot be removed.

➤ Extraction is done by using solvents—like hexane, for example, which is an odorless by-product of petrol—which are often volatile. During this process a wax, or "concrete," which is a solid viscous substance, is obtained. The wax is treated several times, either with a solvent or with alcohol. The solvent or alcohol dilutes the wax and then, when the solvent or alcohol is eliminated—using a repeated vacuum process in the case of solvents—the wax, or concrete, becomes more and more concentrated. When the wax is separated from the perfume using the alcohol process, the perfume is translated into an "absolute," which—unlike an essential oil, which is distilled—is obtained by the extraction process and is an altogether more potent and purer product. The perfumers then work with the essential oil, or with the concrete, or with the absolute. Perfumes created using the wax and alcohol process are usually 10 to 20 percent concentrate and 80 to 90 percent alcohol.

For some plants, extraction doesn't result in anything interesting whereas distillation does, but the reverse is also true. Different components result from the two processes. For instance, the *Rose de Mai* from Grasse is not distilled—the yield would be too small and the price would be too high. But the Bulgarian rose can be extracted into a concrete and then into an absolute; it can also be distilled into an essential oil.

And it is as well to remember that extraction units can be dangerous places. The solvents are so flammable and so volatile that a telephone or a tape recorder can cause an explosion. A journalist once caused a blast with his camera flash in the Laboratoire Monique Rémy. Distillation units, on the other hand, use water and so are far less hazardous.

The following day I arranged an appointment with Frédérique von Eben-Worlee, the commercial director at Laboratoire Monique Rémy (LMR), which has been taken over by International Flowers and Fragrances, the largest perfume company in the world. A typically elegant, petite Frenchwoman, wearing chic black patent shoes and a Pucci blouse, Frédérique told me that her mother had started the company twenty years before and that they specialize in compounds for perfumes, made from natural raw materials, which they buy from all over the world. They also specialize in the most difficult materials, the quality of which varies tremendously. They extract scent not only from the flowers but from the leaves of flowers, and from the seeds or roots; in the perfume trade these parts of the plant are called vegetals. For instance, they extract only the seeds of cardamom and distill only the root, not the flower, of the iris. LMR also distills scents from French vegetals such as moss, blackcurrant, mimosa and violet leaves.

We looked around the laboratory, which is much smaller than Robertet's because LMR specializes in providing perfumers with expensive pure essences made from raw materials; they do not make products for the cosmetic and domestic industries. In the extraction unit—where Frédérique asked me to turn off my mobile phone and tape recorder—there was an acrid smell of ambrette seeds being extracted with solvents. I also saw the clear concrete that was the end product of that extraction.

In the distillation unit petitgrain was being distilled and rectified. Petitgrain is distilled from the leaves and "orangettes" (unripened oranges) from orange trees, and the smell is sweetly cloying, almost mouthwatering and slightly astringent. I asked about LMR's mimosa-scent production, and Frédérique explained that the company produces a very pure essence by removing certain terpenes which color the scent, thus making it purer and more transparent. Like Robertet, LMR uses mimosa from the local fields, but LMR takes more time, uses a more rigorous process of rectification and produces a mimosa absolute (as opposed to Robertet's mimosa concrete).

The storage room was cool and hermetically sealed, lined with shelves of hundreds of aluminium bottles. I longed to unscrew some of the caps to smell their contents, but Frédérique restrained me: many of their products are light and heat sensitive, so they are kept cool and in the dark to prevent the natural components from turning bad. She said that, ideally, we should all keep our perfumes in a cool and dark place, in tightly closed bottles, especially the sensitive citrus oils like mandarin, orange and lemon. And she explained that the heavier products, like patchouli, can improve with age, although they too are best not exposed to air. She told me that LMR's most expensive product was orris root, which they were buying for what I thought was a staggering €30,000 per kilograms.

Frédérique promised to send me some scents and, true to her word, when I returned to England I found a wonderful box of delights. She had sent me LMR's mimosa absolute, which smelled floral and earthy and was as hard as crystal—unlike the Robertet mimosa concrete, which had smelled a little stale, was less potent and a little soft. She'd also sent me vetivert from Haiti, petitgrain oil from Paraguay, jasmine absolute from India, Tuscan orris root and ambrette absolute from Peru. All were very potent and concentrated, and I found I still could not take the ambrette: the acrid smell that I remembered from the factory was too much for me. But the others were tenacious and pure, and so long-lasting that, despite several sessions in the washing machine, my clothes held the smells of vetivert, rose, jasmine and petitgrain for at least six months afterward.

I melted some of the mimosa absolute on my radiator and the lovely smell permeated the room, instantly transporting me far from my damp cottage in the Pennines to the warm, sunny climes of Provence. Its aroma convinced me that—although I know it's not to everyone's taste—I had to have it as a heart note in my own scent.

My final stop in Grasse was the Fragonard perfumery and museum, which is still run as a family enterprise and is managed by the two great-granddaughters of the founder, Françoise and Agnès Costa, known simply as the Fragonard sisters. Françoise gave me a tour of the museum, which houses an exceptional collection of antique scent bottles, flacons and perfumery equipment, copper stills and alembics, including a collection of Carthaginian scent bottles that the present managers' father bought in the 1960s.

In the first room a vitrine was filled with Florentine vases, objects of real beauty. The serpentine shape of the vases enabled perfumers to separate the oil or essence of the flower from the excess water, which was drained out through the long thin necks of the vases. The museum's display of antique bottles, from the ancient Egyptian period to the nineteenth century, came in every conceivable shape and size: some precious, some whimsical, some sober or rococo. There were graceful decanters and the most bizarre forms. There was a slender, hollow Alexandrine sandaled foot with a handle in which to burn perfumed oil; Carthaginian votive oil lamps shaped like heads; miniature fountains of perfume and practical travelling cases made of leather. There were wooden marquetry, tortoiseshell and even sharkskin containers for cosmetics and perfumes; ostentatiously jeweled censers and typical Grasse bergamot pots which were provincial simplicity itself. While the Grassoise were busy distilling bergamot, the tradition of "Bergamots" sprang up: little palm-sized round boxes, hand-painted with charming romantic themes, which sweethearts traditionally gave to each other.

A seventeenth-century collection of silver perfume flacons was embellished with mother-of-pearl, and the collection also included the English "Girl on a Swing" Chelsea porcelain perfume bottles, which were made into separate molds for different parts of the body. I noticed that all the bottles were tiny, and said so. But Françoise reminded me that in the past perfume was much more concentrated, much stronger, more essence than alcohol.

There were bottles made from shells and a most ingenious bottle that doubled as a tiny pair of opera glasses. In the eighteenth century there was a fashion for perfume rings, which had small mechanisms into which a little perfume could be decanted. One of the bottles from the 1700s was a china Cupid, and the scent was poured from his penis!

Throughout history perfume bottles have always been ornamental objects of great beauty, made with craftsmanship and artistry. From the earliest times, beautiful flacons for scent have sought to symbolize the power, mystery and allure of perfume. And perfume vessels often masqueraded as ornaments and figurines in their own right. Bottles and vials were made in alabaster, terra-cotta, jade, crystal, porcelain, ivory, precious metals and glass, and were embellished with jewels, silver filigree and enamel. Perfume bottling is as old as the invention of glass itself. The Egyptians manufactured translucent green glass and balsam pots called "unguentaria," as well as elongated bottles for essential oils which diminished in size according to how precious the perfume was.

The Romans also took to glassmaking, although they were less inventive than the Egyptians. Elongated Roman glass essence mixers, like staffs, were surmounted with birds. Terra-cotta unguent vases were decorated with dancing fauns and racing charioteers. The Christians, in Rome, used glass amphorae for perfume, and the Arabians developed glassmaking in earnest in Antioch. By the thirteenth century, the experts in this field were to be found in Venice and the island of Murano, on the Venetian lagoon, where they made scent bottles in colorless pure glass which was engraved or enameled.

In Florence, from the fourteenth until the seventeenth century, perfume decanters were inspired by Renaissance art and commissioned by the Medici princes. Catherine de Medici and her perfumer, René the Florentine, introduced the decanters to French courtiers. The evil Lucrezia Borgia used tiny crystal and gold bottles emblazoned with skulls, into which she tipped "aqua toffana," a revolting perfume of civet and musk.

Renaissance silver-engraved pomanders were worn around the neck, dangling on a long chain, to ward away the plague and the evil smells. These pomanders came apart in little segments, like an orange, and held different perfumes. Some pomanders came in snail or egg shapes, and the invention of porcelain, in the seventeenth century, greatly influenced perfume bottling. Porcelain bottles were intricately decorated with miniature landscapes, after Watteau, or cameos of the owner. Elaborate stoppers were molded into winged doves or bouquets of roses, and the bottles themselves made charming ornaments. I saw dandies, shepherdesses, swans, cupids and fountains.

The eighteenth century saw the development of glassworks in Normandy and Lorraine. Typical perfume decanters were made of ribbed or enameled glass, some were emblazoned with cameos, others with medallions, and they were embellished with gold and silver. Often they were part of a traveling case, or *nécessaire*, complete with tiny compartments for toothbrushes in which the bottles were squat and flat and made of green-tinted glass with gold stoppers.

In the nineteenth century Lalique made exquisite Art Nouveau perfume flacons shaped like shells, with a naked, crouched lady as the bottle top. He made pocket flasks, bulbs of scent and necklaces of hollowed-out settings filled with a perfume wax. Lalique's Baiser d'un Faune was one of the most beautiful bottles in commercial production, but alas, the scent is no longer produced. Today nothing can compare with the craftsmanship, inventiveness and extraordinary range of materials that were once used for perfume bottles.

As we left Grasse, heading for the Spanish border, I fell into a reverie about the stunning scent vessels I'd seen. I thought about Lucrezia swinging her skull-shaped pomander filled with musk, and the fact that Napoleon poured an entire bottle of cologne over his head every morning. I thought about Catherine de Medici dabbing her wrists with Arabian scents from a decanter, and imagined that if I ever treated myself to a single-note mimosa scent I would keep it in one of Lalique's Art Nouveau perfume flacons, or I'd wear one of his hollowed-out necklaces filled with a mimosa absolute.

CHAPTER THREE

NEROLI AND PETITGRAIN

Morocco

Sharp tasted citron, Median climes produce;
Large is the plant, and like a laurel grows;
And, did it not a different scent disclose,
A laurel were.

VIRGIL
Georgics II.180

IN GREEK MYTHOLOGY THE ORANGE WAS HIGHLY PRIZED. Gaea gave Hera, on her marriage to Zeus, golden "apples" from a golden tree in the Garden of the Hesperides. The site of a real garden at Lixus, just north of the modern port of Larache in northern Morocco, is thought to have inspired the mythical Garden of the Hesperides, and modern Greek scholars believe that those golden "apples" were actually oranges. Certainly orange blossom has symbolized chastity and purity for centuries, and, because the orange tree is an evergreen, it has also always represented everlasting love.

Of all the scent-yielding plants, none has an earthly value equal to that of the orange either. It is hugely profitable, partly because most modern perfumes contain about 12 percent orange flower. It takes four years before orange trees produce their flowers and fruit, but then an average tree will yield 12 kilograms of blossoms a year and, although you need 1,000 kilograms of freshly cut petals to make 1 liter of pure essence, orange trees grow in abundance, so the supply of ingredients easily meets the demand.

Orange trees are native to India and China and were introduced to Europe in the twelfth century by the Moors, who brought them from Syria to Africa and then to Spain. Conquerors and Crusaders also brought back oranges, which took root on the shores of the Mediterranean. Saint Dominic planted the first orange tree in Rome in A.D. 1200; it was the bitter, inedible orange from which bergamot comes, and the tree still exists in the monastery at Saint Sabina, near Rome. Ancient trees of this variety also still grow in the garden of the Alcazar in Seville.

Citrus fruits are complex, yielding many different grades of scent and oil. The preparations vary: some are sweet and some bitter; some come from the blossoms, others from the peel, and preparations are also made from the bark, the leaves, the branches and the twigs. Some preparations are blended together to form eau de cologne, orange water and orange essences. The entire orange tree is harvested to release its fragrant secrets, but the two most distinct odors come from the delicate orange blossoms and from the peel, which is removed and pressed using a method called "expression" that ruptures all the tiny pockets in the peel that hold the essential oils.

Anastasia and I had decided on neroli—with its sweet intensity and its underlying fecal note of indole—as one of the top notes in the first stanza of my bespoke scent. We'd also chosen petitgrain—with its bitter, greener fragrance—as another of the top notes. So I wanted to find out which parts of the orange they came from and something of the legends that surround them.

I had discovered that the flowery neroli is distillled from orange blossoms and that the sweet neroli orange was first cultivated in the fifteenth century. It has a long history as an ingredient in perfume: in 1680 the oil from orange flowers was called essence of neroli because Prince Flavio Orsini Neroli's wife, a French noblewoman, acquired a reputation for perfuming her gloves (and beds!) with the essence of orange flower. It is possible that the Romans had already discovered neroli, and the ill-fated Sabine women who were abducted by the Romans called the oil *nero*, meaning strong, which, compared with its citrus cousins, it is. Orange groves still thrive in southern Italy, where the Sabines lived, and in Pompeian and Carthaginian frescoes there are depictions of citrus fruits that bear a striking resemblance to oranges and lemons. Citrus fruits were coveted for their beauty long before anyone thought to eat them.

The oil of petitgrain is distillled from small unripe fruits called "orangettes," which are about the size of cherries. They fall from the trees just after the flowers, and are called *petit grain*, meaning small seeds or grains, because of their size. Petitgrain is obtained by distillling the leaves and unripe fruit while they are still little grains or orangettes. If you hold the leaf of an orange up to the sunlight you can actually see the globular specs holding the little sacs of oil. There are several classifications of petitgrain otto, too. *Petitgrain douce* comes from the leaves and grains of sweet oranges, *petitgrain limon* comes from the lemon tree, while the *petitgrain bigaradi* is from the bitter Seville orange. I wanted to try petitgrain for its aromatherapeutic properties, one of which is the alleviation of insomnia. There are many types of petitgrain to choose from, and I loved the bigarade. It was pale yellow with herbaceous and woody notes—from the leaves and twigs from which it is distillled.

Four essential oils are derived from the orange—neroli, orange flower absolute, petitgrain and bergamot—and they all smell different. Orange flower absolute is flowery, while neroli and bergamot are aromatically rich compared with the sharper and lighter lemon, grapefruit and mandarin. The lemony bergamot, a rare and valuable essential oil which comes from the peel of a large, greenish, thick-skinned, inedible orange, *Citrus bergamia*, is very popular in perfumes because it lifts and boosts them. It is named after the city of Bergamo in Lombardy where it was first sold.

When the zest of an orange is peeled it permeates the atmosphere with a shower of astringent molecules like sea spray. One hundred orange peelings yield 1 milliliter of essential oil, and the bitterness enriches other bouquets, especially spicy ones. Citrus notes—which are more romantically known as the Hesperides family—give zest and evanescent freshness to the top notes of scents; they make the initial impression before the heartier notes creep up on you. Lemons, bergamot, oranges, mandarins, grapefruits and limes form the upper silvery notes in the first stanza of a scent. Citrus notes always appear at the top of a pyramid perfume formula because they are fresh, vigorous and light.

Many of the citrus notes, including neroli and petitgrain, are cultivated in Morocco and Tunisia, so I went to Morocco to find out what they smelled like in their raw states, to see how they were harvested and to discover the secrets of the extraction of their scents. The morning after we arrived in Morocco, at the port of Tangier, I went down to the medina. The plangent calls of the muezzin echoed across the city from minaret to minaret and, as soon as I was within the old walls of the medina, my nostrils were assailed by the smells of simmering spices in the *tajines* (lamb stews) on the narrow pavements. I heard the clamour of vendors calling out their wares while veiled women—whose beautifully hennaed hands were all you could see of them—and men in hooded djellabas swarmed along the covered corridorlike streets.

I found the topography of the medina confusing, but I

managed not to get lost. There were hidden terraces high above the sea and dark impasses; there were small squares built on sloping terrain and there were tunnels, ramparts and ruins. I found my way to a little square called Le Petit Socco, where cafés spilled out onto the pavement and men sat drinking coffee and mint tea. After asking several people, I found what I was looking for: the Parfumerie Madani. Madani copies perfumes, and when I arrived he was doing a brisk trade. Men and women were queuing up to have scents dabbed on their outstretched, cupped hands. I thought they looked as if they were reaching out for alms.

I tried the perfumes I knew well: Chanel No. 5 and L'Eau D'Issey, but they smelled nothing like the real thing. They were to their originals as Muzak is to Mozart. I remembered Pamela Roberts's warning in Paris: the merchants in the Moroccan souks buy everything from Grasse but pretend it's made in Morocco. I thought the scents I'd just smelled hadn't even come from Grasse but were merely bad copies.

I found another perfumer around the corner, but it was the same story. Klein and Armani copies were being sold in medicine bottles, but when I asked if there was any pure *fleur d'oranger* or neroli essence, the "perfumer" just glared at me and shrugged his shoulders. I began to wonder whether all I was going to find in Morocco was imitation perfume or black-market copies of fashion-house fragrances. Deciding I would certainly find nothing genuine in Tangier, we headed south to the gateway to the Sahara, Marrakech, where I hoped I would discover wild, burned musky perfumes made from genuine ingredients.

Alembics: a Short History

THE EARLIEST ALEMBIC, WHICH WAS FOUND IN IRAQ, IS BELIEVED TO date from 3500 B.C. and was made of clay. Copper alembics consist of three parts. The alembic rests on a furnace of bricks and stones. The flowers are put into the alembic with gallons of water and brought to boiling point. The steam passes through a coiled pipe which is surrounded by cold water in another still above the first alembic. As the steam rises, the volatile oil (or perfume), which is lighter than the water, floats to the top. The oils vaporize in little droplets which are collected in the top boiler. During a distilllation, flasks are used to change the water in the upper still to keep it cool, so encouraging the steam. The oil (or perfume) is then separated from the water by siphoning.

The Arabs improved the distilllation process greatly when they invented the serpentine, which is, literally, a snake-shaped glass tube which catches the heavier water in its curves while the lighter oil flows on out. By the ninth century the Persians were distilling rose- and orange water rather than using the older methods of digestion (boiling the ingredients in liquid) or *enfleurage* (steeping petals in cold-pressed fat). And as early as the thirteenth century a Syrian historian called Uman Ibn al-Adim wrote a guide to perfume making, thus making the Arabs the first to perfect perfume manufacture.

All over the Arab world the same principles of distilllation were developed, and our word "alembic" comes from the Arabic *al-Anbiq*, which means "the still." Early alembics were not only

> made from copper, but from glass or earthenware, and the production of *al-kuhl*, which developed from this thirteenth-century distillation technique, also gave us the word "alcohol."
>
> Modern distillation takes place in factories, but the process is essentially exactly the same as it was when the Arabs invented the serpentine.

As you drive toward Marrakech you catch glimpses of the city through palmeries and olive groves, and the backdrop of the Atlas Mountains floats like a mirage in the heat haze behind it, looking like an immense stage curtain drawn across the sky. The snow-clad peaks seem to tear at the clouds.

Marrakech is a low-lying, terra-cotta city, dwarfed by incredibly high spindly palm trees and the great Koutoubia minaret. It is an oasis city built from what were originally encampments. Tribes from the Sahara and the Atlas Mountains came to trade here, and even though their tents were replaced long ago by houses of stone and brick, and the gardens are full of carefully tended roses, bougainvillea, pale blue plumbago and oleander, there is still a sense of impermanence about it.

We parked the car just outside the medina walls. A "charioteer" then bundled our luggage on to a "chariot" and led us down a maze of alleys to a modest inn built around a courtyard filled with orange trees. Immediately I thought I had a better chance of finding real orange essence here. In a corner of the courtyard French students were smoking kiff (hash) in a huge bong (hookah) while Tarquin looked on fascinated and stretched out his arms for a turn, which, needless to say, I didn't allow him! But I smelled the green narcotic notes.

The next day I plunged into the medina to find the souk El Attarin (the word *attar* is Persian for perfume). I saw the potters' souk, the coppersmiths' souk, the slipper makers," the dyers," jewelers' and sheepskin sellers' souks. I saw the wool merchants' and textile merchants' souks, and a wonderful smell emanated from the carpenters' souk, where craftsmen were making chess sets with hand-driven foot lathes. The woody, luxuriant smell of chippings and the sawdust of cedarwood and cypresswood filled the air. The smell of cedarwood is honeyed, vegetal and animalic, and I discovered later that the women collect cedarwood shavings and put them in a steam chest with wax to make pomanders. Then they attach the pomanders to their clothes and a wonderful aroma fills the air as they walk.

As I passed the spice souk I breathed in the smells of yellow-ocher cumin and deep red cinnamon, of nutmeg, henna, cloves, garlic and ginger as I passed the rows of sacks they were stored in. I found the souk El Attarin sign on a blue tile on a street corner, but it had become a television souk. In my disappointment I almost got lost in a convoluted web of alleyways, but my nose didn't let me down. Following it, I eventually found myself in a lane of perfume sellers who sat behind white cloth curtains that shielded hundreds of vials of perfume from the heat and sunlight. As soon as I showed a glimmer of interest, the perfumers grabbed my arms and hands and dabbed me with scents, and, because oriental scents are not diluted with alcohol, their potent, oily perfumes lingered on my skin.

I was anointed with jasmine, rose from Kelaa Mgouna, musk,

sandalwood, patchouli, flower of the night, neroli and narcissus. Then I explained that I wanted to try all the different petit-grains: there are several major oils distillled from the unripe fruits, twigs and leaves of the citron tribe. The golden apples of the sun, the perfumer told me expansively, give off the odor of angels. And it's true, the golden "apples" of the Hesperides do give off a heavenly aura.

Like an alchemist in his spotless white robes, the perfumer brought down flasks and unstoppered them. The first flask was a petitgrain bigarade, of which only the leaves are distillled. It was pale yellow and smelled a bit woody and quite sweet. This oil comes from Calabria. Next came a strong, bittersweet berga-mot petitgrain with an almost harsh top note. I waved it away. Then the alchemist produced my favorite, the citron petitgrain, which is distillled from the undeveloped fruits of the lemon tree. It was greenish yellow, smelling like a citron pressé and burned sugar with a certain zing to it. It is made in Algeria, Tunisia and Morocco.

We went on sniffing petitgrains, and I wished I had brought some coffee beans to refresh the nose in between smelling ses-sions. (Coffee beans are sniffed between scents in exactly the same way as sorbets are eaten between courses, to refresh the palate.) There was some heaven-sent Algerian mandarin oil, which was dark olive green and intensively sweet and grapelike, but its sweetness, in the end, was too powerful for me.

Just when I thought I had smelled the complete palette of citrus aromas, yet another petitgrain appeared from under the counter. It was a petitgrain *sur fleurs d'oranger*: a codistilllation of petit-grain oil over orange flowers from the bitter orange tree. It was tenacious, and the orange flowers seemed to hover on the top notes; it was by far the most elegant and delicate, but still I decided on the citron petitgrain for my bespoke scent, because I loved its zing.

An overpoweringly mellifluous bouquet sank into the skin of my arms and the palms of my hands. To begin with the smells still seemed too strong, almost vulgar and verging on the unpleasant, but as the hours passed they became balmy, transforming themselves into softer notes on my skin. I began to feel optimistic about the ingredients I would find in Morocco, and the following morning I went to meet Professor Martin, an ethnobotanist in charge of a restoration program for the "regreening" of the medina. Professor Martin was also making extensive records of everything that was sold in the medina, particularly the magic spells, herbs, plants and essences: a formidable task.

We entered the medina by way of the herb souk, where we bought a bouquet of mint, absinthe, sage, marjoram, scented geranium and clary sage. Professor Martin explained that a mixture of these herbs went into the making of mint tea, although he said that he preferred mint tea made simply from mint; he preferred single notes because just one ingredient, like, say, vanilla, clove or tuberose, could be intensely satisfying.

We threaded our way along tiny lanes and, behind a mosque where the ablutions fountain had run dry, came to a courtyard where, Professor Martin explained, the dead are embalmed in cloth soaked with musk before they are buried. Now, as in ancient times, Muslims go into the next world perfumed. A wizened old man walked past us swinging a censer of smoldering frankincense to cleanse and purify the air; I watched him walk away in a cloud of incense. Turning into a square where shops sold spices and perfumes, we stopped at one which must have had several hundred jars of ingredients for perfume, for cooking and for healing potions. In Morocco scent is used as much for cooking and for medicine as it is for perfume. The perfumer lifted a jar of musk from the shelf and took out a lump. He rubbed a bit on my wrist, but, quite plainly, it was not the real thing. It smelled and looked like Turkish Delight, and I thought it would go better in a milkshake than in a perfume. When Professor Martin asked if the perfumer had any real musk he said that fake musk had many virtues, and I guessed that even if he could get real musk he would not have said so, because we were strangers and the trade is now illegal.

We sampled other scents and medicines. There were creams for eczema and essence of orange flower to combat stress; the perfumer showed us jar after jar of potions, poultices and spices—*les plantes medicina*, as he called them. And there were all kinds of curry powders for fish and meat that smelled so delicious I thought they would surely rescue the worst of culinary disasters.

We walked on to the old slave market, where Berber women squatted and talked to each other and to passersby. We found multicolored potpourri made from pomegranate flowers, which are dried and then dyed. Behind was a cupboard of a shop crammed with perfume, spices, pigments in brilliant hues, a caged falcon and a box of rare turtles bound for Belgium. We squeezed in, sat down on little wooden stools and the bouquet of mint and other herbs we had bought in the market was plunged into boiling water to make tea. As we sipped the tea, we had a scent-smelling session. Then the perfumer handed Professor Martin lit crystals of frankincense and myrrh which he told us to pass around. This was a scent I knew well. Its ghostly smoke always takes me back to childhood, when the cool, sometimes dank smell of stone mixed with the heady scent of incense filled my nostrils as I stared at frescoes with my parents. Despite the Moroccan heat I was immediately transported to the cool aisles of Renaissance churches.

Professor Martin asked, on my behalf, about essential oils from real orange flowers, about the neroli that I'd come in search of and longed to smell. The perfumer smiled and produced some neroli which was pure nectar—oily and velvety, like whipped *crème d'orange*. We discovered that ordinary people distill orange flower water and essential oils from orange products in their own houses. But the distilllation of the orange flowers was not something that I was permitted to watch, because the process is still considered a sacred ritual. I wasn't surprised to discover this because, in aromatherapy, the oils are considered to be the soul, the life force, of a plant. In the spring peasants come down from the mountains laden with bales of orange flowers to sell in the medina to the traditional distilling families. The work is done only by the women, who dress in white and must be clean and not menstruating. The ritual of making orange flower water is conducted in silence, and the atmosphere has to be calm because, they believe, at that moment they are dealing with soul.

Since I could not witness the process, the perfumer suggested that I go to see Dr. Belkamel and his aromatic garden in the Ourika valley, outside Marrakech in the foothills of the Atlas Mountains. Before we left the perfumer showed us a piece of nondescript bark which turned out to be the fragrant agarwood. He told us that this particular piece was *Aquilaria malaccensis*, from which gaharu oil comes. It costs $4 a gram, or $4,000 per kilogram, and these bits of apparently rotten wood, I discovered later, are distillled over and over again to make an incredibly rare and costly perfume called oudh. When I got home I kicked myself for not having bought some of it, but, at the time, many ingredients were new to me, and in Morocco I was only just beginning to grasp the peculiar and unlikely conditions in which some scents are born.

Oudh, the Sinking Perfume

AGARWOOD OIL, ALOESWOOD, OR GAHARU OIL, FORMS WHEN THE *AQUILARIA* tree is wounded. The tree grows in the jungles of the Far East, in Vietnam, China, Malaysia, Cambodia, Thailand and Indonesia, and when, for instance, a branch breaks off, the tree reacts by producing a resin to protect the damaged wood. The sticky brown resin then sinks into the tree, and local people regularly tap the trunks of *Aquilaria* trees to gather it. They knock the trunks with a tool, and if the tree contains the resin it makes a particular sound. Gaharuwood is still often obtained from *Aquilaria* trees in secret rituals which women are not allowed to attend, and gaharu oil–filled wood is so heavy that it sinks in water, which is how it got its name: the "sinking perfume."

Once the resin has been tapped it is soaked in water for a long time before it is distillled into an essential oil known as oudh. Oudh gives off an almond–sweet smell and has been compared to ➤

> a blend of sandalwood and ambergris. The older the wood and the more mature the resin, the more delicious the oudh smells. It is sacrosanct in the Muslim world: pilgrims bring it back from Mecca, and it is an extremely expensive and precious perfume. It costs £3,000 to make one little bottle, and so, commercially, it is not economical to produce. Also the *Aquilaria* tree is threatened with extinction: many of the trees have been cut down and, as far as I know, there are no national replanting programs.

As we approached the Ourika valley I looked at the orange sellers by the road, surrounded by pyramids of oranges and necklaces of figs, and I fell into thinking about oranges and their oils. The custom of piercing cloves into the skins of oranges began as an antiplague device—spiced oranges kept pests and the stench of stinking streets at bay. These simple pomanders were the inspiration for the decorative *pommes d'ambre* (pomanders) that Fabergé and Floris produce today.

Essential oils from the citrus tribe are usually cold-pressed, like olive oil, employing the expression method for which a special cylinder shaped like a drum is used. One hundred or so fruits can be thrown into the drum and spun around so that its blades act rather like a juicer. Before such machines existed, a leather glove called an *écuelle*, which was inlaid with pumice and spikes, was used to pierce and squeeze the peel with one hand into a sponge held by the other. The liquid in the sponge was then squeezed into a bottle which was immediately stoppered. The essential oil from citrus fruits is prone to rapid oxidation when exposed to light, so it must be stored in a cold, dark place.

Otto, or essential oil of lemons, is particularly lovely when blended with caraway, cloves and rosemary. Lemon is not much in fashion at the moment, but lime and grapefruit are in vogue, especially in men's colognes. Lime is even used in Coca-Cola, along with nutmeg and cinnamon. I find it amusing to think that one of the world's most popular fizzy drinks uses age-old exotic spices in its recipe.

A pure essential oil also oozes from the zest of the Portuguese sweet orange. The sheer abundance of oil in the peel is obvious when you pinch a piece of peel next to a candle and a spurt erupts and lights up. After the otto has been rasped from the zest, the leftovers from the fruit are cut and mixed with bran and fed to cows. This yields a fine orange-infused latte, the delights of which have yet to be exploited by Starbucks. The famous Lisbon water is made of otto of orange peel, citron zest and a little rose oil, while bergamot mixed with grape spirit is added to these ingredients to make Eau de Portugal.

When the orange flowers are macerated, the oil is extracted using volatile solvents. This product ends up as an absolute called *fleurs d'oranger*. Years ago the blossoms were infused in fat to make a pomatum which was then digested in gallons of rectified spirits. Traditionally *fleurs d'oranger* is a superlative citrus oil, with the strongest resemblance to the smell of the orange flower itself. However, when the orange flowers are distillled with water you get the essential oil or otto known as neroli. The neroli oil that comes from the flowers of the *Citrus aurantium* is the finest quality and is called "sweet neroli" or "neroli petale." The next grade is neroli bigaradi, or bitter neroli, from the blossoms of the bitter bigarade tree.

The residue of the water arising from the distilllation yields yet another citrus category: a delicate and diffuse orange flower water; it's wonderful stuff to splash on the skin as a tonic. Not long ago every self-respecting washstand had a bottle of orange water standing on it. It was thought to cure many conditions, including indigestion, spasms, convulsions, palpitations, anxiety, nervous colic and hysteria. When you step over the threshold of a Moroccan house you will be sprayed with orange flower water, which carries about 5 percent of the actual essential oil. And in this part of the world people often use orange water (and rosewater) in recipes, especially in desserts. According to an eighteenth-century recipe from the first British perfumer, Charles Lilly, just three sugar lumps soaked in Roman bergamot immersed in 15 gallons of water is sufficient to make orange water.

As we traveled we kept a lookout for storks—at least Stephen did—because Dr. Belkamel had told us that storks perched on the tops of his gateposts. But until Stephen spotted one I'd thought Dr. Belkamel had meant ornamental storks. Obviously he hadn't; even the ones on his gateposts were real! After lunch we sat under a canopy overlooking acres of fields of cultivated flowers and settled down for a lesson in aromatherapy.

Dr. Belkamel told us that in a couple of years' time he would be ready to make perfumes from his flower crops, but that he was still working on the chemistry of essential oils. He had five ambience perfumes (room scents) with bases of thyme, mint and sage, and when he sprayed the scent around us it smelled quite natural, as if we were in an herb garden.

The Fragrant Pharmacy, or Aromatherapy

IN THE 1920S RENE-MAURICE GATTEFOSSE DISCOVERED THAT essential oils could penetrate the skin through the blood and lymphatic systems. He coined the term *aromatherapie*, and his book of that name, published in 1937, examined the antimicrobial effects of oils. Since then work with aromatic oils has been called aromatherapy.

It is said that Gattefosse conclusively proved that oils contain therapeutic properties when he burned his hand in a laboratory explosion and then plunged it into a bowl of lavender oil. Others in the laboratory were amazed at the speed of the healing process on his hand, proving that lavender is the most curative of oils for burns and wounds.

All oils are natural antiseptics, and some are antibiotic, antiviral, antiinflammatory or antibacterial; some are stimulant and others are sedative. Oils are collected in different seasons; for instance, pepper oil is extracted from unripe berries; coriander oil when the fruit is ripe; and sandalwood—which is becoming increasingly rare—can be extracted only when the tree is more than thirty years old.

It is a popular misconception that aromatherapy is a relatively new form of treatment and/or a fad. All the ancient civilizations used essential oils, not just for anointing themselves but also as palliatives for pain and as mood enhancers. Traces of cedarwood, clove, nutmeg and cinnamon have been found impregnated in mummies' bandages.

Indian ayurvedic medicine and aromatic massage are three thousand years old. The use of oils spread to Greece and Rome, and around the time of Ovid, when Jesus was born, Rome had as many perfume shops as Greece. Petronius wrote, "Wives are out of fashion, mistresses are in; rose leaves are dated; now cinnamon is the thing."

Hippocrates advocated that, "The way to health is to have an aromatic bath and scented massage every day." During a plague he urged Athenians to burn aromatic oils to protect them from infection, and there are many treatises by ancient physicians and botanists, such as Marestheus, Pliny and Theophrastus, on herbal medicine. The consensus was that the best recipe for health was to apply sweet scents to the brain. Knowledge of oils and their properties was gathered over thousands of years, and, in the eleventh century, a Persian physician and philosopher called Avicenna discovered distilllation and the healing properties of oils.

In the sixteenth and seventeenth centuries several books on aromatherapy were written, often containing advice that is still followed 400 years later. We know today, for instance, that eucalyptus oil can prevent viruses from spreading, just as the famous sixteenth-century English herbalist, Nicholas Culpeper, wrote: "The oil drawn from the leaves and flowers [of eucalyptus] is of sovereign help. Touch the temples and nostrils with two or three drops for all diseases of the brain."

Herbalists passed their knowledge down from generation to

> generation right into the eighteenth century, but then herbalism was eventually replaced by new chemical drugs and was not reinstated until Gattefosse burned his hand in the early twentieth century.

Dr. Belkamel took me on a tour of his aromatic garden. It had been laid out with the flower beds shaped like drops of oil, while the paths curled around in great sweeping serpentine curves. There was a little bed of fragile purple crocuses full of yellow saffron on their stamens, or stigmas, and there were also several types of basil, because Dr. Belkamel wanted to discover which variety contained the best molecules. He had been growing and researching sage for six years—it neutralizes the smell of sweat—in an attempt to perfect a deodorant, and he was cultivating different kinds of *Iris fiorentina* for their roots, which yield the precious orris, or iris, butter—a viscous substance used as a fixative in perfumery. The ubiquitous mint grew in abundance, but because water was scarce the garden looked vulnerable. Dr. Belkamel said that there had been eight years of drought.

Next morning we headed toward the lower slopes of the Atlas Mountains, past juniper, ash, oak and Atlantic cedar forests and golden drifts of broom. The smell was intoxicating until the forests gave way to scrub and bare mountainsides, crowned by the strangest, almost supernatural-looking clouds. The road got narrower, becoming treacherous as we climbed higher and the hairpin bends became more frequent and alarming. Far below, silver threads of rivers meandered through miniature valleys.

Farther up the mountains we found primitive mud villages

with threshing floors; incongruously, they had satellite dishes on the roofs. Women were doing their laundry in the streams, leaving the washing to dry on the lower slopes of the mountains, forming giant patchwork quilts. Old women walked along the road bent double carrying goats on their shoulders, while the unveiled younger ones had lighter loads—their babies wrapped in scarves tied to their backs.

Eventually, having crossed the perilous Atlas Mountain passes, we stopped in a valley of orange groves to watch the aromatic harvest. The perfume of orange blossoms stole up on me in waves, and the voices of the gatherers pulsed in the air. As I watched them I began to appreciate fully the labor involved in culling the oil from the trees. The blossoms were deftly plucked by women and children, who stood on ladders and dropped the blossoms onto sacking spread out below them beneath the orange trees. The blossoms were collected and put into shallow baskets; then the ladders and sacking were moved on to the next tree and the picking resumed.

Following the wadi (valley or water course) and the pastures, we drove on to the pre-Sahara of desert plateaux and steppe land, bereft of any vegetation save a desert fringe of mauve statice. In the distance we could see the Oued Dadès River, but the land around it was parched. We approached Ouarzazate along avenues bordered by feathery tamarisks. Ouarzazate is a frontier town on the edge of the Sahara, which the Moroccans call the "other sea." It is a *Beau Geste* sort of place, a colonial garrison town built by the French in the 1920s.

After hours in the heat of the car, poor Tarquin started to get agitated and began to whimper. I had terrible pangs of guilt as

I wondered why on earth I had brought my little son on such a long and arduous journey. It was weeks since he'd eaten a recognizable—to him—meal. But he soon cheered up when I found him some yogurt and dates and, my guilt assuaged, I thought perhaps he might make a traveler like me.

I mulled over what Dr. Belkamel had told me about the distillation of orange blossoms. He'd said that a skilled picker can pick 20 kilograms of flowers in a day, but that the flowers must be picked on a sunny day, not when it is wet. Wet flowers produce an inferior oil. Also, care must be taken to exclude the leaves from the gathered blossoms because they impart a harsh note to the eventual oil. He told me that some pickers simply resort to shaking the trees or beating the blossoms down with sticks, but this results in a cruder oil and less money for the pickers.

Once the blossoms have been gathered they are spread on sheets and turned over every now and again to stop them from fermenting overnight, before they are distilled. Most neroli oil is distilled in modern stills which hold about 700 liters of water and are charged with 300 kilograms of flowers. The flowers need to float freely in boiling water and must not be steamed, otherwise they stick together and the steam forms channels through the agglutinated mass, escaping without coming into contact with the flowers. It usually works out that about 1 liter of orange flower water is produced from 1 kilogram of charged blossoms in the distilllation process. This, in turn, yields 1 milliliter of neroli oil. The precious liquid neroli gold floats on top of the orange flower water as a yellowish slick and can easily be separated off in a serpentine flask.

A year or two ago, when I was "grazing" in the Harrods perfumery department, wandering aimlessly from counter to counter, unable to find anything I liked, I came across Serge Lutens scents. They were erotic, exotic and pungent, and immediately conjured up the way I imagined that Arabian scents, hundreds of years ago, smelled. Later I learned that Lutens lived in Marrakech and that the source of his inspiration had been the smells of the souk and the attars of the Arab world.

I wanted to find out how he made his scents, but everyone I asked about him was deeply skeptical that I would ever meet him because he is so reclusive. But, just when I had more or less given up hope, a call came through on my mobile as we crossed a mountain pass in the Atlas on our way back toward Marrakech. Lutens said he would be able to see me at the Mamounia Hotel, and I was only mildly disappointed that the meeting wasn't going to take place in his medina house.

Serge Lutens is a slight man, and he is both mercurial and inscrutable. He has a mordant wit and a grave courtesy, and was by turns amused and serious during the interview. He wore a black tie and a black woolen waistcoat despite the soaring temperatures outside, and he quizzed me, through my interpreters Cyril and Cécile Commargue, about why I was writing a book on perfume. He said it must be like writing a history of mankind. But I explained that I'd narrowed the field by simply going in search of the ingredients for my own bespoke scent.

He told me that he'd arrived in Morocco in 1968 with Christian Dior. At that time he'd had no intention of making perfumes—not until the day he went into the souk and smelled all the scents. He said they were overwhelming: the aroma of absinthe as he sipped it; the perfume from a geranium as he sniffed it; the odors from a perfume shop; and the sage, cloves, cumin and saffron from the sacks full of spices. He found the aromas in the souks were a revelation, and the seeds of his Ambre Sultan and Cuir Mauresque were sown that day. Lutens's scents evoke a mood: they capture the Moroccan smells of mint, orange, cedar and musk, and the stronger, heartier notes of rose and jasmine, anchored by sandalwood.

One of his Eaux Anciennes, a *fleur d'oranger*, is made from white orange flower petals with other flowers, including tuberose and jasmine. Cuir Mauresque, moorish leather, is a mélange of amber, musk, styrax (an aromatic gum) and nutmeg and is dominated by the zest of mandarin, which I thought was probably the same Algerian mandarin that I had found in the souk. Orange flower is a heart note in his Tubereuse Criminelle, which is called that because of the inordinate amount of tuberose that is used—so much that it is almost medicinal in its dosage. I remembered Frédéric Malle saying that he and Serge Lutens were the only true *hauts parfumeurs* in the world now, and they are my favorites: the most sophisticated and complex scents that I have come across.

Another of Lutens' perfumes, Black Datura, has a base of Arabic gum with the balm of myrrh and bitter almond, tonka bean, musk, Chinese osmanthus (a small white flower indigenous to Japan), heliotrope, mandarin bark, lemon blossoms, tuberose, vanilla, coconut and apricot. When you first smell it the mandarin bark and the lemon blossoms give it a deliciously strong citrus note.

Lutens told me that he had made a perfume from absinthe called Sheba, and that, as he watched the way the Moroccans perfumed everything, from their mint tea to their clothes and from their houses to their food, he had begun to think quite differently about perfume and thus about the making of scent. He told me that the Moroccans had made him an essential oil of cedarwood, which, I got the impression, made him very proud. And he told me more about the famous sinking perfume, oudh (see page 63), which he said he used in his own personal collection of perfumes.

Lutens said that Morocco grows the best ingredients for perfume and is the biggest producer of essential oils and raw materials. But that is the paradox of Morocco: you can't find much in the way of actual bottled perfume. It is usually imported from other countries like Saudi Arabia and Pakistan. In Morocco they burn essences to make entire rooms perfumed, and very rich families actually eat perfume: they put a grain of musk in hot milk in the mornings and drink it, so that their whole body smells of scent from within—the body creates the perfume with just a *petit grain* of musk. Lutens also told me that it was the ancient Chinese who invented the exquisite custom of feeding courtesans bland food laced with musk, so that during love-making their consorts could enjoy the scent of their bodies as they sweated pure perfume.

When musk was introduced to the Arabs by the Persians, the Arabs thought it was a kind of salt and used it for meat stews. But it became highly esteemed as a potent scent in which to soak silken robes, to rub into the skin and even to mix in mortar for muscadine walls. Perfume, in the Arab world, is ornamental, like jewelry, and it has never been completely natural. The Arabs practiced alchemy and developed chemicals to mix with perfume.

Beautiful perfumed roses were cultivated in Granada; they even had an indigo rose and they invented L'Eau de Rose there. They also had very sophisticated methods of distilllation. However, re-creating old scents is difficult because, as Lutens explained, the secrets of those ancient perfumes were written down in formulas and recipes that were kept in the libraries and archives in Granada by the Moors and, sadly, all the records were destroyed by the Spanish when they, in their turn, defeated the occupying Moors. As I left Lutens, my mind was full of thoughts of musk-swilling aristocrats, large pieces of wood billowing incense, moonlit groves of jasmine grown in the king's gardens and indigo roses.

A flock of storks rose above us as we left the Mamounia and headed north toward Fès. The sunset was dramatically golden as it filtered through the tamarisks and, by the next morning, we were driving through the cedar forests of Azrou. Dr. Belkamel had told me to contact Monsieur Rashdi once I reached Azrou. He met us at a petrol station in his tracksuit. He was handsome with soft brown eyes, shy and unusually tall for a Moroccan. We followed him out of town to a derelict warehouse, passing donkeys and goats tethered to trees. When we arrived I thought it the most unlikely place to find £30,000 worth of oak moss.

La mousse de cèdre, or *mousse de chêne*, sounds like a delicious pudding, but it is in fact a moss that grows on the forest floor and around the bark and trunks of oak and cedar trees. The cedar tree itself yields lovely, aromatic oil, while the moss is redolent of seasons of compressed vegetation and the scents of the damp forest floor. Oak and cedar mosses, which grow throughout Morocco and the eastern Mediterranean region, are used as a fixative in perfumes; the earthy scent of cedar moss haunts all chypre perfumes, which are strong, powdery and spicy.

In the courtyard of the ancient, ruined stone warehouse was a huge compressor. It looked like a medieval battering ram, but it served its purpose well. It takes one harvester one day to pick about 50 kilograms of moss, and they pick by hand, all year round. The moss is gathered in the woods up in the hills behind the warehouse and brought down in horse-drawn carts, put into the battering-ram compressor and pressed into 50-kilogram blocks (about the size of a regular cardboard box), which are weighed and stored. Then it is shipped to Grasse by truck, where the first phase of extraction with solvents takes place in the factories of companies such as Robertet, Charabot and Charvet, who pay about €25 for each compressed block of moss. After this, it is often transported all the way through the Balkans, for instance to the Robertet factory in Turkey, for the second extraction process. Finally, the mosses are shipped back to Grasse and incorporated into finished scents as fixatives.

In the inner sanctum of the warehouse, a huge storeroom under lock and key, towers of compressed bales of moss soared up to the roof. Monsieur Rashdi gave us bags of gray-green, curly, seaweed-frilly moss, and he told us that he also had a factory where the aromatic oils from thyme, verbena, oregano and clary sage were distilled. I wished we had time to visit it.

We drove up to the fragrant cedar forests to see where the moss grew. It was everywhere, like a lawn beneath our feet, strewn all over the stone walls in wisps and hanging in the leaves of the trees like fragrant cobwebs. The air was powdery and narcotic. I noticed the workers were calm and contented. One of them made us mint tea while the others shoveled moss on to wheelbarrows and Tarquin got a ride on one. We walked along narrow paths through the forest to find the moss growing in abundance. Coming to a clearing full of conical, wickerwork huts, I thought they looked like something out of a fairy tale, but I soon discovered that the moss was stored in the huts during the day's gathering.

The sun was low in the sky and the woody moss smelled of hay on a hot summer's day, or of an aromatic bonfire gently smoking, but also of verdant coolness as it was torn from the forest floor. The mossy atmosphere reminded me of old libraries and the mustiness of ancient, leather-bound books, and then I had a euphoric memory of the days after Tarquin was born. It didn't take me long to work out the association. I'd spent a long time in bed, breast-feeding, and my bedside table is made of cedar wood.

Chypre

CHYPRE, WHICH IS PRONOUNCED "SHEEPRA," ORIGINALLY CAME from Cyprus, the birthplace of Venus. (*Chypre* is French for Cyprus.) It was a blend of styrax, which gave it a sweaty smell, sweet rush, which emits a bitter and spicy scent, and a balsam amber. During the Crusades, when Richard the Lionheart assumed the title King of Cyprus, a famed Eau de Chypre was brought back to Europe. People probably smelled the Crusaders coming home before they saw them, because chypre is one of the most potent odors ever made; at that time it was made of, approximately, a pint of musk, half a pint of vanilla, some tonka bean, orris and ambergris, and 2 pints of esprit rose triple. (This

> recipe comes from *The Art of Perfumery* by G. W. Septimus Piesse, 1857.) Over time chypre has evolved into a more subtle mélange characterized by bergamot, patchouli and oak moss.
>
> François Coty refined and revived chypre when he launched Cyprus in 1917. Then the Corsican perfumer called it "an olfactory oak-moss bouillon." It also contained orange, spices and geranium and, according to Coty, it was much loved by women he called "racy."

We drove on toward Fès for my last Moroccan scent mission, to go to the royal bigarade orange orchards. The hills outside Fès looked like stripy Berber carpets, with plots of plowed land alternating with fallow. Drifts of narcissi, chamomile like snow, and miles of delicate asphodel formed carpets of perfume. The roads got narrower, and a flock of a rare breed of sheep that looked like mythical beasts blocked our way.

The Roman ruins of Volubilis appeared beyond a deep gorge on a fertile plain of olive groves. We sat by the triumphal arch, and Tarquin listened to the echo around the ruins, screeching with delight at the sound of his own voice coming back to him, while the clouds raced above us. As we approached the ruins of Lixus—believed to be the ancient site of the Garden of the Hesperides—we breathed in the scented air and it had a near-sedative effect. There were miles of orange groves, and the aroma of their blossoms was heady and sweet. The avenues of orange groves stretched away toward the horizon, casting long scented shadows in the evening light which gave the groves a remote and magical quality. In the distance I watched a Berber woman in flowing robes cantering sidesaddle on her horse through the groves. I walked between the trees smelling the sharp notes from the blossoms as they effervesced in the air.

I had come in search of petitgrain and neroli because I knew that I wanted a mysterious, haunting note in my bespoke scent, although I wanted the initial impression to be of the assertive, astringent bittersweet nature of the fabled golden "apples" of the Hesperides. In the end I had decided on neroli because it gives the impression of fullness and it is the kind of smell that permeates everything with which it comes into contact. It gives off a sense of opulence, heavy and rich, but at the same time it is fresh. And I had chosen the citron petitgrain in contrast for its zing and cool iciness.

In Morocco I had discovered a land impregnated with scent, from the fragrant forests of oak moss to the miles of orange groves and the myriad mingled smells of the medinas. The Moroccans know how to interpret the mysteries of perfume: they consider the making of perfume a path to the soul, but it is also part of daily life and ritual—like the centuries-old customs of burning incense and embalming the dead with musk. The Moroccans cure illness with oils and unguents, and on the street corners hawkers wave wands of incense under your nose, while the aristocrats drink musk milk shakes for breakfast.

We took the night ferry from Tangier. At the port the customs smelled my oak moss suspiciously—I was sure they thought it was kef. As they took the bags away I protested that it was only *la mousse de chêne*, and, after making us wait for a nail-biting hour, we were finally allowed to board the boat for Bilbao with our bags of pungent oak moss safely on board.

CHAPTER FOUR

DAMASK ROSE

Turkey

Venus, night and day. Daughter of Jove…
All the corpse o'erlaid with roseate oil,
Ambrosial.

HOMER

O F ALL FLOWERS, THE ROSE IS THE MOST UNIVERSALLY loved, especially for its scent, and this has been true since the dawn of civilization. In Homer's *Iliad* Aphrodite anoints Hector's dead body with ambrosial rose oil; chaplets of *Rosa sancta* have been found on mummies; and roses have decorated Cretan vases since 1600 B.C.

Herodotus wrote that King Midas introduced a many-petaled scented rose to Macedonia in the seventh century B.C. Theophrastus, an early Greek philosopher and botanist (372–287 B.C.), describes roses with many petals in his *De historia plantarum* (*A History of Plants*) and discusses the advantages of propagation by cuttings over the more usual cultivation from seeds. In one of his many perfume recipes, Theophrastus recommends that the scent of roses is best absorbed by sesame oil because of its viscid nature. He also writes that rose petals impart a sweet taste to wines.

The cult of the rose has reached both the heights of extravagance and the lows of decadence. The Persians had a passion for the rose; they perfected the art of distillling rosewater and they (and the Sybarites) even stuffed their mattresses with rose petals, so giving rise to the expression "Life is a bed of roses." The Sybaritic Emperor Heliogabalus is known to have bathed in rose wine and absinthe.

The Romans were equally fond of the rose, to the point of obsession. The Emperor Nero's rose banquets were celebrated to the sound and scent of fountains of rosewater; the ceiling of the dining hall was hung with rotating discs which scattered perfume and petals down over his guests; rose petals were strewn in fragrant carpets on the floors and cushions were stuffed with roses; the guests wore garlands of roses in their crowns and around their necks.

So enamored of roses were the Romans that Horace worried that the craze would cause farmers to neglect their vineyards and olive groves. Pliny describes the decadence of the Romans who sprinkled rose petals and rosewater on their food, and Virgil in his *Georgics*, Horace in his *Odes* and Pliny the Elder in his *Historia Naturalis* all describe and praise *Rosa damascena*, *Rosa centifolia*, *Rosa alba* and the twice-flowering *Rosa bifera* which grew in Roman gardens.

Roses also played an important part in the magic of antiquity. In the *Golden Ass* by Apuleius, Lucius is turned into an ass, and the only way he can return to his human condition is to eat roses. During a rite he is ordered to devour a crown of red roses, after which he metamorphoses back into a human.

Early Christians disapproved of roses and their inherent air of luxury: they were a reminder of Roman paganism. But, slowly, the rose transformed from pagan symbol to become the emblem of the Virgin Mary. The rose symbolizes love, and many religions consider it sacred. The Virgin Mary was sometimes known as the Mystic Rose, and the rosary was originally made of one hundred dried roses threaded on a string; later on the roses were replaced by precious stones. So the term "rosary" not only refers to rose gardens but to the chain used to say Ave Marias and to worship the Virgin Mary. In Avila in Spain, Carmelite nuns still make rosaries from dried roses.

Avicenna, the great Arabian philosopher and physician who lived between A.D. 980 and 1037, observed that roses were widely cultivated in Syria and then distillled for rosewater. He describes the damask rose as the Roman commercial rose, the rose of Paestum, *Rosa bifera* or autumn damask. By the twelfth century the damask rose was growing in Spain, no doubt flourishing in the exotic Mogul gardens in the Alhambra at Granada. The damask rose was also brought back to Europe from Damascus, in the form of cuttings, by the Crusaders.

Perfume, and roses in particular, pervaded all aspects of the Islamic world. The Arabs invented rosewater, and in the hammams (Turkish baths) clay soaps scented with rose oil were used, as they still are today. We know that thirty thousand bottles of rosewater were delivered to the treasury in Baghdad from Faristan (the center of rose production on the Gulf of Persia) in A.D. 810. Arabic and Persian rosewater was sold from as early as 1381 in the infirmary of the convent of Santa Maria Novella in Florence. Rose otto was first mentioned by Geronimo Rossi in Ravenna in 1574 when he found droplets of it on rosewater. Father Catron, in his *History of the Moguls*, testifies that a further discovery was made when, in 1612, the Persian Grand Mogul Emperor Djihanguyr filled the canals of his garden with rosewater. When one of the princesses was out rowing she noticed a strange scum on the surface of the canal, which, when skimmed off, was found to be a stunning new perfume. (The scum was, of course, caused by the heat from the sun separating the water from the essential rose oil. It was skimmed off with the blade of a sword lily.)

The Origins of Perfume

THE ORIGINS OF PERFUME ARE AS LAYERED AS THE "NOTES" IN A classic scent. Some say scent was discovered in Mesopotamia, others that it originated in Arabia, which is still known as the "Land of Perfumes." The earliest records date from Egypt, in 2000 B.C., when incense was offered at the burial of mummies and perfume was believed to be the sweat of the gods.

So, when man first discovered scent he used it as an offering: aromatic gums were burned on altars and the word "perfume" (from the Latin *per*—through—and *fummum*—smoke) aptly evokes its earliest use, but it wasn't long before men and women began anointing themselves with unguents. Chinese maidens gathered aromatic grasses for fertility rites, and Pharaonic courtiers wore wigs perfumed with unguents of lilies. In Kodo, the Japanese art of perfumery (which was introduced to Japan by the Chinese in A.D. 500), the main ingredients were cloves and nutmeg blended with sandalwood, musk, fennel and the prized agarwood.

The first record of the secular use of perfume appears in a passage that describes a "chest of perfumes" that accompanied Alexander the Great on his campaigns in the fourth century B.C. The first record of trade in perfume—in the form of incense—is in Genesis, when Joseph's brothers sold him to merchants who arrived bearing "spicery, balm and myrrh down to Egypt." It is said that Cleopatra immersed herself in clouds of incense, while Alexander the Great was said to smell naturally of musk—hence his attraction to women. ➤

Walls were sprayed with scent, and musk was often mixed with mortar to make muscadine walls in the hammams. In Mecca, the mosques were drenched in perfume. When the Temple of Minerva at Elis was built, the plaster was mixed with saffron and milk so that—even today—if you wet your thumb with saliva and rub it onto the plaster it will give off the taste and smell of saffron.

The *Ramayana*, an ancient Indian epic, recounts that nobles were perfumed with sandalwood and warriors carried perfumed powders as part of their battle kit. The perfumer, or *attarwalla*, was a pillar of the Indian community, and effigies of Hindu gods were washed down with musk, sandalwood and agarwood water.

Much of our knowledge of early Arab perfumes comes from a book of perfume recipes by Yakub al-Kindi (A.D. 803–870) called *The Book of Perfume Chemistry and Distillation*. In seventh-century Persia, under the Abbasid caliphate which ruled until the thirteenth century, perfume making was refined into an art. The caliphs who controlled Persia traded with India, the East Indies and China, bringing back new materials from which to make perfume. Baghdad became the center of the seventh-century perfume trade—there were fifty perfume shops and some fifteen hundred public baths in the city—and Arab perfumers traded all over the Arab empire. Returning Crusaders brought back Arab perfumes to the Christian world, and, as late as the Elizabethan era, Shakespeare's Lady Macbeth bitterly complained that "All the perfumes of Arabia" could not wash her hands of the blood of the murdered King Duncan.

The Persians invented the distilllation process, and the philosopher Avicenna was one of the first to apply the principles of chemistry to perfume and preserve the volatile aromas of flowers by distilllation. By the thirteenth century Persia was producing most of the raw materials for scent. These were exported to Venice, from where they, together with exotic merchandise and spices, were traded with the Middle and Far East.

The enduring quality of Egyptian perfumes was recognized when Tutankhamen's tomb was excavated in 1922. The archaeologists found oily unguents that, after three thousand years sealed from the elements, still gave off a sublime smell. The most significant of these perfumes was the Egyptian sacrificial oil called kyphi (thought to be spikenard, whose literal translation is "Welcome to the Gods"). Pliny thought kyphi allayed anxiety and made dreams vivid. The priests made kyphi from sweetflag (odorous roots similar to iris roots that smell of aniseed), aromatic grasses, a tree resin, cassia, cinnamon, peppermint, juniper, mimosa, henna and raisins, all of which were steeped in wine for days with a mixture of honey and terebinth, a resin to which myrrh was added. Plutarch also records a recipe for kyphi which includes twenty-two ingredients: it must have had an overpowering intensity.

The Roman *unguentum Parthicum Rhodicum* was described by Dioscorides in his *Materia Medica* as a pomander of roses. This is his recipe:

Of fresh roses, beginning to fade but without any dampness, forty dragons; of Indian nard [spikenard], ten dragons; of myrrh, six dragons. When all these have been pounded, they must be shaped into little balls and then laid up in jars of clay and left to dry. Two dragons of costus [an aromatic northern Indian incense] and as much again of iris of Illyria may also be added.

The Florentine Medici family encouraged research into the medicinal properties of plants, and Italian perfumers increased their production of scent compositions for the rich and mercantile classes, while Italian aristocrats also invented new scents. The Medici and the Dukes of Ferrara collected alembics, made essences and aromatic waters and hundreds of recipes were exchanged.

"Frangipani"—made by the old Roman family of the same name—which is a powder of every known spice added to orris root, with a touch of civet, became popular when Mercutio Frangipani, a learned botanist, sailed to the New World with Columbus and, as they approached the shores of Antigua, he breathed in the delicious scent of the sweet-smelling flowers that were called *Plumeria alba*. They were subsequently renamed *Frangipani*, after Mercutio, who distillled the flowers and made the perfume long-lasting with rectified spirits of wine.

Perfumers were also spice sellers and alchemists, and perfume was bought from apothecaries. There were hundreds of therapeutic perfumes with as many as sixty ingredients each, which were burned as incense. During the plague in Venice in

1504, Venetians applied damask water made from a dozen aromatics together with civet and musk; and the Italian alchemist Girolamo Ruscelli made a perfumed oil for the hair and for beards from rosewater, damask rose oil, cloves, cinnamon, gum Arabic, musk and civet. In the sixteenth century, when the clergy and doctors ordered the closure of public baths because they thought that baths encouraged the spread of epidemics, bodily smells had to be counteracted by perfume. Courtesans carried sponges impregnated with musk, amber and civet between their thighs and under their armpits and their garters were soaked in scent. Perfumed sachets were sewn into their clothes to mask the smell of their unwashed bodies, while rosewater acted as a disinfectant.

In the twenty-first century, we are apt to underestimate the role that scent and incense played at a time when foul odors pervaded the world and clouds of sweet-smelling smoke were required to mask them. As recently as the eighteenth and nineteenth centuries London's air was foul and the gentry carried scented handkerchiefs and pomanders to disguise the smells. Burning incense was often used to scent clothes, spices were used to scent bedding and were burned in houses to drive out reptiles and pests. And through the ages scent has always had as much to do with sexual attraction as with rituals and rites. Plutarch said that most men would make love to their wives only if they were powdered with spices and scented with ointments.

Perfume has also always possessed curative powers. In ancient times, frankincense and myrrh were known to have fumigating and cleansing properties, and an old Chinese proverb stated that "a perfume is always a medicine." The ancient *Persian Pharmacopoeia* has hundreds of perfumed preparations for healing; narcissus was used to treat melancholia, while Megalium—an ancient Greek perfume made of myrrh oil, sweet rush (which is redolent of sweet basil) and cassia (which resembles cinnamon)—was thought to be good for wounds.

An antidote to poison, prepared for Mithridates of Armenia in about 80 B.C., included thirty-six ingredients. Among them were frankincense, myrrh, cassia, cinnamon, pepper, saffron and ginger mixed with wine and honey. It was said that poultices of spices had a healing effect on wounds and tumors.

The first eau de cologne was made in the seventeenth century by a young Milanese commercial traveler called Paolo Feminis, who eventually settled in Cologne, from where he sold his Aqua Mirabilis. When we think of citrus smells we associate them, rightly, with eau de cologne. Feminis's cologne was a divinely citrus aroma of spirit of rosemary, essences of bergamot, neroli, citrus cedrata (lemon zest) and lemon.

Guerlain opened for business in 1828, and this perfumer's attempts to evoke moods and reproduce atmospheres, especially sensual ones, through scent were revolutionary. In focusing on the philosophy behind the making of perfume, Guerlain changed the way perfume was made, and others followed his ideas. L'Heure Bleue, which is made from roses, iris, musk and vanilla, was inspired by that crepuscular time of day just before sunset, while the bewitching Shalimar conjures up a Mogul garden.

There are over ten thousand species of rose, and there are subtle variations in their scent: no two species emit exactly the same smell. *Rosa arvensis* is myrrh-scented; *Banksian* recalls violets; *Desprez* is fruity; *Eglantine*'s leaves are like jasmine; *Macartnean* smells like apricots; *Marechal Niel* resembles raspberries; *Moschata*, which grows wild in Tunis, is musky; *Muscosa* is moss-scented; *May* recalls cinnamon; *Socrates* is reminiscent of peach; *Souveraine* resembles the melon; and *Unique jaune* emits an odor of hyacinths. The *Rose de Mai*, *Rosa centifolia* and *Rosa damascena* are oil-bearing roses and are used in perfumery. But the damask rose or, as it is also known, the Bulgarian rose, provides the bulk of the world's production of this volatile oil, and Anastasia and I had chosen it as one of the four middle notes in my bespoke scent.

The rose, the undisputed queen of flowers, harbors the richest and most complex of fragrances, some four hundred volatile components making up its inimitable scent. The most common aroma concentrates of rose otto (or rose oil) and rosewater are extracted by steam distilllation, while rose absolute is made by solvent extraction. Rose oil and rose absolute—with its deep, spicy, musky aroma—is used extensively in perfumes of high quality. Both are also used in creams, ointments and lotions. In its unadulterated form the cloying odor is sometimes too strong and does not always appeal, but when rose oil is blended with other ingredients, such as sandalwood, neroli, orris root, patchouli, musk or ambergris, it comes into its own: there is nothing quite like its long-lasting, refined and, sometimes, austere aroma. It takes about 5 tons of rose flowers to produce 1 liter of essential rose oil, but the proportions vary depending upon the potency of the rose flowers—so, for instance, fewer *Rose de Mai* flowers are needed to yield the same amount of oil because its blossoms are so potent.

Fossil evidence and archaeological digs show that roses have existed since prehistoric times. The damask rose is likely to have been flowering as long ago as the Neolithic era in southern Anatolia in Turkey. Over the centuries botanists have attributed lots of common names to this old rose, including York and Lancaster. According to some rosarians, the York and Lancaster roses, which were used as symbols of the Wars of the Roses, are believed to be the parents of today's damask rose.

The damask rose—which gives off a slightly musky smell—is called *Rosa damascena* because it originally came from Damascus but is cultivated most intensively today on the plateaux of Bulgaria and Turkey.

It was therefore to Turkey that Stephen and I went in early June to catch the rose harvest. I decided not to take Tarquin with us because I knew that—just as in Morocco—there would not be much food that he'd happily eat, and I was worried about finding suitable accommodation. So I left him behind, but I missed him.

I love arriving somewhere I've never been before at night and waking up the next morning in a strange land. In the old quarter of Antalya it felt as if we had flown in by magic carpet rather than by charter jet. I threw open the wooden shutters to see old timber Ottoman houses, their balconies adorned with necklaces of peppers and chilies. I breathed in the fragrant scent from gardens of orange trees and I saw narrow cobbled streets, towering minarets and the full-breasted domes of mosques and hammams. The cooing of doves and the clatter of carts broke the silence of an otherwise sleepy Turkish morning.

Venturing from our room we went down to the garden in search of breakfast. The hotel was an old Greek Orthodox town house with a glassed-in veranda. Some tortoises crept around the garden, white rabbits were suspended in cages hanging from the orange trees and we were served olives, melon, feta cheese, apricots, jam and some coffee from a doll's tea set: a little eccentric by British breakfast norms, but delicious.

We wandered around the old quarter of Kaleici until we came to the Roman walls and Hadrian's marble arch: the soffits of the archways had coffers carved with rosettes. Then we had a Turkish bath and, in our altered state, after the steaming and scrubbing, soaking and smoothing, we wandered around the old town, which was eerily empty: there was only a trickle of tourists.

Next morning we left Antalya and the Mediterranean to drive inland. It was then that I felt that the real Turkey began to unfold before us as we climbed the western Anatolian plateau into the rose-growing region of Isparta. Snowcapped mountains appeared in the distance, there were drifts of wildflowers, cornfields covered with a sea of purple larkspur and plantations of opium poppies. Women in pantaloons were hoeing in the fields and, beyond the orchards and plantations, towering rocky outcrops were honeycombed with houses carved into the caves.

Soon we saw the rosebushes stretching out before us. At daybreak in late May and early June, Isparta's rose fields are a flurry of activity as women and children hurry to pick the blooms before the sun hits them. Harvesting has to start before daybreak, at five or even four in the morning, while the dew is still on the petals. The roses are gathered daily so that the buds, which open during the night, retain their freshness. The ephemeral and ethereal smell in the blooms must be caught before the sunshine vaporizes their odor away. A day under the hot sun will destroy their fragrance and leave the petals lifeless.

Picking is very labor-intensive, and even the best pickers have never managed more than 6 kilograms of flowers an hour. Every bloom is picked by hand, without the aid of secateurs, right at the base of the flower. A hectare (2.5 acres) of rosebushes yields 3,000 kilograms (6,600 pounds) of rose petals. As much as a 100 kilograms of freshly picked petals will make only 10 milliliters of essential oil: imagine a laundry basket full of petals yielding 1 milliliter of rose oil. The plucked blooms are placed in willow baskets, which are then emptied into sacks, weighed and rushed to local distillleries before the fugitive smell vanishes in the heat of the coming day. It is a Herculean task.

Damask roses were introduced to Bulgaria by the Ottomans in the seventeenth century. However, the Bulgarian *Rosa damascena* thrived so well and produced a rose oil so superior to its Anatolian cousin that cuttings of the Bulgarian species were brought back to Turkey from Kazanlik in Bulgaria a century later, in 1878, just after the war between Russia and Turkey. New rose plantations were established in Isparta province, where the climate and deep sandy soils are perfect for this oil-bearing rose. The *Kazanlik damask*, which is probably a hybrid of wild *Rosa gallica* and *Rosa phoenicia*, is a highly scented floriferous rose which is perfect for perfume. These damask rose scents are very stable, and the scent from their low-growing shrubs carries on the air for some distance, drawing bees to the flowers for essential pollination.

Today, 90 percent of Turkey's rose fields are in Isparta, stretching from Lake Burdur to Lake Egirdir. However, because Turkey no longer has its own perfume industry, barely a drop of rose oil or rosewater stays in the country; 90 percent of it is shipped straight to Grasse, where it is treated again and sold on to the noses and perfumers. The remaining 10 percent goes to Saudi Arabia, with just a fraction of that being sent to Turkey's capital, Istanbul.

Middle Eastern Perfume-making Traditions

THE PERSIANS HAVE ALWAYS BEEN HIGHLY PERFUMED. ALEXANDER the Great, in his campaigns against the Persian King Darius, recorded that the Persian soldiers carried supplies of scent as part of their battle kit, and rosewater played a great part in festivities. Hosts sprayed their guests with rosewater and invited them to dip their fingers in bowls of rosewater. Servants offered the stronger scents of civet and musk to rub into coiffures and beards, just as we might hand around canapés. To complete the scented gathering, guests were ushered into rooms filled with the gently billowing smoke of ambergris or aloeswood. The rarer the scent— just as, for us, the older the vintage of wine—the better the party.

The first Ottoman perfume factory to produce *kolonya*, the Turkish for cologne, was set up by Ahmet Faruki in 1882. The most widespread kolonya is lemon, but there are regional specialties. ➤

Antalya produces a bittersweet orange kolonya made from the Balikesir white lily; in the Black Sea area a tea-scented kolonya is produced; while in Trabzon they produce an anchovy-scented kolonya which smells like a salade niçoise. And, of course, there is rosewater.

But now that the giants of the French perfume industry have taken over, fewer and fewer Middle Eastern families distill their own rose petals. Until quite recently rose oil production was a cottage industry in Turkey, and the *itir* of roses, from the Turkish word for scent, was made in *imbiks* which are traditional log-fired stills. (These Turkish words themselves derive from the Persian *attar* and Arabic *al-Anbiq*.)

In Turkish the rose absolute, otto, attar or oil is called *Gul yagi*. *Gul suyu* is the name given to the rosewater that arises from the steam, while the name for the actual damask rose is simply *Gul*. But most of the rosewater in Turkey today is synthetic. I was given a bottle of *Gul yagi* which smelled mulchy and rotten-sweet at first, but as it sank into my skin the smell improved and I detected the beginnings of a delectable scent. The *Gul yagi* concrete is treated again with alcohol and transformed into an absolute in Grasse. And in Iran, attar of roses is still prepared for use in the mosques.

The traditional local family distillleries were called *Gulapana*, and a few still exist. *Gulapana* were built near streams or rivers, and housed copper boilers and wooden vats in which kilos of petals and liters of water were distillled over and over again. It was a lengthy, repetitive process which yielded only a few liters of rosewater or otto, and because the method was rather inefficient and produced low-quality oil, state-supported cooperative federations known as *Gulbirliks* were established in the 1950s.

Modern production techniques have been steadily increasing yields to the point where output now exceeds world demand for oil. So the expansion of rose cultivation has been discouraged to keep the prices up. It is estimated that the production of rose oil and concrete from Bulgaria, Turkey, Morocco and, in smaller amounts, France is between 15 and 20 tons a year—a considerable commodity.

We stopped by a lakeside café for breakfast and in the shop found hundreds of bottles of rosewater and kolonya. I bought kolonya and sprayed some on Stephen, who then grabbed the bottle and poured the rest over my head, just as Napoleon, who loved perfume, did every morning. The scent permeated our hot car.

In Turkey there is a charming custom. Wherever you go you are liberally doused with rosewater. No matter how short your bus journey, conductors will spray you with kolonya, and you will be sprayed when leaving a restaurant or a café. This custom dates back to the time when the Persians perfected the art of distillling rosewater.

As we drove on, I craned my neck to stare at the green rose hedges with their masses of pale pink buds. The sun was high in the sky and the fields were deserted. I was trying to focus my zoom lens on them when Stephen asked where exactly we were going. I had been dreading this question, because all I had was a very sketchy map on a faint fax with directions to the rose factory. The names of the nearby towns and villages bore no relation to the names on the map. So I bluffed. I said we had to follow the railway line out of Senirkent and we'd find the factory beside a lake—we would see the big blue "Robertet Turkey" sign. According to the almost illegible map, the factory was just outside the town, but we drove into and out of Senirkent and around the outskirts four times without seeing a lake or a factory.

We gave up, parked the car and found a taxi driver who, on seeing our directions, gesticulated wildly that the factory was a long way back down the road that we had been traveling along. We stopped at the next village for more directions and had coffee in a café full of backgammon players and people playing games of Turkish dominoes. They waved us on back down the Isparta road, where we stopped at a motorway café and rang the factory. They gave some more directions to the waiter, who pointed us on to the right road. Eventually a smiling man in a car roared up to us, sounding his horn, and we followed him.

It was raining when we arrived at the distilllery, and a dusty, earthy smell of rose, reminiscent of potpourri, hung in the damp air. Monsieur Allard, the man who had rescued us, was in Turkey from Robertet Grasse to oversee the rose harvest. His number two was a Turkish man in his late fifties called Mr. Timour. They gave us supper of bean salad, beef kebabs, pasta, honeyed baklava and apple tea while lightning and thunder flashed and trundled across the Anatolian plateau. After supper Monsieur Allard showed us around the distilllery.

In a building the size of an aircraft hangar, a sea of damasked (flecked with white spots) pink petals had been laid out to air. For one ecstatic moment life really was a "bed of roses": I longed to throw myself onto them and luxuriate in their heady, intoxicating scent. The men tossed the petals with wooden pitchforks and as the petals fluttered in the air they looked as if they were performing a dance.

It struck me as ironic that something as romantic as the rose—symbolic of friendship, pleasure, pain, beauty, love and war—should begin its long journey from flower to essence to scent bottle on a gritty factory floor. I watched robust bare-chested workers beaded with sweat shovel petals into steaming stills, boiling cauldrons and vats of noxious chemicals to capture the musky smell of the roses while they were still drenched with fragrant dew. There is probably no organic matter which so rapidly absorbs oxygen as a mass of freshly gathered roses, and for this reason the journey from field to factory must be *vite, vite, vite,* as Monsieur Allard said, clapping his hands: *"Le plus vite, le plus meilleur."* The workers were to continue the grueling task of shoveling the petals into sacks and loading them into the extraction units all night long; it seemed a Sisyphean task. I thrust my hand into one of the sacks. It was a delicious sensation; the petals felt like ripples of satin and silk.

In the warm, steamy air we climbed a spiral staircase to a mezzanine above the distillation vats as the vapors rose the way they do in a Turkish bath. We inspected glass demijohns of translucent rose oil which reminded me of liquid gold, and it occurred to me that this precious oil probably was worth more than its weight in gold.

The Language of Flowers

IN THE EARLY EIGHTEENTH CENTURY THE TURKISH SECRET *Language of Flowers* was introduced to Europe by Lady Mary ➤

Wortley Montague, wife of the British Ambassador to Constantinople. She brought the book back to England in 1716. It was also translated into French as *La Langue des Fleurs,* and was printed with over eight hundred floral designs. A later English edition, published in Victorian times, was toned down because of the sexual content of much of the language.

Perfume, especially the scent of roses, is connected with desire and romance. The smell of a loved one's perfume stirs the odoriferous wings of desire and helps us fall in love. The damask rose especially represents love, and its scent is often used in perfumes because it is a sexual attractant. In Victorian times, when it was considered improper for young men to express such feelings in direct words, the language of flowers was substituted, and certain flowers were invested with particular meanings. Suitors sent flowers not only for their beauty but for the silent message they delivered.

A white rosebud represents a heart ignorant of love; a thornless rose represents early attachment; a Provence rose implies "My heart is in flames"; and a Christmas rose conveys the message "Relieve my anxiety." There are combinations, too. The giving of a Moss rosebud (which derives its name from the mosslike growth that covers the buds) and a piece of myrtle is a confession of love. The person to whom the confession is being made may answer "yes" by bringing the petals to the lips, or "no" by picking the petals off.

Some meanings are fairly obvious: for instance, the tuberose denotes dangerous pleasures because it has a carnal quality; witch hazel suggests a spell; the daisy implies innocence; and the words attributed to the dandelion are "I am very cheap."

The following morning carts loaded with sacks of freshly picked rose petals arrived at Robertet, drawn by donkeys or by tractors. Entire families, including babies strapped to their mothers' backs, were perched on the sacks in extremely cheerful moods because they had achieved a good morning's work. At the peak of the harvest about thirty-five cartloads come in every day.

In Isparta's rose-growing province there are about four hundred villages with rose plantations, which do not need much tending, apart from pruning, and although the traditional methods of distillling in *imbiks* (log-fired stills) in family houses have now given way to much larger factory distilllation methods, in the cultivation of the damask rose an ancient and beautiful culture endures: almost every family owns a donum, or smallholding, and is paid $135 for three sacks of freshly plucked petals. Four harvesters can pick three sacks in an hour, and it is thanks to their practiced skill that the scent of the *Rosa damascena* remains intact. On each donum of land (one donum is about 1,000 square meters) there are roughly one thousand rosebushes, each bush producing 500 milliliters of distilled rose oil per season.

We were taken into the steaming distilllery, where the air was heavy with the rich deliquescence of roses as dewy petals were loaded into the vaporous stills. Mr. Timour explained that they use two techniques for processing the roses: steam distilllation and extraction. In Turkey, it takes 4 tons, or 400 kilograms, of blossoms to extract 1 kilogram of rose concrete, but a much larger quantity—3,500 kilograms—to distill 1 liter of essential oil. It takes a champion rose picker one hour to pick 6 kilograms of rose petals, so, if he picks for five hours, he will amass 30 kilograms and yet this produces only a few drops of rose oil. And because rose oils and absolutes are so expensive—about £10 per milliliter of rose oil—substitutes are made, although they bear no comparison to the true scent and they have none of the added psychological and emotional effects that leave you feeling soothed and uplifted.

About one-third of Robertet Turkey's harvest of rose petals is extracted while the other two-thirds are distillled in the boiling cauldrons. The extraction process takes about twenty minutes, whereas distilllation takes several hours, and then the remaining rosewater is distilled yet again until all the precious oil is recovered. The essential oil is obtained from the petals by steam distilllation from the boiling water in which they are steeped. The waxy constituents of the rose oil that float to the top of the water are decanted, while the remaining condensed water is transferred to a more efficient still and distilled again to recover any remaining oil. The apparatus has three parts: the still itself, and an oval-shaped vat on top of which is a head shaped like a swan's neck linked to the condenser, which is made up of a heated metal coil inside another vat filled with cold water. This encourages the steam.

The rose petals are loaded onto perforated shelves, and the water in the bain-marie, or false bottom of the vat, is brought to boiling point. The agitation associated with boiling prevents the rose petals from forming a compact mass and coagulating. Steam laden with the fragrant rose molecules escapes through the swan's neck to the condenser, where it becomes liquid and flows into the collecting flask, known as a Florentine flask. The water drains to the bottom of the Florentine flask while the essential oil floats to the surface and is siphoned off. The leftover rosewater, still imbued with some essence of rose, is also drained off.

Damask roses have a rich mixture of more than a hundred different components, but the most important one recovered from the blossom is phenylethyl alcohol. Because of its solubility, some of it gets lost in the distillation water, but that is then collected as rosewater. When rose absolute is made by the extraction process the phenylethyl remains in the superior absolute, which has been refined from the concrete and is therefore "superior"—of finer quality than essential oil. The absolute tends to be used by the noses for their perfumes, while the essential oil is preferred by aromatherapists. The other rose alcohols are geraniol, citronellol and nerol, and when you smell *Rosa damascena* you can detect geraniums, citronella and neroli orange blossom. Many of the other components are present only in trace quantities, but they are all important for the overall quality of the oil. One of them, the compound *damascenone*, is important even though it is present only in minute amounts, because it adds potency and gives the oil its character.

While the rose petals were being loaded straight into the distillation stills, other bales of rose petals, which had been laid out the night before to be aired, were ready to be extracted with a hexane solvent to produce a rose concrete. The extraction units were darkened chambers with low-wattage lightbulbs. I was asked to switch off my tape recorder and refrain from taking any photographs—just as at LMR in Grasse—because the chemicals and solvents are so volatile that any battery-powered equipment could cause an explosion. The atmosphere was quite different from that of the distilllation units: there were no rose oil vapors and all was calm and orderly because of the extreme danger of the chemicals in their airtight vats.

I watched rose petals being shoveled onto tiers of circular trays steeped in hot solvents so that the wax and oils could be dissolved. The mixture was then siphoned off, and the remaining spent, scentless rose petals on their tiers looked like a bizarre wedding cake. It is an incredibly complex process to strip the roses of their perfume. Huge, 3,000-liter stainless-steel vats are filled with trays of rose petals so that the solvents can circulate freely around them. There are successive solvent rinses; then the solvent saturated with scent is decanted to remove excess moisture. At this point it is transferred to a vacuum still, where it is evaporated, retrieved and then recycled, leaving a pastelike mixture composed of fragrant molecules, pigments and waxes at the bottom of the vat: this is the concrete.

The concrete, along with the rose oil produced by Robertet Turkey, is dispatched to Grasse in wax-sealed copper flasks called *kumkuma*. The concrete is refined in machines called *batteuses*, in which it is rinsed in alcohol several times to dissolve the fragrant molecules. As wax congeals at low temperatures, the concrete-alcohol mixture is frozen and filtered again to remove all traces of the wax. Finally the mixture is distillled gently at a very low temperature; the alcohol evaporates, leaving what is aptly called an absolute, which, in its absolute purity, is the jewel of the essence.

A Turkish Robertet employee sat in a cubicle on a platform beside the vats with samples of olibanum, cucumber, tobacco, fenugreek and rosemary. *Le chef de l'extraction* shyly presented me with a tiny bottle of terra-cotta-colored, waxy rose concrete.

Rosa damascena in Morocco

ROSA DAMASCENA WAS TAKEN TO MOROCCO BY THE GREAT seafaring Phoenicians from Persepolis in Iran. It grows at Kelaa Mgouna, which is on the edge of the Sahara desert, although it feels more like the edge of the world. When you get into the Sahara you notice the silence and the absolute stillness, but the area around Kelaa Mgouna is fertile from the Dadès tributary, and thousands of acres of roses are cultivated for their rose oil. The oil is then exported to Grasse.

The rosebushes grow in the oases, planted out as tiny hedgerows which divide plots of barley, maize and mint, and all are shaded by olive trees and tamarisks. It is miraculous to see these crops, particularly the *Rosa damascena*, growing in the ir-rigated sub-Saharan desert. Aerial photographs testify that there are 42 kilograms of these low rose hedges in the region.

The rose petals are picked early in the morning, only in May, at dawn, before the blooms shrivel up in the heat. It is too hot in the desert for a harvest in the succeeding months.

During the May and June harvest in the Turkish province of Isparta, Robertet employs fifty workers on twelve-hour shifts; the amount they earn in two months keeps them and their families for the rest of the year. The annual rose harvest lasts a minimum of twenty-five and a maximum of forty days, and women, chil-dren and even older relatives pick more or less around the clock,

but it has to be efficient. A badly organized harvest can ruin an entire year's crop and spoil the scent. Carefully controlling how and when the crops are picked, and maintaining high standards in the distilllation and extraction processes are essential.

Every day, at harvest time, 38 tons (over 35,000 kilograms) of rose petals are distillled and 8 tons (over 7,000 kilograms) are extracted. In just two months the factory produces 800 kilograms of rose concrete worth $640,000 and 140 liters of essential oil worth $700,000. It is a lucrative harvest.

Mr. Timour described the other ingredients that Robertet produces when the rose harvest is over. Some I found difficult to place in a scent, like fenugreek; it is a rather bitter herb that I have only ever tasted in Yemeni lamb stews. Even tobacco is extracted; although I thought its smell revolting, it has a sub-liminally addictive effect, just as nicotine does, and you want to breathe it in, just as you sometimes want to breathe in someone else's cigar smoke. There were also lovelier ingredients. As Mr. Timour held one vial under my nose, the smell was very famil-iar, reminding me of summer, especially an English summer. I thought of freshly cut lawns, billowing marquees and Buck's Fizz. It turned out to be cucumber absolute—no wonder those images had come to mind: all those cucumber sandwiches, the very quintessence of an English summer.

Outside, a putrid effluvium from the residue of spent rose petals poured from the distilllery, and a lake of rose residue was congealing and baking in the sun, but none of it goes to waste. The local farmers collect it and bake the residue into little bricks which they burn as faggots in the winter. I imagined winter eve-nings in rooms filled with the smell of summer roses.

It falls to the Turks to deal with the huge bulk of rose waste, but it is in Grasse that the Damask otto has to pass the acid test. At the beginning of every harvest a sample is sent to Grasse so that the great noses can approve it before the Turkish extraction and distilllation process can proceed.

The damask rose is mainly made into concrete, just as is the rare *Rose de Mai* in Grasse. The *Rose de Mai* is lighter, with a lemon sherbet note; the damask is more suited to making the rose essential oil favored by aromatherapists, while perfumers prefer the concrete or absolute to work with. When I got back to England I tried some Turkish rose absolute that had been sent to me from the International Flowers and Fragrances group in Grasse. It was from the previous year's crop, quite possibly from the very spot I had traveled to. I compared the IFF sample with the *Gul yagi* I had been given in Isparta. It was like comparing a mature wine with a young one: the IFF rose did not smell as crude; it had been refined into a more velvety odor, although it retained the distinctly musky rose smell.

As a parting gift, Mr. Timour gave us some rose-flavored Turkish delight and a pot of rose jam. We spread the jam on chunks of delicious fresh bread, and the mellifluous elixir made me feel as if I were eating the smell of roses. Then we opened the Turkish delight, and after I had eaten the aromatic jelly I exhaled smells of lemon and roses. I began to understand the tradition in the Arab world of consuming fragrant food in which smell (perfume) and taste become synonymous.

Fragrant Food

ROSEWATER IS USED AS A FLAVORING IN MANY RECIPES, AND ROSE fragrance plays a great role in much Middle Eastern cuisine. The Persians were a sophisticated race of epicureans, and their customs spread throughout the Arab world. They made delicious nonalcoholic drinks, called sherbets or juleps, flavored with roses and violets. (The Persian word *"serbet"* means draft or drink, while *julab* means rosewater.) The word "julep," as in mint julep, was also used for any medicinal aromatic drink. Partridges were cooked in frankincense and wine was spiced with frankincense and myrrh, which could be characterized as the ancient equivalent of cigarettes or cocaine. An aromatic "rush" plainly produced a druglike euphoria, and the ancients were as addicted to the stuff as some of us are to our own drugs.

Food was cooked in scented water, and a rose pudding was presented for the guests' delectation at the Emperor Nero's banquets, where rose wine was served to wash it down. The Medici family is known to have used a rudimentary method of *enfleurage*, by which layers of rose petals were alternated with layers of pure cocoa to make a rich aromatic chocolate. And the consumption of roses is not confined to the distant past: in the twentieth century Elizabeth David adapted a recipe for sautéed rose petals from the futurist art movement in Italy.

In Turkey and the rest of central Asia roses and rose oil are used to flavor all kinds of sweets. The Turks dissolve *lokum*, a sweet scented with rose, in their coffee. In Iran honey and jam ➤

are suffused with rose flowers. Iraqi rice dishes, called *machboos*, are flavored with rosewater.

Over the centuries ambergris has been used, in small amounts, to flavor alcohol. One grain of ambergris is sufficient to give a fine bouquet to a hogshead of claret, and when cocktails came into fashion during the 1920s, and at the time of prohibition in America, many bartenders used ambergris as an aromatic additive. It is particularly delicious in hot alcoholic drinks, like punches. It was also added to aqua vitae and to rye whisky. The recipes sound mouthwateringly good, intoxicating and quite lethal.

The great French gastronome Brillat-Savarin's recipe for a restorative ambergris chocolate milk shake sounds delicious, and, if you're feeling a bit low, try adding a knob of ambergris no larger than a small bean (if you can find it . . . see Chapter 9), pounded with sugar, to a strong cup of chocolate. I've found it helps enormously.

In Tuscany, orris (iris) root extract is not only used as a fixative in perfume but also to flavor cakes, and the *contadini* (peasant agricultural workers) put the rhizomes into vats of Chianti wine. Iris extract can be found in a Sienese walnut tart and in an ice cream and, when I was in Tuscany researching the iris, Signora Casalini, an iris enthusiast I met there, told me that she put a tiny droplet of iris essence into her trifle.

Elizabeth David wrote that no Italian kitchen is complete without *noce moscato*, or the musky nut: nutmeg. She wrote that it is "as necessary as Parmesan cheese and oregano and, for that matter, salt." The Italians use nutmeg in their cream cheese and

➤ spinach stuffings for cannelloni, tortellini and ravioli, while the English, David observed, use nutmeg in "puddings and cakes and sweet creams . . . grated over milk junkets, cream curds and the Christmas brandy butter." Chaucer's Sir Thopas and Shakespeare's Falstaff drank their ale sprinkled with nutmeg, and eggnog has its origins in the sack posset, a warm wintry drink which was a sort of alcoholic custard of nutmeg, milk, eggs and strong ale. The French add a pinch of nutmeg to give a subtle nuance to Forcalquier pastis.

On our way back to the coast from Isparta, we drove past villages where, in every square, people were weighing sacks of rose petals on scales. I thought about the long journey that the damask rose petals were about to be sent on, across the 3,000 miles to Grasse, which, with its perfume brokers and hermetically sealed laboratories, is as distant culturally as it is geographically from Isparta province. I doubted if, in this rural Turkish backwater, the local rose pickers and workers would ever smell the expensive bottles of scent that their precious rose otto haunts.

We descended 1,000 feet from the plateau to the coast, the heat strengthening the resinous smell from the pine forests that clung to the cliffs. Down by the sea we arrived at Side, which, in ancient Greek, means pomegranate. It was once a great port, but on that day the sea breezes carried the smells of the wild herbs and it was like being presented with a gigantic bouquet garni. Among the olive groves I found basilicas, some ancient baths and a nymphaeum. I lay down in the shade beside an ancient Temple of Fortune, just able to make out a carving of a naked man and a swan on the dome of the Temple. It was wonderfully peaceful and fragrant, and I remembered that near the rose-residue lake in Isparta I'd seen fields of a Spanish species of rosemary, which would eventually be distillled into essential oil. I'd heard that, in its native Spain, the rosemary grows on the coast and can be smelled at sea long before land is visible.

Continuing westward along the coast, we drove eventually down a dramatic gorge scattered with Lycian tombs to the beautiful bay of Cirali beneath Mount Olympus. In a hamlet with small pensions and fruit orchards, we saw fishermen putting their nets out to sea. We had stumbled upon the ancient city of Olympus, where, in the seventh century B.C., the Phasilians— whom Demosthenes described as scoundrels—founded a colony called Phaselis. They had excellent harbors and made scents and ointments from the wildflowers and roses in the heavily wooded hinterland. Now the ruins of Olympus are buried in undergrowth.

Dusk was falling and a full moon was rising as we walked along the gorge to a clearly marked path up the mountain. The crickets were singing and the air was filled with the smells of wild sage, thyme and pine. We walked along the shingle path 900 feet up the mountain and, as we approached the mountain rock face, we saw, beyond the trees, a cluster of lights. It was a wild and otherworldly place where dozens of little flames leaped from crevices in the ground. I poured some water from my bottle onto a flame, but it reignited seconds later. It was, I discovered, a natural phenomenon: a combination of gases which is thought to contain methane. The ancient Greeks called the constantly burning flames "the Flames of the Chimaera" and thought that they were caused by Hephaestus, god of the forge, who, it was said, lived at Cirali. I watched the flames blacken an ancient Latin inscription on a broken plinth and imagined vestal virgins and high priestesses wreathed in ambrosial clouds of smoke as they burned offerings of resins and myrrh to their gods.

In antiquity pirates and sailors would have been able to see the fire from the sea because the flames were much higher then, but over the intervening millennia they have lost their height and power. Although there must have been about thirty people on the mountainside that evening—tourists just like us—not one of us spoke. We were witnessing natural phenomena, but I fancied we all imagined ancient rites.

On the way back down we passed a wandering bard or *asiklar*. *Asiklars* recite and sing their own poetry and songs while playing the *saz*, a Turkish mandolin, and their tradition is centuries old. Their ballads are sad songs of love and life in Antalya, but some modern ones are about Turkish politics, so they sometimes find themselves in trouble with the police.

Next day we traveled farther west, deeper into Lycia, and found the ruins of Arycanda perched on the mountainside. The baths were constructed from polygonal masonry, and the arches seem to defy gravity. The theater commanded stunning views across the mountains—it was one of the most beautiful sites I have ever seen. I recited some verses from *Antony and Cleopatra* to test the acoustics; Stephen said he could hear me from the top tier. When Antony summons Cleopatra to Tarsus (in southeastern Turkey, not far from Arycanda), she sails in a perfumed barge:

> *Like a burnished throne,*
> *Burned on the water;*
> *The poop was beaten gold.*
> *Purple the sails and so perfumed that*
> *The winds were lovesick with them.*

We headed back east, crossing the mountains that surround Antalya, which were a cerulean blue in the heat haze. The next day we would head to Syria.

As we didn't have visas, we stole across the border, in a taxi, into Syria. We traveled through Qalat Semaan—where Saint Simeon Stylites, the anchorite, lived on a column for forty years—and passed Alawite and Druze villages. Along the way, we saw Bedouin living in Byzantine ruins. In the evening we reached the Baron Hotel in Aleppo.

The following morning, in the burning heat, we made for the shady souk and, wandering through the medieval labyrinth, smelled our way along the pungent spice street, where hessian sacks burst with multihued spices and aromatic coffee laced with cardamom. We smelled the sickly-sour milk from sheep's cheese wrapped in sheep's dung, felt the heat of the anvils and saw their flying sparks. The Christian quarter was filled with bolts of silk damask, and among the carpenters we smelled linseed, cedar wood and sawdust. We peered into khans (courtyards) hung with vines, where cooling fountains splashed, before reaching the perfumers with their little libraries of bottles and old-fashioned makeup, lipsticks and weighing scales.

Ancient Syrian scents were made from unguents of lilies and compounds of cinnabar, honey and wine, and whiffs of Syrian thyme and myrtle once wafted over the agoras of Imperial Rome. We sat down with one perfumer and had a glass of tea with him, while he held a powdery unguent made from the lily—both bulb and flower—under our noses. He asked me how many children I had—Syrians love children and always ask about yours. I told him that I had one son, and was planning to have at least one more child. The perfumer advised that the best oil for child-birth, for the womb and for rubbing over one's swollen belly to prevent stretch marks, was rose oil. He said that the rose petal had the ideal texture, fine and delicate, exactly as you would wish for your skin, and that when you touch a rose petal you can sense its graininess. We talked about how the rose's scent is, at first, like dew in the morning; then it reveals a richness and sweetness that refuses to sink into other scents. We agreed that the scent of the rose cannot be overpowered. The perfumer sold me several Syrian rose oils, some of which had been blended with other ingredients: one had been infused with honey, an-other with dried figs and another with mint.

When we left the perfumer, we threaded our way back along cobblestones flecked with pools of light from the apertures in the vaulted roofs, passing teeming crowds of baggy-trousered Bed-ouin, Druzes, brown-cloaked Iraqis, women wearing the hijab and Shiites wrapped in red-and-white-checked cloths. All the time I clutched my Syrian rose scents.

Driving back to Antalya the following day we passed mile after mile of partially built, abandoned resorts. Half the coast-line seemed to have been cemented over and its wild beauty destroyed. Most of the once-romantic and mysterious ancient cities that now lie half-buried in the sand have been turned into major tourist attractions. But if you look hard enough there are still beautiful, wild parts of Turkey to be found.

As we left Turkey I thought that if the country were a perfume it would be a bouquet of dates, figs, pomegranates, roses in jam and Turkish delight, rounded off by the aniseed from the cloudy glasses of potent raki. My lasting impressions of Turkey are of a girl wearing the hijab standing on the baking hot beach while her brothers splashed her sandaled feet from the sea; the ruins wafting with the scents of sage and thyme; the eternal flames of the Chimaera on Mount Olympos; and I shall never forget the explosion of perfume from the sea of rose petals laid out to dry beside the Robertet factory in Isparta.

To me, the damask rose is like a grand dowager. I knew I wanted a slightly haughty, old-fashioned, even dusty scent to haunt my own bespoke scent. It is an elegant smell, too. Noses say that you skip a generation and tend to like a scent that your grandmother wore. My grandmother's Chinese bedroom smelled of roses, and whenever I stayed with her I would climb into her bed of damask sheets every morning—she never got up until midday—and she would read *The Last of the Mohicans* to me. The damask rose takes me back to those mornings.

Armed with boxes of Turkish delight, attars of *gul* and rose-infused jam, we flew back to the welcome coolness of England and to Tarquin. I was longing to see him, and so glad I could take him with us on the next leg of my scent trail, to Tuscany, where I grew up.

CHAPTER FIVE

IRIS

Italy

Fenced up the verdant wall: each beauteous
   flower,
Iris all hues, roses and jasmine,
Crocus, and hyacinth, with rich inlay
Broidered the ground, more coloured than with
   stone
Of costliest emblem.

MILTON
Paradise Lost

ORRIS, THE DRIED RHIZOME OF THE TUSCAN IRIS, IS A precious fixative in perfume. It strengthens the odor of other fragrant ingredients with its earthy vineyard smell and smooth buttery mellifluence. The odorous roots smell of Tuscany to me: of chestnuts, cypress, pine, meadows of mint, basil, thyme and sage, and their perfume haunts Italian linen chests. The Italians also use it in toothpaste, to perfume face powder and to flavor Chianti. As mentioned before, it can even be found in a Sienese walnut tart and an ice cream.

The iris flower was originally called *giglio* and is still commonly referred to as *ghiacciolo*, which means icicle, because the white iris which grew on the banks of the Arno was tinted a pale violet blue, exactly like ice. The name *giaggiolo* (iris) derives from *ghiacciolo*.

In Greek mythology Iris is the messenger of the gods. She travels between heaven and earth on the rainbow and, in Greek, her name means rainbow. The iris was also used as a decorative emblem on Egyptian bas-reliefs and on Arabian funeral urns. Pliny records that the Egyptians grew irises in the Nile valley and that they made an essential oil from the rhizomes. The Greeks and the Romans used the rhizomes in medicine as well as in perfume, and Macedonia and Corinth were renowned for their iris unguents, which were made by pulverizing the root. Theophrastus relates a story about a perfumer who kept an iris perfume for twenty years; it was still as good as, if not better than, freshly made perfume all those years later.

The iris is symbolic of the flowering of the fledgling Florentine city-state, and the standard of Florence, the *Iris fiorentina*, became its emblem. It was, once, a white iris on a red field, but after the Guelphs banished the Ghibellines in 1266 they reversed the colors. To this day the iris remains the enduring emblem of Fiorenza (the city of flowers). It was stamped on florins and appeared in garlands around the dancing wood nymphs of Botticelli's *Primavera*; the *Iris germanica* is visible in Ghirlandaio's *Adoration of the Magi* in the Sassetti Chapel; and in Drer's *Madonna of the Irises* there is a species of iris called the Trojan iris whose rhizomes came to Europe from Constantinople. The old masters used *verd'iris*, a varnish made from the juice extracted from iris leaves, which imparted a luminous quality to the paint.

Irises grow all over the rugged Tuscan hills. The most aromatic is the *Iris pallida*, which, unlike most other flowers, conceals its scent within its roots. The scarcity of iris scent is due to the fact that it takes nearly six years to manufacture. It requires three years of cultivation, with frequent hoeing by hand to avoid damaging the rhizomes before they can be harvested, followed by a fortnight's drying in the sun. Then, for two more years, the rhizomes dehydrate in sacks where a chemical reaction occurs, releasing the chetone alpha irone, which is distilled into an essential oil for which there is no synthetic substitute.

The rhizomes are then pulverized, macerated in cold water and distilled over and over again for six months, when, after a bit of moderate heating, they eventually produce a rich, buttery concrete known as orris butter, which is further refined into the absolute. It takes 40 tons of rhizomes to extract 1 liter of absolute. The scent is both subtle and powerful; it is deep, soft and warm, reminiscent of violets and the kind of old-fashioned face powders our grandmothers might have worn. The rich, smooth, costly heart of the Florentine iris is prevalent in Chanel No. 19; it rounds off and smoothes the sharpness of galbanum, the green scented oil from the gum of Iranian grass. In the Middle Ages pulverized iris roots formed the base of many European powdered perfumes; they were packed in sachets and dangled from the body, dusted into hair, and the orris roots were peeled into fragments to make rosaries.

Scent: Sacred and Secular

ACCORDING TO THE VEDIC TEXTS, SOME OF THE WORLD'S MOST ancient documents, in ancient India fragrant woods were lit and fed with consecrated perfumed ointment and offered to the Hindu gods. In Hindu mythology there are five heavens and they all abound in perfume. The Jupiter of the Hindus, Indra, is always portrayed with his breast tinged with sandalwood, while Kama, the god of love, had a bow and arrow tipped with flower blossoms. The god Brahma was born from a lotus flower which grew from Vishnu's navel, and the principal ornament of Brahma's heaven is the blue champak flower, which, on earth, is white and belongs to the *Magnoliaceae* family. It has a lovely, overpowering scent and is still cultivated for perfumery.

In the first millennium B.C. the priests were the perfumers, ➤

and the skill of grinding up pastes to make incense and unguents, using hundreds of ingredients, was considered a mysterious and esteemed art. High priests kept the sacred fires burning by sprinkling incense on charcoal in censers at the altars. At Heliopolis the sun worshippers burned gum resins at dawn, myrrh at noon and kaphi (more commonly spelled "kyphi"), a mixture of aromatics, at sunset.

In Europe, in the Middle Ages, gardening was restricted—because of the constant threat of invasion—to protected places. Aromatic and medicinal plants were cultivated in the cloistered herb gardens of the monasteries, where the monks and nuns manufactured scent for its medicinal properties. Their knowledge of alchemy and their recognition of the curative powers of scent helped them in their development of new recipes for perfume and medicine. Monks had their own distilling equipment, and various orders like the Dominicans, the Carthusians and the Franciscans vied with one another to make the best scents and herbal extracts. When they began to distribute them, their perfume preparations made their monasteries famous throughout Europe.

Perfume has been made by the Dominican monks at the Officina Profumo-Farmaceutica at Santa Maria Novella, in Florence, since the 1220s. It is the oldest pharmacy in the world and was founded when the friars began to distill herbs and flowers to make essences, fragrant waters and elixirs. The perfumery and pharmacy still exist, and as you walk into the Officina Profumo the aroma of the herbs, leaves and flowers of the Tuscan countryside, its woodsmoke, lilacs and pine, the twiggy smell of rosemary in summer, the herbal mimosalike smell of the yellow broom and the wild woody smell of the cypress haunt the vaulted chapel.

The preparations made in the monastery became celebrated not only in Italy but throughout Europe, and medicines were ordered from as far afield as China. Over the years each new abbot set out to devise a new recipe to add to the fame of the order. In the middle of the nineteenth century the Officina was handed over to the Italian state, but all the original recipes—which the friars invented and perfected over the years—are still kept there. In the fifteenth century Fra Angelo Paladini made an almond paste, a lily water and a cosmetic vinegar, which were very popular with the Tuscan courtiers. In 1707, another abbot, Fra Ludovico Berlingacci, discovered and made his famous "Life Elixir," which included viper flesh.

During the seventeenth and eighteenth centuries the scents were bottled and put into small boxes or cases shaped like books, whose covers were embossed with ornamental devices in gold or colored pigments, and in *Pepys' Letters* it is recorded that his nephew John Jackson, who was making a grand tour of Italy, sent his uncle "one small book of Florence essences."

Curative potions made by the monastery, such as "Vinegar of the Seven Thieves," which restored those prone to fainting, and an antihysteric water, are all still made, as are all kinds of scented and antique pharmaceutical preparations—from pomegranate soaps to rose elixirs—made from every ingredient you can imagine. There is an iris toothpaste, a myrrh mouthwash and colognes made from *Aqua sicilia*, mimosa, honeysuckle, tobacco and Spanish leather. A medieval potpourri was also made which was left to mature for months and lasted for years.

The Greeks and Romans were known to have anointed different parts of the body with appropriate scents: mint for the arms, palm oil for the breasts, marjoram for the hair, ground ivy for the knees; perfume extracted from vine leaves kept the mind clear and white violets were used to help digestion. Saint Hildegarde, in her twelfth-century book *Le Jardin de Santé* (*The Garden of Health*), wrote about the therapeutic properties of sage, aniseed, thyme, rosemary and, above all, lavender. Plant and animal substances were researched for their uses to combat plagues, and, in the fourteenth century, Olivier de la Haye recommended spreading aromatic plants and sprinkling vinegar and wild roses on floors, as well as burning incense pans of rosemary and juniper berries to disinfect houses. People with maladies disinfected their mouths and hands with an aromatic wine flavored with pepper, cinnamon, ginger, musk, cloves and mace. Then in 1370 a remedy for many illnesses appeared. It was called a *boule de senteur*—literally a ball of scent—and was made from aromatic vegetals and animal extracts which people inhaled. These *boules de senteur* later developed into the more sophisticated pomanders.

Directions for making holy oil can be found in Exodus 30:23–4: "Take thou also . . . three principal spices. Of pure myrrh, 500 shekels, and of sweet cinnamon half so much, even 250, and of sweet calamus 250 shekels. And of cassia, 500 shekels, and of olive oil a hin." A shekel is an ounce and a hin is a gallon, so this is a huge quantity. Incense was made from pulverized spices—especially cinnamon and perfumed cyprinum, the odoriferous leaves of henna—into psagdi (pastilles of incense), which were tinted green with extracts of henna flowers. Cinnamon also infused holy anointing oil.

In the Middle Ages, perfume was also, naturally, used in the churches of the orders that made it. At Mass, resinous incense billowed from censers, and vases of scented water were used at baptisms. But perfume also came into general use. *Maisons de bain*, or bathhouses, were built and filled with aromatic herbs and perfumes. A sybaritic scene from a medieval miniature of one of these public bathhouses depicts couples immersed in huge wooden tubs of water, while servants dispense flacons of wine to the bathers. Beside the bathers another couple lies resting in a four-poster bed.

Banqueting rooms were filled with chaplets of roses on feast days, and by the fourteenth century violet, orange and lavender waters were used by ladies of noble birth. In 1365 Charles V of France planted a garden of sage, hyssop, lavender, roses and violets. Musk, amber and civet, and oriental cinnamon, benzoin and sandalwood were also much in vogue. Agnès Sorel, the mistress of Charles VII of France, was so enamored of ambergris that she had her cloaks soaked in the stuff. One of the most popular scents of the time was made from a mélange of chypre, damask rose, sandalwood, aloes, musk, ambergris and civet. Iris roots were also ground into a powder that gave off a soft violet scent, which responded well to the smell of skin and was thought to be an aphrodisiac.

I love Italy. But most of all I love Tuscany, where I spent most of my childhood. All the smells from my childhood are bound up with Tuscany: the dusty smell of geraniums, the citrus scents of potted lemon and orange trees, the scented powdered iris sachets between the sheets and the hot pans of smoldering charcoal to warm the beds. The split, rotten-sweet tomatoes lying in the sun, the resinous green soapy smell of pine, the musty, mildewy-sour smells of wine fermenting in the cellar, the piquant smell of the olive harvest and the nectarous, cloying aroma of jasmine hanging limply in the heat of the summer. And there were the herbal smells of the brackish green lake choked with weeds that I used to swim in, and of basil and oregano simmering in sauces on the stove. I remember picking muscadine blackberries in the autumn and the smell of woodsmoke that hung in my hair in winter.

I could never understand why we moved back to England, and I lived for the holidays when we could return to my beloved Italy. So when my father—who is a professor of modern history and lectures at universities in Italy, traveling often between his apartment in Florence and his flat in London—told me recently about an exhibition of ancient scents in Rome, and the fact that you could even have perfume cocktails in a bar off the Piazza del Popolo, Stephen, Tarquin and I were soon driving along the Appian Way toward Rome beneath the umbrella pines that cast long shadows in the crepuscular light.

We booked into a family-run hotel in Trastevere, where the kindly grandma stroked Tarquin's head and asked him what his name was. She looked horrified when I told her—because of the bloody reign of the Tarquins in Rome. The last king's son,

Sextus Tarquinius, raped his cousin's wife, Lucretia. She committed public suicide and her husband, Lucius Collatinus, paraded her bloody corpse through the streets, exhorting the citizens to rise up and drive the Tarquins from Rome. They did and the Roman Republic was established. Despite his name, and in a fairly short space of time, my Tarquin's sweet nature won the kindly grandma over.

During the night we were so hot it was difficult to sleep: Rome was in the grip of its worst heat wave for ages. The only person who was unaffected by the heat the whole time we were in Rome was Tarquin, tempered by an ice cream every now and then. We left him at a Roman nursery the following morning and took a taxi to the Museo d'Arte Orientale to see "Aromatica," the exhibition my father had told me about. It began with some jars of spices: coriander, juniper, sticks of cinnamon and cumin seeds, fragments of myrrh and crystals of incense that the curator had found in the basement of the museum. Vitrines of unguentaria, ancient glass vials, bottles, incense burners and display panels were sandwiched between the museum's permanent collection. Then I found test tubes of ancient scents that you could smell, if you put your nose right up to them. (Had the scents escaped into the rooms, the smells would have been too overpowering and we would not have been able to savor and differentiate between them.) Some of the scents had been reconstructed from ancient recipes by a perfumer called Laura Tonnato: she'd re-created the ceremonial unguents of ancient Greece and Rome.

The curator, Dotoressa Serafina Pennestri, took me round, speaking rapid Italian, and admitted that the space was not really big enough for such an exhibition. We sniffed the vials: there was Egyptian kyphi, the sacrificial oil made from cassia, cinnamon, juniper, acacia and myrrh; a sublime ancient Greek perfume made from laurel and myrtle; a heavy frankincense from Imperial Rome and *unguentum Parthicum Rhodicum*, which was made from roses and was used at Roman banquets.

Then we went to the scent bar for our perfume cocktails. Only in Italy, where *la bella figura*—a serious interest in one's image, fashion and the latest trends—is of the utmost importance, could a scent bar be taken seriously. The Olfattorio opened in April 2003, and during "il happy hour," instead of the usual Prosecco or Campari, both men and women are served with perfumed aperitifs.

Stefania Zuccotti, the vivacious barmaid, served cocktails to resuscitate and stimulate jaded olfactory senses. We sat at a long steel counter on bar stools while she handed us bottomless paper cups shaped like cocktail glasses called *moujettes*. She aimed an atomizer at the cups, sprayed and we sniffed. She mixed a spritzer and told us that it contained mint, lemon and basil. She sprayed fluted paper champagne cups and said that, at the Olfattorio, they were trying to promote a perfume culture founded more on smells than on brand names and marketing.

My cocktail cups were piling up and, in a cloud of perfume and feeling tipsy from fig, amber and roses, I accepted Stefania's offer of some sobering coffee beans to clear the palate. I dug into my bag for my wallet but was told that the perfumes weren't sold at the Olfattorio. Instead I was given a card with a list of twenty-eight shops in Rome that stocked the scents. The scent tasting or, I should say, scent smelling, was free too, and Stefania gave us one for the road, which, she said, was for those in search of a more androgynous scent. It was called Dzing and was a mixture of animal smells, leather, sawdust and caramel. It reminded me of a passage in Jean Cocteau's autobiography, in which he eulogizes the smells of the circus:

> *The smell of the circus, the smell of the Nouveau Cirque, the great marvellous smell. Of course you knew it consisted of horse manure, tanbark, stables and healthy sweat, but it also contained something indescribable, a mixture which escaped analysis, an amalgam of expectation and excitement that caught your throat, that habitually preceded the show.*

We picked Tarquin up from the nursery, where he had learned to say, "Ciao!," and caught the Eurostar Pendolino train to Florence.

Whenever I arrive in Florence I always feel a sense of excitement and my mind is filled with flashbacks. My heart is in my mouth because I'm coming home. The geography of Florence is engraved on my heart. My father's apartment, a lofty suite of rooms with frescoed ceilings and heavy oak Florentine furniture, is on the *piano nobile* of the Palazzo Pandolfini, a stone's throw from Dante's house. From my father's bedroom window you can practically touch the Bargello, the huge civic fortress that was once a prison and is now a museum of Tuscan sculpture.

The following morning, to begin my research on irises, I went to see the Florentine perfumer, philosopher, author and alchemist Lorenzo Villoresi, whom I'd met several years before. Dr. Villoresi has a doctorate in ancient philosophy and biblical philology, and during his postgraduate research he traveled extensively in the Middle East, studying the correspondence between Seneca and Saint Paul. But he got sidetracked, seduced by the great souks in Egypt, Jordan, Sudan and Morocco, and began collecting exotic oils and essences to bring home. It was not long before friends were asking him to concoct scents for them.

Dr. Villoresi officially founded his perfume house, LV, in 1990, which breathed new life into the forgotten Renaissance traditions of Florentine perfumery. Dr. Villoresi has also written two books on perfume, one on the culture and history of perfume and another on the art of bathing. His atelier is on the top floor of a fifteenth-century palazzo that has belonged to his family for centuries. A mélange of rich scents lingers on the stairwell and gets stronger when you enter the alchemist's attic, but his atelier is shabbily elegant, with none of the swanky look you might expect of a perfumer. It is full of family portraits, photographs and worn silk cushions, and there is a great recessed alcove where there is a sofa bed and piles of books on perfume. Going to see Dr. Villoresi for a scent tasting is more like going for a chat with your tutor or your shrink: the atelier exudes learning rather than commerce, and very little seemed to have changed since I'd been there three years before.

On Villoresi's desk were fans of blotters, an ultrasensitive pair of weighing scales, test tubes, glass alembics and Florentine flasks, and the walls were lined with cabinets and wooden shelves containing almost a thousand meticulously labeled amber glass vials and bottles of essences, absolutes and oils—an archive of every conceivable aroma you could think of. I was particularly struck by the "fresh-cut grass," the "sea breeze," the "tobacco," and a peculiar "wet fur," which emanates from the indole in jasmine and really does smell like a wet fur coat. Beyond the atelier was a drawing room and a glassed-in loggia that overlooked the green Arno and the Ponte Vecchio, austere palazzi and the misty blue hills fringed with spires of cypresses.

Dr. Villoresi politely pretended to remember me. He is affable, bearded and distinguished-looking, and he was dressed in Burberry slacks, yellow socks and sneakers. I asked him if he still used orris-root butter from the iris in his perfumes. He sighed and told me that orris absolute was now worth three times more than its own weight in gold and cost about $40,000 a kilo. He said he had some orris essential oil, but he no longer used orris-root butter because it was just too expensive, unless it was for a scent for a very rich private client.

Villoresi has composed fifteen signature scents from natural essences. The emphasis is on single notes such as a sublime patchouli blended with lavender and oak moss, or Mysorian sandalwood and an earthy vetivert with notes of celery, nutmeg and mint. And, of course, a scent inspired by a Tuscan garden which he has called Spezie. It is composed of pure herbs: laurel, oregano, sage, thyme, rosemary, lavender, fennel, tomato leaves, cut grass and fir, enriched with juniper and cloves. He sprayed some on my arm and, as it evaporated, I was transported back to the garden of my childhood.

Villoresi told me that he kept notebooks to help him transpose memories into scents and that it took him about two years to make a scent. He said it was very important that the ingredients did not vary and that once he had made the final compound, the mixture had to be diluted in alcohol and, because the effect could change a great deal, it had to be left for a few days, or even weeks, before it could be evaluated. A good perfume, he explained, should give the wearer a sense of well-being, the sensation of being complete, and should also please other people around the wearer. He also told me that customers who wanted their own signature scent have to come for consultations—an olfactory analysis—which can last for hours. Villoresi questions his clients—just as Anastasia Brozler questioned me—about their dreams, and he delves into their psyches in order to conjure up an inimitable, custom-made scent for them. The sessions cost £300, but that includes a bottle of your very own scent, although prices soar if you choose rare ingredients like Bulgarian rose, pure jasmine or orris root.

Villoresi told me that not everyone is able to give a clear indication of what they want in a scent, but he is always careful not to make assumptions. What some people think of as depressing smells—such as those of cypress, tuberose or magnolia—can induce happiness in others. But he said that most people's awareness and knowledge of smells is limited. This sentiment is echoed by Italo Calvino in his short story "The Name, The Nose," in which he writes:

> But the vials, ampoules, the jars with their spire-like or cut-glass stoppers will weave in vain from shelf to shelf their network of harmonies, assonances, dissonances, counterpoints, modulations, cadenzas: our deaf nostrils will no longer catch the notes of their scale.

Most people want aphrodisiacs in their scents. Sometimes Villoresi's scents are so infused with carnal notes of musk, ambergris and oriental accords that they attract unwanted attention. He told me that an American customer who had asked for an aphrodisiac laughingly complained that packs of cats were following her around the neighborhood whenever she wore her new scent. He also told me that the most unusual request he had ever had was from a woman who wanted to immortalize the scent of her beloved dead dog. Villoresi said that he knew he'd been successful when the woman left his studio wearing her scent and all the stray dogs in the street started howling and following her. I asked whether she was English and when he nodded we both burst out laughing.

Serenissima, Scent and Glass Scent Bottles

BY THE THIRTEENTH CENTURY VENICE HAD BECOME THE GATEWAY to the Orient, the unrivaled medieval trading post between East and West. It had also become the capital of perfumery. Venetian merchants traded with those from Libya, Armenia and Syria, and with merchants from as far away as India and China. Venice became the great marketplace for spices and scents such as musk, rosewater from Persia, balms, amber, pepper and camphor. Merchants were either *apothicarii*, who sold medicinal ingredients, *speciarii*, the spice sellers, *herbarii*, who sold herbs, or *aromatarii*, who sold aromas and perfumes. There were also specialists in musk, known as *moschieri*, who sold little lead boxes of musk pods or civet bladder.

➤

The rich and fashionable developed a passion for scent, dousing not only themselves, but their cloaks, shoes, socks, furniture and even their money and their mules with perfume. Baths were filled with musk and hairpins were decorated with balls of amber.

Throughout the Middle Ages and the Renaissance, Venetians also manufactured glass containers for their perfumes, on the island of Murano in the Venetian lagoon. So rigid was the control of glassmaking that the glassmakers were not allowed to emigrate; if they did they were tracked down and executed.

As early as 1224 *oricanni* (little scent bottles) were presented to the doges of Venice by the glassmakers of Murano. The glass the *oricanni* were made from was colorless, crackled and clear, tinted and, sometimes, sanded with gold, filigreed or enameled. Perfume containers were also made by cutting colored rods of glass into tiny pieces and carefully melting them together into a mosaic effect known as *millefiori* (a thousand flowers). These bottles were ground and polished and the end product was so beautiful that there was a great demand for them. Unfortunately, by the nineteenth century, bad reproductions had cheapened the aesthetic value of the *millefiori*—but if you search hard enough you can still find the real thing in antique shops.

Murano glassworkers also produced glass pearls from which chaplets and necklaces were made. Andrea Viadore, a sixteenth-century perfumer, came up with the idea of injecting the pearls with a few drops of scent that would then evaporate once they came into contact with the warm skin of the neck. Some small scent bottles were also designed to be worn as jewelry.

After my conversation about the astronomical cost of orris-root butter with Dr. Villoresi, we headed out into the Tuscan countryside in search of it. We drove along below the Certosa monastery, leaving Florence behind us and, as the suburbs receded, a landscape of hills covered with cypresses, vines and olive groves, framing villas and towers, unfolded before us.

Valeria Rosselli, chair of the Iris Society and keeper of the Iris Garden in Florence, had put me in touch with Signora Serni Casalini in Panzano, a woman with a lifelong passion for irises. Because I had grown up with the local children and learned the Tuscan dialect, when I met Signora Casalini she showed me several *stornelle* (rhyming couplets about Tuscan life) which used to be recited during the long hours of cleaning and peeling orris roots. She told me that *gallozze*, or *zolla*, were the Tuscan dialect names for the roots once they had been cleaned and peeled with little curved knives called *roncoli* or *roncollini*. She said that you peeled the roots like potatoes, until they were clean and white; then they were rinsed, soaked in water and left to soften in terra-cotta pots. The water in which the rhizomes were soaked could be used as an excellent disinfectant. Once the rhizomes were all spread out on cane mats to dry, great care had to be taken not to let them get wet again, because, at this stage, even a small shower could ruin the whole harvest; if there was any threat of rain they had to be brought indoors. Signora Casalini remembered how strong they smelled—damp, earthy and not at all floral, but more like honey and fennel—and how they filled the house, spread everywhere, all around the kitchen and even spilling over into the bedroom. Even if the *gallozze* were wrapped they could become moldy if the roots had not dried properly, and the smaller roots had to be separated from the larger ones—a task which the older people and the children took on, as they sat in the shade under a loggia or canopy of vines. But these days, Signora Casalini told me, the harvests were *pocchissimo* (very small) and there were hardly any *contadini* (peasant agricultural workers) left to grow and harvest the irises. There was a time, she told me, when a *contadino* could earn ITL 24,000,000 a year growing irises.

In the middle of the nineteenth century, Adriano Piazzesi from San Polo realized the potential of farming irises intensively for their roots. Piazzesi traveled all over Europe to establish a commercial trade in the orris root and, from the end of the nineteenth century until the 1930s, this area of Tuscany—San Polo and Pontassieve—was devoted to iris cultivation. Every farm and estate set some land aside, and the rhizomes from Pontassieve were the best quality in the Mediterranean. All agricultural activity revolved around the iris between June and September—the period reserved for the long, delicate operation of digging up and preparing the rhizomes. But after the Second World War Pontassieve iris cultivation went into decline, and crops were grown in parts of the world where manual labor was cheaper, like Morocco.

However, as I know from my childhood, irises are still cultivated in the area, and Signora Casalini and I talked about the sea of violet iris blooms that covers the land in May. As a parting gift she gave me a rhizome which is still at the bottom of my handbag giving off its musty, buttery smell.

Next I tracked down a young farmer of irises, Gianni Prunetti. I could hardly believe my ears when he said that he lived in San

Polo, which is the nearest village to Villa Tizzano, where I used to live as a child. My father was captivated by the villa when the shutters were thrown open to reveal fields of irises blooming in a haze of violet in the soft, early May sun. He took the villa for ten years, and I remember halcyon days under the Tuscan sun when I would watch, fascinated, as the irises were dug up and the *contadini* peeled the roots and threw them into pails of water. But I never thought, then, to question what they were for. I had no idea that the roots ended up in perfume. To me, it was just another harvest like the *vendemmia* in September and the gathering of the olives in late October by the men and women who climbed up tapering ladders to shake the olives from the branches onto the sacks spread out below them.

I met Gianni Prunetti in the village square. He was a typical blue-eyed blond Tuscan; he could have been a Virgilian shepherd. He was twenty-four but he was wise beyond his years, and determined to keep the *giaggiolo* business alive. We drove a few miles out of San Polo to his family's *fattoria* (farm). The crickets were singing as we scrambled up to the fields of irises, which were wilting under the midday sun. Gianni dug up a few of the flowers to show me the roots. He explained how the top part of each root is saved to replant, as a bulb, in September. He asked me if I remembered the iris harvest and the festival of irises in May; I did. Gianni told me that his family and all the other farmers in the region used to send sacks of rhizomes directly to Grasse; there were once special trains that left from Florence for Grasse carrying the rhizomes. But, he said, in recent years scientists had discovered a chemical synthetic iris scent which was very similar to the scent of orris root, and the Grassoise perfumers now used that instead of natural Tuscan orris roots.

His expression was gloomy as he told me that virtually no *aziendi* (companies) or *podere* (farms) work with the *giaggiolo* any longer—there are only a few iris farms left and the tradition is vanishing. There are, however, still a few companies that prefer the real orris root to the synthetic version—but even their orders have shrunk from three hundred sacks of rhizomes to thirty each season, and, now that the major French companies which had once sustained Tuscan iris production no longer want Tuscan rhizomes, Gianni said he knew that they had to find new clients. He was keen to revive the idea that perfume should come from natural materials; he thought that would help the Tuscan orris-root industry.

Gianni also told me that since the shooting of porcupines had been banned in the 1990s, wild irises are also vanishing because the porcupines dig them up to eat the roots. When it was legal to shoot porcupines—and they were eaten as a delicacy—many more wild irises survived.

We sat in the shade under a trellis of vines, where the peeling and soaking of the rhizomes is done. Gianni showed me the typical *roncoli* curved knife, but he said that there was only one artisan left who made them and, whereas the farm used to employ twelve peelers, now there are only three. He explained that the roots shrivel to one-third their size as they dry in the sun and that, on their carpets of straw mats, they resemble chipolatas under the broiling sun—just as I used to think as a child. Behind the *fattoria* was the "warm room," a stiflingly hot wooden shed with a tin roof, just like a sauna. Gianni showed me the superior-quality roots that had been peeled and those of lesser quality that had not and explained that they were left to dry in the "warm room" for two years. He was worried, however, about what the demand for rhizomes would be in two years' time. The rhizomes—when they are ready—are transported whole; otherwise they lose their scent. As the sweat poured down my body, I tried to savor their smell, inhaling deeply, but Gianni explained that the fresh rhizomes do not smell.

Then we went into the *fattoria*, where it was deliciously cool, and Gianni led me into the *salotto*, a room reserved for guests and special occasions. It smelled of beeswax, mothballs and a whiff of iris from the sachets laid in the chest of best linen. *Salotti* are still the sepulchral places I remember from childhood, and this one was like all the others, furnished with heavy Tuscan oak furniture, kitschy glass ornaments, doilies, a lace tablecloth, a crucifix or two and heavy brocade curtains which were drawn to keep out the harsh sunlight.

As I left I realized that I had found the last fields of irises in Tuscany just in time, and I wondered how long it would be before even an enthusiastic young man like Gianni eventually abandoned iris cultivation and began tilling his land for the more lucrative olive oil and wine. The bucolic Tuscany of my childhood has changed. It is not even "Chiantishire" anymore; it is more like the Hamptons. Medici villas have been transformed into health spas or places where exclusive cooking courses are run, and the towns are littered with delis stocked with wine, lavender, honey and oil. Azure swimming pools have taken the place of the threshing floors, and tumbledown villages have been turned into restored showcase hamlets.

When I met Benedetta Alphandery—a tall, handsome woman

dressed in black and wearing a pair of flip-flops decorated with pearls—she presented me with a small book she had written on the iris. Benedetta Alphandery runs the Santa Maria Novella (SMN) perfumery with her father, the managing director, Signor Alphandery. SMN continues the perfumery traditions begun by the Dominican monks in the thirteenth century. The traditions were handed on to the Stefani family, and the Alphanderys are now the directors. When the taxi driver realized where I was going—to SMN's new laboratories in the suburbs of Florence— she flourished a plastic bag of SMN's potpourri and said she kept it on the dashboard all the time.

Benedetta introduced me to their in-house chemist, and I asked if real iris scent is still made, but I heard the same story about the difficulties: fewer fields of orris root and the length of time it takes for the roots to mature. Benedetta explained that *burro di giaggiolo* has to be distilled for twenty hours or more and that the resulting gooey butter can only then be extracted with solvents and refined into an absolute. It takes around 100 kilograms of rhizomes in powdered form to make 100 milliliters of essence.

As we walked around the pristine laboratories, Benedetta told me that they still used recipes that hadn't changed since medieval times. She also said that a preference for natural scents was returning, partly, she thought, because natural perfume smells different on every individual's skin, whereas the big-name brands' synthetic-based products smell the same on everyone. At SMN, Benedetta said, they use essential oils as the base notes, and those oils come from all over the world. They use bergamot from Calabria and vetivert, patchouli and sandalwood from Indonesia, Ceylon and India. A young chemist told me that they'd been testing a rosemary essence from Spain for three years.

I saw one of SMN's medieval recipes for potpourri being packed into terra-cotta bowls shaped like pomegranates and, as the herbal and floral aromas mingled in the clean cool air, it struck me that, whereas French scent is very rich and sophisticated, Italian scents are more innocent, aromatic and herblike, pure-smelling and immediately identifiable. I prefer the Italian smells, although I do find that it depends on the time of day. Italian scents suit the daytime because they are uplifting and possess a certain clarity; they go with linen and cotton. French scents, on the other hand, suit nighttime better because they're more seductive and erotic; I think they suit satins and silks.

Renaissance Beauty Treatments

HUNDREDS OF INVENTIVE RECIPES FOR PREPARATIONS FOR MAKEUP, using perfumed ingredients, appeared in the Renaissance. To us, these beauty preparations read more like culinary recipes and some seem quite repugnant, not to mention faintly irrational and not at all what you might find on a Clarins makeup counter in the twenty-first century.

However, Caterina Sforza—Countess of Forli and Imola and an alchemist, who marched with her soldiers to defend her small kingdom—recorded hundreds of these recipes in her treatise *Experimenti*, which was published posthumously in 1525. Among them is a mixture for a rejuvenating mask which was composed of lilies, terebenthine (fragrant resins), honey, breast milk, ➤

camphor, fresh eggs, pigeons and swallows—all distilled together! Another recipe for a face mask for "fresher complexions" seems positively to be the work of a sorceress. It is stomach-curdling and cruel, requiring a young crow to nest, hatch its eggs and nurture the chicks for forty days, after which time the chicks are killed and then distilled with myrtle leaves, talc and almond oil.

Caterina Sforza's recipes also included suggestions for overnight facials. You could either put a raw veal escalope soaked in milk on your face, or a mixture of egg whites beaten with flour. Strictly for nights alone, I think!

When we drove back to the center of Florence, Benedetta showed me around the ancient pharmacy at Santa Maria Novella and I imagined the scents that had once haunted the cold, dark, austere cloisters for centuries. Signor Alphandery conducted us around the *sala verde* (green room, because it is lined with green frescoes), where all kinds of medicinal preparations were sold to satisfy the whims of hypochondriacs. In neo-Gothic, carved walnut cabinets were displays of sixteenth-century filigreed thermometers of spun glass, tin and copper stills, and massive bronze and marble pestles and mortars. One of the pestles was so heavy that it had to be tied to a rope fixed to a bow that hung from the ceiling before the apprentice could handle it. Perfumery techniques made great strides in the Renaissance, as testified by the equipment in Santa Maria Novella's *sala verde*.

We walked out into the old *spezeria* (spice shop), where, until recently, all the preparations were made. The room was empty, but one old iris mill had been left behind which, once, had been used to grind the rhizomes. It resembled a giant mouli-légume. Beside it was a basket of discarded dried-up iris roots, all whorled and white, and I wondered how many decades they'd been lying there emitting their elusive scent: the scent of Renaissance noblemen.

The tour ended in the old monk's cell that is now Signor Alphandery's office; it overlooked the cloistered courtyard and, as the bells rang for vespers, Signor Alphandery told me that there were only nine monks left in the monastery. I thought that there probably wasn't a single monk left in Tuscany who distilled aromatic waters any longer.

I asked Signor Alphandery whether he thought certain scents appealed to different nationalities. He immediately said that the Japanese loved mint, the Americans loved old-fashioned pot-pourri, and tuberose, he said, was very popular with "il gays." He said that mimosa was popular too because it smelled of pure Tuscany. As I left, Signor Alphandery handed me a box tied with ribbons containing some almond soaps and a pomegranate scent.

As I wandered back from the Via della Scala along the stone streets, I came across another old pharmacy with a great carved wooden shopfront just off Piazza Signoria. It was called Dottore Bizzari. I went in and tried some unadulterated iris essence. As a droplet evaporated on my arm it smelled buttery and earthy, like the scent of grass or new-mown hay, and I breathed in the scents of countless herbs and flowers scattered across fields, stirred by the wind and warmed by the sun. As it settled on my skin I waited for the next scent layer to make itself known, but it never did, because natural iris butter is not strongly perfumed. Its delicacy makes it a perfect fixative to enhance other scents. I also chose an almond oil—*olio di mandorle*—infused with mandarin and eucalyptus.

As I left the pharmacy the bells of the Duomo rang out and a wave of melancholia washed over me, as it always does whenever I am about to leave Italy. But I knew that the iris note in my scent would always remind me of Tuscany and my childhood there. I was also lucky enough to be sent some orris absolute from the Monique Rémy laboratory in Grasse; it was like the hardest toffee imaginable, but when I melted it down it became really sticky and its perfume soaked into my clothes—which I loved. It smelled sublime.

If you grow up in Tuscany, as I did, her rugged terrain becomes part of your soul, and I knew that I had to have the perfume from Chianti's iris roots, which spring from that terrain, in my bespoke scent. The scent of the iris root is not floral; I don't even think it smells like violets, as some people think it does. To me it is distinctly rooty; it smells as the air smells after a summer shower. It has aromatic overtones not unlike fennel and—in my bespoke scent—it will ground the floral notes with its uncompromising masculine aura and its bouquet that echoes a Vino Nobile, and the noble scents of the Renaissance.

As Stephen, Tarquin and I drove away from Florence I began to wonder what nutmegs looked like in their natural state and to look forward to finding out about Asian spices. I was impatient, excited and curious about seeing the place where I was going to find these raw ingredients: Sri Lanka.

CHAPTER SIX

NUTMEG: THE BROKEN WORMY PUNKY

Sri Lanka, a Spice Island

The earth is a jewel case; the herbarium is
a perfume burner: cinnamon, mace, nutmeg,
ginger, opium, hashish, rose oil, betel nut,
capsicum, date sugar, Himalayan tea, aloes,
saffron, indigo from Salem and Madras:
does this all not resemble the spice mountain
of which Solomon spoke?

THEOPHILE GAUTIER
The Orient

I DECIDED TO TRAVEL ON MY OWN TO SRI LANKA AND INDIA, partly for budgetary reasons but mostly because taking Tarquin to Morocco had been more difficult than I'd thought it would be. I had fond memories of my own mother bundling my brother and I into her Saab and thinking nothing of driving to Turkey with us, but there was always a nanny in tow then—and I was anxious about the effect of the climate on Tarquin, not to mention worrying about malaria. So, unlike my carefree mother, I left my son happily ensconced in a nursery school in England; he was two and a half by then. Also, because it isn't difficult for a woman to travel on her own in Sri Lanka or in India, I left Stephen behind to look after Tarquin and I set off.

Nutmeg is a strange ingredient for a perfume, you might think, but I first came across it in a scent made by Jo Malone called Ginger and Nutmeg. I became as addicted to it as I am to nutmeg itself. My love of cooking and grating nutmeg into béchamel sauces to accompany fish and fettucine also inspired me to include nutmeg for a tenacious and spicy note in my perfume.

Nutmeg, or *Myristica fragrans*, has a definite musky smell. The nutmeg tree grows up to 60 feet tall and it is an evergreen. Its plumlike fruit splits open to reveal a scarlet lacy wrapping—the mace, a separate spice—enfolded around the nutmeg itself, which is the seed of the fruit. Oil of nutmeg is steam-distilled and adds a spicy or masculine note to a scent.

The etymology of the word "nutmeg" is quite complicated. One theory is that when nutmeg became familiar to the Byzantine traders—who obtained it from the Arabs—they may have used the name that derives from the Arabic word *mesk*, meaning musk. Another theory, which seems more plausible, is that the French term for musk—apart from *muscadier*—was *muguette* and, when combined with *noix* (nut), formed the phrase *noix muguette*. Early English derived *notemuge* from the French and, eventually, *notemuge* became "nutmeg." The botanical name, *Myristica fragrans*, sums up the scent; it means fragrantly musky. The ancient Indians and the Chinese called it by the Sanskrit names of *Jati-kosa* (for the mace) and *Jati-phala* (for the nutmeg), and they wrote up the taxonomy of the nutmeg in their medicinal treatises.

In Elizabeth David's anthology, *Is There a Nutmeg in the House?*, she writes that Joseph Nollekens—famed for his eighteenth-and early nineteenth-century busts of well-known people, including one of Laurence Sterne—was so partial to nutmegs that he stole them from the Royal Academy dinners. Again according to David, "the nutmeg appeared in England at least as far back as Chaucer's day—he mentions it in connection with ale." In the eighteenth century, people carried nutmegs everywhere—as an amulet to ward off evil and as a spice to flavor punches and rum—and they took portable nutmeg graters with them wherever they traveled. Silver nutmeg graters and boxes were intricately decorated, becoming essential items for eighteenth-century gentlemen along with their hip flasks, their snuffboxes and their traveling three-pronged forks. Dickens, in the nineteenth century, carried a monogrammed pocket nutmeg grater in his waistcoat.

Nutmeg probably arrived in medieval England when Arab merchants began to trade it in the Middle East and in the Mediterranean in the thirteenth century. And we know that nutmeg came to Constantinople as early as the ninth century, because Saint Theodore the Studite let his monks sprinkle it on their pease pudding on nonmeat days. Today nutmeg is used in hundreds of perfumes, particularly men's colognes; it is also used in medicines; and, as I discovered, it crops up in some unlikely quarters.

In the early sixteenth century Master Alexis of Piedmont, an alchemist, wrote that "To make a verie good perfume against the plague you must take mastich [a gum resin that smells like varnish], chypre, incense, myrrh, aloes, musk, ambergris, myrtle, bay, rosemary, sage, rose, cloves, mace and nutmegs. All these stamped and mixed together you shall set upon the coals and so perfume the chamber." What a heady and protective aroma it must have been.

I traveled to Sri Lanka—the island whose spices promise miracle remedies, oils and unctions to help us live longer—in the languorous heat. When I arrived the aroma of spices, of vanilla, of cloves, cardamom, cinnamon, nutmeg and pepper, lingered in the hazy tropical midnight air.

I had arranged to stay with a friend's mother, who owns a hotel in Kandy, the main nutmeg-growing region in Sri Lanka. I was shown to my bedroom and collapsed onto a four-poster bed under a black mosquito net suspended from a gold crown, where I slept fitfully until the morning light streamed through the bright orange curtains. I had breakfast on the terrace overlooking Kandy, which was laid out below me like a garden city spreading over steep hills that plunged down to an ornamental lake. The vegetation was lush, there was a profusion of flowers and trees and, as I drank it all in, my jet lag began to evaporate. It was like waking up in paradise.

I swam in a refreshingly chilly pool and then, as I studied some old sepia family photographs in the hotel, I saw my friend's grandmother—who had championed women's rights—standing with Nehru, and her grandfather, who had been the mayor of Kandy. When Helga Perrera Blow, my friend's mother, was seventeen she eloped with Jonathan Blow, the son of the architect Detmar Blow, who at one time rivaled Edwin Lutyens. There were press cuttings from the *Tatler* and color supplements about the Blows, who have an inimitable style: a combination of exotic Sri Lankan blood and English eccentricity.

I headed out to Matale, where there are over one hundred spice gardens with names like Diamond Spice, Greenland and Lord Paramount, run by salesmen who, even if you are feeling fine, will convince you that you have some ailment in order to sell you a cure. I chose the government-approved Regent Spice Garden and, on entering it, I was given an on-the-spot ayurvedic massage. Anointed and rubbed with different oils for my feet, head and legs, I felt the remains of my jet lag and exhaustion ebb away. Much revived, I toured the garden.

Every plant was labeled, and the earth around each one, a damp clay soil, was packed down with circles of coconut shells. I was told by the custodian that almonds are good for face creams; the roots of ginger are effective against asthma; aloe vera protects against the sun's harmful rays; cinnamon counteracts earache; lemon and lime reduce weight; and red coconut oil gets rid of pimples. He also told me that, in Sri Lanka, ginger, vanilla, pepper and cinnamon are used in perfumes and that the fruit of the nutmeg tree is made into marmalade. I discovered later that the outer casing of the fruit is actually made into jam but that in large quantities it is poisonous, while the nutmeg itself can be a potent drug.

Nutmeg Power

THERE IS NO DOUBT THAT NUTMEG, IF TAKEN IN SUFFICIENT quantities, can make you as high as a kite. It is added to organic ecstasy and can be taken neat (two tablespoonfuls, freshly grated, is the dose, apparently). It can also be added to iced cocktails, especially a daiquiri, or made into a "space paste," which is, I gather, four parts nutmeg mixed with other spices and Magimixed with maple syrup, then spread on toast or gulped down in a cup. If you drink several cups you can, apparently, remain high for days.

Nutmeg's natural high is similar to a hashish buzz—too much of it produces wild hallucinations, even astral traveling. The courtiers of ancient India, China and Imperial Rome carried small ivory boxes of freshly grated nutmeg powder to sprinkle into their wine for its hallucinogenic effect, and when sea trade routes were established, slaves—who knew that a few large seeds would give them a euphoric buzz—were punished for eating the nutmeg cargo.

Nutmeg is a recreational stimulant, and it is legal in U.S. prisons. Before his conversion to Islam, Malcolm X chilled out on nutmeg when his supply of marijuana ran out. In his autobiography he wrote, "I got high in Charleston prison on nutmeg. It ➤

had the kick of three or four reefers." When I got back to England I experimented with nutmeg grated into a glass of port and it certainly had a mildly trippy effect.

Nutmeg is also lauded for its aphrodisiac and magical powers. A sixteenth-century monk advised men to spread nutmeg oil over their genitals to increase virility, and William Salmon, a seventeenth-century doctor, recommended that nutmeg oil rubbed into the genitals would arouse sexual passion. Nutmeg was once widely used not only as an aphrodisiac but also as a cure for frigidity and impotence. It was, you could say, the first Viagra. As late as the eighteenth century it was still the custom for English newlyweds to be sent to their marital beds with a posset of wine, milk, egg yolk, sugar, cinnamon and nutmeg. Nutmeg is also a mental stimulant which blends beautifully with citrus oil, geranium and ylang-ylang.

Nutmeg has many other properties, and magical powers have been attributed to it; it is sometimes thought of as a sorcerer's scent and is one of the ingredients of a magical perfume described in *The Key of Solomon the King*—a book of black magic.

More colloquially, in football, to kick the ball between an opponent's legs is to "nutmeg" him—possibly from the slang use of the word "nutmegs" for testicles.

When the custodian had finished showing me around the Regent Spice Garden he took me to the shop and I smiled, wanly, as he wafted a sickly pineapple-and-banana essence under my nose. I asked him where nutmeg perfume oil was made but he did not appear to know. I noticed some interestingly named tinctures: "Slamming drops to bring down weight from bees honey"; "King Coconut oil stops hair dropping"; and "Red oil massage with your finger lips." I was persuaded to buy some sandalwood powder toothpaste after the custodian told me my teeth were gray(!) and I bought some ginger syrup tincture for my roll-up induced cough. (I hadn't been able to find any cigarettes in Sri Lanka, so I'd resorted to a packet of Old Holborn that I'd found in the nether regions of my bag.)

The Regent Spice Garden did not really suggest the powerful appeal of spices, nor the power struggles that were caused by the spice trade. Traces of cedarwood, cloves, cinnamon and nutmeg had been found impregnated in mummies' bandages, and as early as 1000 B.C., a scroll had listed over eight hundred medications, incenses and perfumes that used spices. The merchants of Imperial Rome developed trade routes to India and Arabia—sailing with the monsoon winds on the Arabian Sea past the Gulf of Aden and the island of Socotra, south to Kerala in India. Trade with India, however, was a serious drain on the empire's resources, because what came back was almost entirely luxury goods for the rich: brocades, rare spices and jewels, and even exotic pets like monkeys and peacocks. And the Romans paid in gold.

The Arabs capitalized on European ignorance of the origins of spices by inventing wild stories to protect their market, to satisfy curiosity and to discourage competitors. They described how cinnamon grew in deep glens infested with serpents and how great birds used cinnamon sticks to make their nests; brave villagers, said the Arabs, raided the birds' nests to collect the cinnamon. Cassia, they said, grew in shallow lakes guarded by flying snakes. But Pliny the Elder wrote that the tales had been invented for the purpose of enhancing the price of the spices, which, of course, was true.

It was not until the fourteenth century, after the Crusades, that luxuries like nutmeg filtered back into Europe and became popular once more. In 1393, one pound of nutmeg was worth seven fat oxen. London procured its spices from Venice, and the merchants traveled overland. Their routes linked with the Silk Route, which began in Petra, in Jordan, and continued to Persia, Afghanistan, India and finally to China. By the year 1500 major sea routes had also been established across the Indian Ocean: the longest was from Aden in southern Yemen to Malacca in Indonesia.

Vasco da Gama's arrival in Sri Lanka and the Spice Islands in 1498 heralded the Portuguese monopoly on the spice trade, which lasted for over a century. However, the Portuguese failed to take Aden, the gateway to the Red Sea, and despite their dominance over the Indian Ocean, their rule declined; what was left of the Portuguese spice trade was finally destroyed when the Dutch seized the Spice Islands and Sri Lanka in 1621. Dutch control was itself broken when a Frenchman nicknamed Peter Poivre stole nutmeg and clove seedlings and established them on Mauritius in 1762.

I visited a few more spice gardens but failed to discover the exotic fragrances or ingredients I was looking for. I realized that what I needed to find were the spice merchants and nutmeg plantations, so I hired a driver to take me to Dumballa, where I saw the great golden temple with its colossal gold-leafed Buddha glittering in the sunlight. The driver and I, accompanied by a boy guide, climbed 150 meters up a vast sloping rock face, polished by centuries of pilgrims' bare feet. From the top we saw curvaceous hills, undulating verdant valleys and inky-blue mountains stretched out below us, shimmering in the heat haze.

The sculpted folds of the Buddha's robes were so delicate that it was difficult to believe they had been carved from rock. In each of the six caves I saw hundreds of Buddhist images painted with natural pigments, mixed with an extract of jungle plants and lime, and I discovered that a paste of tamarind and teakwood shavings mixed with honey had kept the murals intact for hundreds of years. The airless caves were full of the smell from the wilting sweet-scented jasmine and frangipani petals that were scattered over the altars.

On the way to Dumballa we passed cricket fields where boys were playing the great national game, and I saw girls who looked like bridesmaids, wearing long white dresses with garlands in their hair; I discovered later that this was their school uniform. I also saw men bathing in the rivers while women did the laundry on the riverbanks. Dumballa was one great landscaped garden of flowering orchids, rhododendrons, trees draped with Spanish moss, fruit trees, mangos and papayas. Shallow lakes were interspersed with paddy fields, and duckboards had been laid across the ponds and swamps. The region was covered with dense undergrowth and a tall canopy of hardwood trees, including teak, ebony and silkwood, and the Gothic railway stations and wooden villas with their gabled verandas were reminders of the colonial past. However, I failed to find any nutmeg plantations, let alone spice merchants, and I returned to my friend's mother's hotel feeling despondent.

But, as I walked into my bedroom, the telephone rang. I was told that there was someone waiting for me downstairs in the bar. I couldn't think who it might be, but when I got there I found Julian—yes, she really does spell her name that way—West, whom I hadn't seen for years. She is half–Sri Lankan and half-English, and after three grueling years as a war correspondent she had returned to Kandy to write a novel. She'd heard that I'd been asking around about spice merchants and nutmeg plantations, and she told me I needed introductions. She invited me to stay with her and put me in touch with Link Natural Products, the Sri Lankan producers of essential oils near Colombo. They, in turn, put me in touch with a spice merchant. Another of Julian's friends rang to say he could arrange for me to see a distant cousin of his who owned a nutmeg plantation.

At last I felt I was getting somewhere, but I also felt a little foolish. I shouldn't have presumed that I'd just be able to find the spice merchants and the nutmeg plantations on my own. The trade is controlled by the merchants, or middlemen, and they don't talk to just anyone. Also, the spice gardens—which I had thought would reveal all—turned out, essentially, to be tourist attractions rather than places where I could find the answers to all my questions about nutmeg.

I woke up the next morning at dawn and, after a luxurious breakfast in bed, I went to meet a Muslim spice merchant: all merchants and middlemen in Sri Lanka are Muslim. In the pouring rain I found Mr. Bougari, a jovial, burly man, and we sat at his desk to look at samples of his spices. He told me that nutmeg was used in face creams and that it prevented black-heads. Then he showed me the grade of nutmeg that is used in extraction and distillation to make nutmeg oil. He also told me that the Sri Lankan slang for nutmeg is the "broken wormy punky," because the grade of nutmeg that is used for distilling and extraction is often broken, and sometimes it will have been infested by pests, whereas the grade used for cooking is whole and pest-free. The nutmeg concrete, or butter, is prepared in oblong cakes which are wrapped in palm leaves.

Nutmeg and mace are two distinctly separate spices and separate essential oils are distilled from them. Nutmeg, the seed, gives the best oils and highest yields. Otto of nutmeg is a beautiful transparent fluid which smells intensely of the nut: spicy, warm, aromatic and sweet and, as its name in Italian—*noce moscato*—suggests, it is musky and resinous, rather than overtly spicy, and so is somewhat mysterious. Oil of nutmeg blends particularly well with bergamot, sandalwood and lavender, and the nutmeg also yields an unctuous fat oil which is made into soap under the brand name Bandana, or Banda, after the archipelago where the nutmeg trees grow. (Sadly, I discovered that the December 2004 tsunami badly affected more than half the smallholder nutmeg plantations there: I do hope they recover.)

Mace, the crimson leathery covering which forms the layer (the aril or membrane) around the nutmeg seed, yields a strong-smelling oil that is useful for scenting soaps but not scent, while nutmeg oil is used in frangipani perfume. The odor of mace is spicy, as nutmeg scent is, but there the similarity ends. Otto of mace is procured by distillation, as is nutmeg otto, but the different parts of the nutmeg tree, like the orange tree, yield distinct fragrances.

The Nutmeg Trade

FEW FRAGRANT SUBSTANCES HAVE HAD MORE COMMERCIAL importance than the nutmeg. At one time it was considered such a valuable commodity that the battle to secure the nutmeg trade grew fierce, sparked a war between the British and the Dutch and, indirectly, led to the birth of the most glamorous city in the world. The Dutch and the British fought for decades in the East Indies over spice-trading rights, and the spice they coveted above all was the nutmeg.

Nutmeg is indigenous to the Isle of Run in the remote Banda archipelago in the East Indies. The Banda islands were the nutmeg gardens of the world, and Run was central to the battle between the Dutch and the English. The Isle of Run is still thickly forested with nutmeg trees, and you can smell the island long before you see it: its languorous scent hangs in the air over the cliffs where the willowy nutmeg trees set down their roots and burst into flower each spring. The flowers are small, bell-shaped and light yellow, but they are not used in perfume. Enough nutmeg was harvested to fill a flotilla of ships every year, making Run—which is rich in volcanic soil and has a microclimate that is perfect for nutmeg trees—the most lucrative of all the Spice Islands, although the devastation caused by the frequent hurricanes means that nutmeg trees are all too often destroyed, and Run is no longer the most lucrative of the Spice Islands.

Run was seized by the British, and when Nathaniel Courthope, an English spice merchant from the East India ➤

Company, was besieged there by the Dutch, European nutmeg supplies were cut off. Recounting these events in his book *Nathaniel's Nutmeg*, Giles Milton tells how Courthope faced starvation as he and his men held off the Dutch navy for four years between 1616 and 1620. Eventually they had to surrender, but Courthope's great courage brought the British the most wonderful bargain (at least for a while). The 1667 Dutch-British treaty awarded Run to the Dutch, while, in exchange, a piece of valueless land on the other side of the world, which was then called New Amsterdam, was given to the British. It was, of course, renamed New York.

The British recaptured the Banda islands in 1796, and the East India Company, over the following two years, imported 129,723 pounds of nutmeg and 286,000 pounds of mace into England alone. By 1814 the annual consumption of nutmeg in England had risen to 140,000 pounds.

Giles Milton wrote: "Nutmeg was the most coveted luxury in seventeenth-century Europe . . . [it was] a spice held to have such powerful medicinal properties that men would risk their lives to acquire it." The "withered little nut," as Milton described it, became as sought after as gold. In London, nutmeg commanded fabulous prices: with a markup of 60,000 percent, it cost 90 shillings (£4.50) per pound. A sackful could set a man up for life.

Nutmeg began to be used in perfume preparations in England in the early nineteenth century. The English uprooted hundreds of nutmeg seedlings from the Isle of Run and the Moluccas, and transported them to their colony, Sri Lanka, thus sounding the death knell for the Bandanese economy.

Mr. Bougari led me into the warehouse, which was filled with the luscious pulverulent smell of *Myristica fragrans*. I saw rows of women, young and old, sitting silently shelling and sorting good nutmegs from lesser-quality ones and sizing them into piles of small, medium and large. The warehouse echoed rhythmically with the rattling and tapping of the workers' wooden mattocks as they split open the shells. After the nutmegs have been shelled they are dried on straw mats in the sun. At this stage they have no scent—unless you get extremely close to them—because the smell is still encased inside the nut and is released only when the nutmegs are grated.

I asked Mr. Bougari how many hours a day the women worked, and was told that the law prohibited more than an eight-hour day, but that machinery to do the job would cost much more than the manual labor. Mr. Bougari broke open a shell to reveal an oval nutmeg seed. It was a marbled mixture of light and dark brown, like a praline chocolate, and a pungent, musky, nutty smell emanated from it.

In the shop, which was on the street in front of the ware-house, men were weighing spices and baling them into sacks. Mr. Bougari told me that mace, cardamom, coriander, nutmeg, cloves, pepper and even the resinoid fenugreek are used in perfumery.

We drove out to the plantations of stately nutmeg trees, which soar to 40 or even 60 feet. Nutmeg trees are either male or female and they are insect-pollinated, although to this day no one is quite sure which species of insect does the pollinating. Some say it is a moth, others a beetle or a bee; yet others suggest it is simply the wind. But what is known is that the imperial pigeon is the main disperser of nutmeg seeds; it is attracted to the nutmeg by the purple arils (the mace). All nutmeg trees bear mostly female flowers, and the pollen from one male nutmeg tree guarantees a harem of twelve female trees bearing fruit. Beneath the nutmeg trees a warm, pungent, slightly sweet smell hung in the damp motionless air. The aroma of the fruit is likened to fragrant blossoms and is so heavy that birds become intoxicated as they fly by.

Harvesters pluck the fruit by hand, and the nutmegs that they can't reach are knocked down with long wooden poles. Nutmegs are harvested all year round, each tree yielding about eight thousand nutmegs a year. But the harvesting can begin only seven years after the tree has been planted, and the tree reaches its maximum potential when it is between seventeen and twenty years old; so, although the harvest is continuous, it requires long-term investment.

The main area for nutmeg trees is around Kandy, where there are hundreds of "home gardens," or smallholdings, with nutmeg groves. Nutmeg gatherers collect the nutmegs from the smallholdings; the harvest provides a small income for both growers and gatherers. Mr. Bougari took me to see a family of nutmeg growers on their smallholding. Mothers, toddlers and babies came out of their huts, and one of the men picked a fruit and peeled back the crimson outer lacy covering—the mace—to show me the seed.

The fruit of the nutmeg tree resembles a small peach, but in place of the peach's flesh is a thick, fibrous husk underneath the outer skin. Inside the husk is the thick layer of lacy material that produces the mace, and this surrounds the seed shell. The seed itself is the nutmeg. When the nutmeg fruit is ripe the husk splits apart, revealing the crimson-colored mace inside. At this point the fruit is harvested. The mace is carefully peeled away from the seed shell; as soon as it is removed the blades of mace are spread out to dry. The nutmegs, on the other hand, are left in the shell and dried until they rattle when shaken. The shells are then cracked open and the nutmegs removed.

Mr. Bougari told me that nutmeg fruits glow like lightbulbs in moonlight, and that people used to put nutmeg under their armpits when they went to festive gatherings, presumably, I thought, so that the nutty, musky smell combined with underarm sweat would act as an erotic deodorant.

Images of nutmeg fruits glowing like Chinese lanterns filled my mind as, after I left Mr. Bougari, my taxi driver drove me three hours "up-country" to see a 48-acre nutmeg plantation with some nine hundred nutmeg trees. The countryside got wilder and more beautiful. I saw iguanas wander across the red earth of the dirt track, and carefully tended gardens fenced in with young trees that had been woven together. It started to rain heavily; the smell of the rain-sodden earth, the cloves, coconut, mildew and mold, cinnamon and orange rising in the mist, conjured up mince pies and Stilton. I felt sudden pangs of nostalgia for past Christmases.

A German family owned the plantation. They lived in a colonial lodge with a long, deep veranda, where I found some of the family poring over huge logbooks, doing the accounts. The owner, Gunther Helm, told me that his family had been there for twenty-five years, that 20 percent of the population cultivated spices and that most of the plantations were smallholdings.

Unfortunately it continued to rain so heavily that it was impossible to go out to see the trees, so we discussed flower cultivation in Sri Lanka, and Mr. Helm told me that, up in the Nuwara Eliya region, they grew carnations and the best roses, all in different colors.

Resigned to the fact that I wasn't going to see a second nutmeg plantation, I traveled to the capital, Colombo, where I went to Link Natural Products, the only distillers of essential oils in Sri Lanka. One of the directors picked me up from the Galle Face Hotel and drove me past swamps and lagoons into the spice-growing hill country. As soon as we got out of the air-conditioned car the profusion and concentration of spices from the distillery and warehouses almost overwhelmed me. I felt as if I were sinking into a vat of mulled wine.

Pepper Money

EDWARD GIBBON WROTE, IN *THE DECLINE AND FALL OF THE ROMAN Empire,* that pepper was a favorite ingredient in the most extravagant Roman cookery. Pliny the Elde—who always disapproved of the Romans' decadence and apparently unquenchable appetite for luxury—complained that, "There is no year in which India does not drain the Roman Empire of 50 million sesterces." Black pepper was, once, worth its weight in gold. In the fifteenth century, Europeans consumed about one quarter of all Asian spices, but the greatest consumer of pepper was China. In the sixteenth century, Europe's consumption of pepper increased and its price rose considerably. At source it cost 1 or 2 grams of silver, but

➤

that amount rose to 14 grams of silver in Alexandria and to as much as 30 grams once the pepper reached Europe.

For centuries pepper has kept the wheels of trade turning. It became such an important commodity in ancient Greece, Egypt and Rome that a duty was levied on it at the borders. In the Middle Ages Venice imported 1,000,000 pounds of pepper each year, and the Portuguese more than 2,000,000 pounds. In the fifteenth century, its exorbitant price drove the Portuguese to seek a sea route to India so that they could monopolize the pepper trade, and Lisbon became the center of pepper trading for a while. Although trade in pepper is far smaller now than it was then, it still accounts for a quarter of the world's spice trade.

In the seventh century, when spices were first traded commercially, they soon became recognized as a universal currency in the way that credit cards are now. In the Middle Ages a man's liquidity was judged by his pepper assets. There are records of serfs buying their freedom with peppercorns, and they were so valuable that even a few of them would pay the rent, as we know from the expression "a peppercorn rent." Even as late as 1937 the King of England received from the mayor of Launceston in Cornwall the sum of 100 shillings and 1 pound of pepper in rent.

It is a popular misconception that, in the Middle Ages, pepper was used to disguise the smell of rotting meat, though it was used in all manner of drinks and food.

Pepper was first used in antiquity along with other spices in unguents and perfumes and incense. It was also used in colognes. In the last century it was reintroduced to perfume by Guerlain. Today, Yves Saint Laurent's Opium contains pepper.

I learned how Link Natural Products use environmentally friendly technology combined with ancient ayurvedic wisdom to distill their essential oils of cinnamon, cloves, vanilla and nutmeg. They export their oils to global perfume companies, like International Flowers and Fragrances, and since 1982 they have also been making health care products, essential oils and oleoresins. (All spices contain oleoresins, which are a mixture of oil and resin. These are extracted from the spices with solvents and separated. The volatile essential oil is steam-distilled into its purest form; the nonvolatile waxes, fatty oils, pigments and tannins—from the resin—are used for flavoring and coloring in cooking.)

I was shown into the conference room, where fans whirred, and introduced to the managing director, a graduate of Manchester University. He told me that the biggest consumers of nutmeg oil these days are Coca-Cola and Pepsi, each of whom buys 400,000 liters a year. I wondered whether nutmeg was the secret of their twenty-first-century success. Both Coca-Cola and Pepsi were once made with cocaine, but when it was banned nutmeg was substituted; it occurred to me that perhaps it is the nutmeg that induces the mild high that people who drink Coca-Cola and Pepsi can experience. I also wondered whether that was why both companies still keep their recipes secret, although I had discovered—see Chapter 3—that lime and cinnamon are also ingredients in the recipes. I know, from watching my small son when he's stolen sips from my Coke when I wasn't looking, that it does induce a mild hit.

An elderly man showed us around the distilleries. The vats were squeaky-clean and steam and pressure controlled. On the day I was there they were distilling cardamom, the camphorlike smell of which took me straight into the souks of the Middle East and the coffee that they lace with cardamom. (Cardamoms are small, squiggly pods, and the end product, after distillation, is a lemony-colored liquid whose scent is a little more tenacious in oil form.) Then we were taken up to the flat roof of the distillery, where the raw materials are dried before the oils and resins are extracted and distilled. We stood on the roof breathing in the warm, pungent smell of the cardamom as it bubbled away beneath us in the distillery. The atmosphere was heavy with the smell; I could almost taste mulled wine. There were other smells too, of mothballs and rum, mint and molasses, and my nose sent some funny olfactory messages to my taste buds. I had the odd sensation that I was eating After Eight mints. On the way back down, on the top floor of the distillery which is used for grinding and husking, I saw a huge stainless-steel nutmeg grinder with a jagged set of dangerous-looking teeth. Broken, wormy, punky nutmegs are ground before the oil is distilled from them.

At Link Natural Products they purify the distilling water so that, when the water goes back into the ground, there is no effluent. I saw the big purifying plant behind the distillery. All their raw materials are stringently quality controlled and tested in the microbiology laboratory before the oils and other products are extracted. Link Natural Products have also perfected a postharvest technology for herbs and spices. Every sample is monitored and given a fingerprint by each grower so that the ingredient can be traced from the grower all the way to the bottled product.

Link sources their herbs and spices from large estates and from smallholdings, but they insist that the raw ingredients they buy are organically grown. They select the growers and teach them organic farming methods, if necessary, and they do not buy from farmers who use pesticides. From four hundred types of medicinal herbs, they make 250 ayurvedic medicinal products. They make wine tonics, herbal teas, toothpastes, muscle gels, herbal balms, *ashwagandharishta*—an energy drink—and *balarista*, which is a sleeping draft. They also make *ashayarista* syrups for hemorrhoids and even some Sihini Slimdrops, which—supposedly—help you to shed a few pounds.

Ayurvedic medicine has a five-thousand-year history. Link Natural Products follows its methods, but they combine ayurvedic recipes with new technology: ayurvedic doctors work with Link's scientists to develop and improve the products. Ancient ayurvedic healers understood that herbs are the most concentrated and powerful natural medicines. Researchers today are confirming that herbs contain the richest mixtures of phytochemicals, which correct imbalances. Link's most successful product is a sort of ayurvedic Lemsip, only it is much more effective; Link sells 400 million sachets each year. As I discovered from a box of sachets they gave me, you dissolve the mixture in hot water exactly as you would with Lemsip, but this product really works. By the time I got home I had a streaming cold, so I dosed myself with it—it doesn't taste of saccharine and is spicy. It knocked ordinary old Lemsip for six.

Ayurveda

AYURVED IS A SANSKRIT WORD MEANING "KNOWLEDGE FOR PROLONG-ing life." It is a five-thousand-year-old medical system, which is still practiced throughout India and Sri Lanka. Ayurvedic herbal and spice preparations include soaps, herbal wines, tisanes, shampoos, herbal balms, massage oils, cosmetic face creams, skin ointments and sun lotions. The essential teaching of ayurvedic medicine is that many diseases are psychosomatic. Disease and/or illness are regarded as symptoms of imbalance in the system, so it is the imbalance, rather than the disease or illness, that is treated with herbal remedies, helped by yogic cleansing.

Ayurved is yoga's sister science and it stems from the same Vedic philosophy. The Maharishi Mahesh Yogi—who founded transcendental meditation and taught it to the Beatles—also promoted the understanding of ayurvedic medicine, which, forty years ago, was almost unheard, of in the West but is now an integral part of alternative health practice and holistic healing. The whole system of ayurvedic medicine is based on a vegetarian diet of the three elements laid out in the Hindu *Bhagavad Gita*. The first element is Sattvic, the foods of which are fresh and pure—such as milk, fresh fruits, vegetables, grains, legumes, nuts and seeds—and on which the diet should largely be based; the second is Rajasic, the foods of which are bitter, sour and salty, hot and spicy—such as coffee, tea, meat, fish, eggs, spices and butter; and the third element is Tamasic, the foods of which are fermented and overripe, for example cheese and alcohol.

➤

> The Aveda company produces a line of Pure-Fumes based on ayurvedic principles. These scents and other products are mind-and mood-enhancing and they boost energy levels. Aveda's Pure-Fumes follow ayurvedic preparation methods and are classified according to the doshas (elements). The three doshas are Vata (Air and Ether), Pitta (Fire and Water) and Kapha (Water and Earth). Aveda research the ingredients for their chakra aromas in India and are well versed in the ancient ayurvedic texts. A classic ayurvedic incense recipe which represents all the elements is:
>
> **Air** (leaves) patchouli **Ether** (fruits) star anise
> **Fire** (flowers) clove **Water** (stems and branches) sandalwood, aloeswood, cassia, frankincense and myrrh
> **Earth** (roots) turmeric, vetivert, ginger, costus root, valerian, spikenard

Back in the warehouse, three hundred women were sorting out bags of herbs by hand; some were to be ground and some boiled and, in the bottling-plant warehouse, women and girls were bottling vetivert shampoo. I lingered there because I love vetivert. It is a most uncompromising raw material; it stands on its own and is rather solemn and stoic. In the shampoo I saw being bottled, essence of vetivert was being blended with coconut oil, which was the carrier oil: it imparted a certain fairground sweetness to the product.

Outside, copper cauldrons of coconut and almond massage oil

were gently simmering away—the smell reminded me of cakes—and I was told that the copper oxidization from the cauldrons preserves the green color of the plants. Up in the laboratory, on the top floor, the scientists showed me their different oils. There was oil of nutmeg, which was golden, and there were oils of black pepper, clove, cardamom and cinnamon. They were bottled like preserves and were limpid and pure, and treated like liquid gold. The oil of the nutmeg was the most transparent. They carefully gave me a few samples on blotters and even now, a year later, all the spicy scents impregnate the pages of my notebook; but by far the most delicate and ethereal is the musky note of nutmeg.

The oil of the "broken wormy punky" is versatile and magical. It is a scent, a medicine, a drug, an aphrodisiac and a delicious culinary flavoring. And nutmeg oil reflects how tastes have changed over the centuries: its earliest use was for embalming the dead to prepare them for the afterlife, and its curative properties are still said to promote longevity, but, as we have seen, the twenty-first century's greatest consumer of nutmeg oil is the Coca-Cola company; and one has to question how far civilization has come. Despite this, nutmeg oil is also used in dozens of perfumes, though rarely as a single note. Calvin Klein's Obsession has notes of nutmeg and clove; Diptyque's L'Autre has notes of coriander, cardamom, pepper, cumin and nutmeg and is quite literally the olfactory equivalent of curry!

Serge Lutens's Fleurs de Citronnier leaves a trail of neroli, wine, honey, tuberose and nutmeg in its wake; it is the nutmeg oil that, according to Lutens, gives the perfume its elusive sensuality. Similarly, his Arabie is a mysterious mélange of cedar and sandalwood, enriched with dried figs and dusty dates, nutmeg, cumin and clove: it is delicious. Jo Malone's first creation was a homemade batch of ginger-and-nutmeg-scented bath oil. She made it as a present for her clients when she worked as a beautician, but it was such a success that they all wanted more. She has never looked back, and I still think it her best scent.

I thought nutmeg would add mystery and a little nuance to my own bespoke scent and, perhaps, prove holistically healing. I thought also that it might make my scent slightly narcotic. When I put a few drops of nutmeg on my pillow one night I dreamed in Technicolor of the steaming valleys of Sri Lanka, forested with nutmeg trees releasing their aromatic vapors. Nutmeg vividly brings back the warm spicy air that blows offshore in Sri Lanka and the almost unearthly fragrance that reaches those sailing toward the Isle of Run.

Nutmeg would, I hoped, smolder beneath the other ingredients in my scent, just as a pinch of nutmeg adds a subtle nuance to Forcalquier pastis. As I sat on the plane and breathed in the musky nutmeg scent from msy notebook, I thought how well it would temper the exotic jasmine top note in my scent. I looked forward to putting the two together in my next destination, India.

CHAPTER SEVEN

ZAMBAC JASMINE AND VETIVERT

India

In the summertime the beautiful women
of the court perfume their breasts with
sandal oil, their hair with jasmine oil,
and the rest of their bodies with rose
oil. They are ready for love.

KALIDASA
The Seasons

THE SMELL OF JASMINE IS A QUINTESSENTIAL PART OF Indian life. The Hindu poets call jasmine "Moonlight of the Grove" because it is a night-blooming flower. The Arabs call it *yasmyn*, and the plant became indigenous in Europe after the Moors brought it to the gardens of the Alhambra in Granada. Several varieties of jasmine are grown in India; the most widespread is *Grandifloram*. Zambac jasmine is native to Arabia and grows wild in India, and a high-yielding clone of Spanish jasmine has recently been developed at Tamil Nadu Agricultural University in Coimbatore. The plant grows like a small bush in well-irrigated soil and produces tiny blossoms. Jasmine also grows in Tunisia, Morocco and Egypt.

About eight thousand flowers are needed to make just 1 milliliter of jasmine absolute, or 1 ton of flowers to make 1 liter of absolute. It is, literally, like getting blood out of a stone. Harvesting takes place as dawn breaks so that the blossoms retain their odor before the sun's heat spoils the scent. The flowers have to be plucked individually—a dextrous and time-consuming skill. A good gatherer can pick about 1 kilogram an hour. Once picked, the flowers are put into a special flat basket so that they aren't crushed and are then taken to extraction sites on wooden carts drawn by oxen.

In the 1930s perfumes consisted of about 10 percent jasmine absolute; today concentrations are much lower, at about 2 percent, but according to the blenders no great perfume is made without it. Jasmine is the most widely used of all the white flowers in perfumery because of its indole, which is one of the strongest odors around and which, on its own, smells curiously like wet fur, making the jasmine carnal—which marries well with our own bodily smells—and mysterious. Jasmine is known as the king of oils, rivaled only by rose oil, and is said to cure depression and anxiety; it also eases labor pains by strengthening contractions. Jasmine is the sweetest of smells and is powerful enough to scent a whole room. The list of notes associated with jasmine include flowery, warm, animal, spicy, fruity and rich.

In France jasmine used to be treated by *enfleurage* but now it is extracted; it is too delicate to withstand the heat in steam distillation. It is percolated in a solvent of purified hexane, which is eventually removed with a special vacuum pump or evaporator. However, in India, jasmine flowers are still sometimes distilled in the traditional method on the banks of the Ganges. Clay stills are filled with twice the amount of water to jasmine flowers and the mixture is left to cool overnight. By morning the otto, or essential oil, has congealed on the surface and is carefully skimmed off. Sandalwood shavings are added to facilitate the skimming-off so the jasmine otto becomes infused with a heavy sandalwood aroma. An Indian perfume called Chameli Ka Tel (fragrant jasmine oil), which has existed for at least a thousand years, is made by macerating jasmine flowers in sesame oil.

Sanskrit treatises on perfume and perfume compounds classify the fragrance families as *vargas*. They include sublime mixtures of holy basil, saffron, cloves, nutmeg, pepper, musk and camphor. There are also all kinds of recipes for perfumed waters, incense, powders, oils and some quite advanced technical processes such as *Bhavana*, which was a method of saturating perfumed powders with liquid.

India's rich resources of natural perfumes, such as cinnamon, cassia, saffron, valerian (which yields spikenard) and pepper, were important trading commodities in antiquity. As early as 200 B.C. cardamom, pepper, nutmeg, cloves and cinnamon were sent out into the world from Kerala, and sailors spoke of how, when their ships approached the southwestern coast of India, the sea breezes brought them gusts of scented air, of pepper and other spices, from the land. (Everyone I met in India eulogized about the euphoric smell of mace and other spices that still emanates today from the warehouses at Cochin in Kerala.) In the first century A.D. trade between the Roman empire and India reached its zenith, and gems, silks, gold, fragrant woods and many perfumes and spices such as bdellium (an aromatic gum resin, pronounced "delm"), cassia, cinnamon, costus (an aromatic root), cardamom, cloves, spikenard, ginger and sandalwood flowed into Roman markets. The two great civilizations continued to trade and exchange customs, although they were suspicious of each other. The Romans exploited the East and the traders made large profits. Roman women imitated oriental women by putting henna on their fingertips, like nail varnish, and rubbing musk into their bodies.

Attar is a vital part of modern Indian life and is used as a perfume concentrate, especially by the Muslims, who are particularly fond of a scented powder called *abeer*, a heady mixture of sandalwood, aloes, turmeric, roses, camphire (a kind of henna) and civet. *Attardans* (rosewater sprinklers) are circulated at weddings; smart Indian women wear musk and saffron, and ointments to make hieratic signs on the face are infused with sandalwood. In their scents, the Hindus tend to prefer light, fresh notes, especially those made from freshly cut flowers.

Perfumes are still used in modern Hindu worship too. Incense is burned in ceremonies, and some temples are covered, daily, with freshly gathered blossoms. At the Krishna festival a red powder is dissolved in rosewater and squirted over passersby from syringes. Hindu marriages are celebrated under a canopy where a sacred fire is kept going by throwing sandalwood and scented oils into it.

India has changed since I traveled to Kashmir and Ladakh in 1986; in the intervening years it has become much more Westernized and organized, which is both a good and a bad thing. But some things never change. As soon as you arrive in India you experience an assault on all the senses, especially the olfactory sense. The smells are foul and fragrant, the foul making the fragrant all the more beautiful. If you happen to pass a cesspool it matters far less if you are wearing a garland of jasmine and marigolds around your neck. The acrid smell of bidi smoke and betel nut juice, rancid curds, fatty ghee and rotting rubbish intermingle with sweet-scented jasmine and wafts of coriander, sharp-smelling tiny onions, pyramids of sweet-smelling tomatoes and the smoke from the ubiquitous incense sticks. All float and mingle in the heat and dust, but the potent Indian perfumes are often the strongest smells. You can smell aphrodisiac musk and patchouli, oleaginous sandalwood and grassy vetivert. After a year my bags and summer clothes are still suffused with the scents of India; they just don't seem to fade.

I went first to the temple town of Madurai, where the air is thick with incense and filled with the scent of cartloads of freshly cut flowers destined for the temples as offerings to the deities. Madurai is a city of pilgrims and beggars, and there is an overwhelming atmosphere of devotion and excitement. Towering *gopurams* (spires) of Dravidian baroque, the size of modest skyscrapers, dominate the skyline.

I went into the Sri Meenakshi temple by the east gate, leaving my shoes at the door. I saw the garland makers heaping mountains of jasmine and marigolds onto scales and then dextrously threading them into necklaces and bracelets. Close by were a cluster of attar wallahs (perfume sellers) plying their wares. They sold ointments, attars and incense. In India the perfumer serves both men and gods, the physical and the spiritual.

A procession of saffron-robed priests playing cymbals and drums wove its way between the shrines like a caterpillar, and thousands of pilgrims, anointed with aromatic yellow marks on their foreheads, offered garlands of jasmine and roses at the shrines. Temple music, sometimes mournful and sometimes frenetic, echoed under the coffered ceilings. The air was heavily suffused with the scent from emollients burning in clay bowls, and clouds of incense and dustings of saffron and crimson pigment floated by.

Outside the temple walls I paused to watch a procession of seminaked *sadhus* (Indian holy men) whose skin was tinted orange from the saffron ointment that they rub in. Orange has always been a holy color in India, and saffron has sacred associations.

Saffron

SAFFRON IS THE MOST EXPENSIVE OF ALL THE SPICES. IT IS extracted from an autumn-flowering lilac crocus and at least 100,000 stamens, or stigmas, yield only 1 kilogram of dried saffron. These days its fragrantly scented potency is most commonly used to flavor paellas and other dishes. The Greeks, however, believed that Zeus slept on a bed of saffron, and wealthy Romans scattered saffron on their beds and stuffed cushions and pillows with dried saffron stamens. *Dormivit in sacco croci* (he has slept on a bed of saffron) also implied a passionate night of lovemaking.

In Roman times saffron from the province of Cilicia in southern Asia Minor was used in great quantities. Statues were washed down with saffron-perfumed water, and saffron-perfumed rivulets ran in small gutters down stairways, around the sides of chambers and into fountains. Saffron also has a cooling effect, and during the Hindu Mariatta Codam festival, saffron-perfumed unguent is rubbed into the skin of those who pass through the crowds collecting alms; people who make donations receive scented sticks of sandalwood in return.

Today saffron is to be found in only two perfumes. The French company Diptyque makes Opone, which has lots of saffron in it, and Ormonde Jayne's Taif has top notes of saffron, as well as dates and pink pepper. Otherwise saffron is an ingredient that is no longer held in such esteem in scent, or as an aphrodisiac. Rather, it is the expensive ingredient that you show off in your kitchen spice rack and scatter on your bouillabaisse.

I mused on what I'd discovered about the Indian floriculture industry. It is booming. Almost 80,000 hectares of land are devoted to the cultivation of roses, jasmine, marigolds, chrysanthemums and tuberoses. Production is estimated to be an astonishing 300,000 tons of loose flowers each year, and by the 1990s India was exporting 3,536,553 million rupees' worth of attars and perfumes. There is a huge demand for freshly cut flowers, because at Indian ceremonies and rituals, and for almost any occasion, an abundance of flowers is essential. Every day Indians buy a fresh garland of jasmine, as we would buy a newspaper. Truck drivers hang garlands on their mirrors, women wear bracelets of fresh jasmine and plait the delicate stems of jasmine into their hair. Almost 3,500 kilogram of jasmine flowers are transported daily between the major cities by air—part of the great crosscurrent of flower transportation across India: lilies are sent from Kashmir, chrysanthemums from Bangalore, roses from Madurai, tuberoses from Bihar and jasmine from Karnataka.

The heavy, hypnotic smell of patchouli is particularly evocative of India and conjures up images of the hippie trail; it is also used to scent Kashmiri shawls and pashminas. G. W. Septimus Piesse's *The Art of Perfumery* has this to say about it: "The essence of patchouli . . . when smelled in its pure state . . . is far from agreeable, having a kind of mossy or musty odor . . . or, as some say, it smells of 'old coats.' " I rather like patchouli because it reminds me of my teenagehood and my old 1970s haunts, when I sat with my friends on beanbags and listened to the dirges of the Grateful Dead. We smoked hashish and it reminds me of that smell, too; patchouli has an aromatic buzz that is woody and sweet.

The oil of vetivert, which is known in India as *khus*, comes from the rhizome of an Indian grass. It has an aromatic and spicy smell, with an orrislike sweetness and hints of myrrh. It is often associated with ascetics and priests. Vetivert oil is not just a perfume, but a medicine and a natural coolant. In the heat of the summer it is added to bathwater and applied to the skin to reduce the effects of heat, and the dried roots and reeds are used as an ingenious scented, organic herbal kind of air-conditioning. (If only all air-conditioning systems could be like this.) The roots are woven into floor mats and into screens that are hung over the windows in the summer months to stave off the heat and keep the air cool. During the day, these *khuschiks* (or *tatties*) are sprinkled with water so that when any chance breeze blows through, a sublimely cooling aroma is released. Ancient royal palaces were kept cool in this way, and in the sacred city of Nathdwara in Rajasthan, the temple of Shrinathji is covered with *khus* mats. An army of water wallahs keeps the mats moist, while large *khus* fans rotate when the cords attached to them are pulled by the punkah wallahs. Handheld fans are also made from *khus*. (Miniature pavilions, like dollhouses made from *khus*, are sold to pilgrims both for worship at Shrinathji and so that they can set them up in their own houses as altars.)

Clay water pots wrapped with *khus* roots also work as air-conditioning units: as the water cools in the pots and slowly evaporates from the tiny pores in the clay, the roots absorb the moisture and scent the interiors of houses with their aromatic vapors.

The dry aromatic roots are made into curtains, blinds and awnings too. Quentin Crewe, in a book about his travels in India, described being driven in taxis whose drivers had rigged up their own perfumed air-conditioning system. The roofs of the taxis were strung with mats made from vetivert, which, when they wetted them from time to time, emitted a deliciously refreshing scent that made you forget about the heat, at least for a while. No wonder the oil of this mysterious, magical monsoon marvel is known as the "oil of tranquillity."

Essence of vetivert was much admired in the early days of English perfumery, in the seventeenth century. In colonial India, British women used vetivert as a handkerchief scent; the famous and deliciously named Mousseline des Indes took its name from the vetivert-scented muslin and mosquito nets, and linen, which kept the moths and insects at bay. Vetivert also haunted Maréchale and Bouquet du Roi. In its distilled form it is a fine fixative, with a gingerlike aroma, and is used in several modern perfumes.

In the middle of my travels in India I went to visit a friend, Francis Fry, who was staying with his father, Jeremy, on his coffee and cardamom plantation in the Palani mountains in the south, where lemon-scented bananas are grown. Jeremy Fry, who sadly has died since my visit, was a man of few but well-chosen words, and when I asked him about vetivert he handed me a book on the grasses of India. Sitting on the Frys' veranda sipping a *chota peg* (small drink) cocktail and breathing in the sweet, spicy air of cardamom and coffee, I found much that I wanted to know about wild vetivert in the pages of the book.

Vetivert grass grows in northern India and has fine, spongy, fibrous roots. Botanists call it the "seedy vetivert," because it spreads itself through its seeds. Most noses know about the cultivated varieties of vetivert that grow in the former French colony of Réunion, a perfume island in the Indian Ocean, and in Java and Haiti, and how it gives scents a deep, mysterious, rich and earthy resonance. But wild vetivert rarely reaches commercial Western perfume counters; it is used solely in India and is four times the price of cultivated types. To a sharp Indian nose it is quite possible to distinguish the wild vetivert from the cultivated.

I began my quest for wild vetivert, or *Anatherum muricatum*, by taking an overnight train to Delhi; then I took a train on to Kanpur, from where I was driven, in an Ambassador taxi, to Kannauj. A strong tradition of perfume making has thrived at Kannauj, by the banks of the Ganges, since the seventh century, when Kannauj was the capital of the Mogul emperors. As the taxi bumped along past dust-laden acacia trees, wandering barefoot children, clusters of sari-clad women and village elders lying listlessly on *charpoys* (Indian rope beds) beside the road, I spotted strands of vetivert growing in the marshes. It was a tough, wiry grass, and it was impossible to guess that it yielded one of the most exotic aromas imaginable. In its raw state, the sublime synthesis of the scents of the monsoon just looks like a tough old weed.

Vetivert is deceptively rich in oil: it is one of the most complex oils known to man. Scientists have isolated more than 150 molecules from it, and there are still more mysteries to be unearthed from its roots. The delicate strands of the roots of vetivert extract the rare molecules from the earth and feed them into its vascular system, which, in turn, transforms them into a myriad more molecules, and they produce the rich, multilayered aroma of *khus*.

At Kannauj, I went in search of a traditional distillery, where, after a few false starts, I chanced upon a world I would not have thought could still be found in the twenty-first century. In the distillery I saw rows of copper stills perched precariously on earthenware wood-fired ovens. Each still had been loaded with 454 kilograms (1,000 pound) of marigolds which were submerged in water. Bamboo pipes from the top of the stills connected them to other long-necked "receiving" stills which sat in water baths. The smaller receiving vessels held the soft, creamy sandalwood into which the marigold vapors condensed through the pipes to make a marigold-suffused sandalwood attar. The attar smelled woody and luxuriant, making me think of stately homes full of antique furniture carved from old and precious woods that had just been polished with beeswax.

The attar wallahs diligently watched the fires, stoking them to keep them at an even temperature, without the aid of a temperature gauge. If the heat is too high the water evaporates too swiftly and the flowers singe, ruining the velvety, creamy smell of sandalwood. The water baths were also kept under constant observation to make sure that the water never got too warm; fresh cold water was added whenever it was needed, to ensure proper condensation of the vapors. The whole operation was conducted in a silent, almost spiritual fashion. The atmosphere was serene and calm, which is exactly the effect of the marigold-infused sandalwood attar that was being cajoled from this archaic apparatus.

I discovered that this very same equipment was going to be used, the following day, to distill and make ruh—the pure hydrodistilled oil of vetivert. But for the ruh there is no sandalwood in the receiving vessel, and the bamboo pipes are disconnected. I watched as presoaked chopped roots of vetivert were loaded into the big copper still above the oven. Slowly the oil sacs in the vetivert roots open up, and it is precisely this low-pressure distillation that allows the release of the more delicate molecules; this would not happen in modern high-pressure distilleries. The gentle distillation continues for twenty-four hours until, finally, when all the essence has been teased from the vetivert roots and the receiving vessel in the bath is saturated with *khus* oil, the oil separates from the water, floats to the top and is skimmed off skillfully with a special brush which absorbs the oil. The oil is then squeezed from the brushes into bottles. I was given a precious bottle of ruh as I left.

I had not timed my visit for the vetivert harvest, which begins in earnest in October, in the heart of Uttar Pradesh. But I knew that wild vetivert thrives on the vast tracts of uncultivated land in India and that when the monsoon is over the roots are left to dry in the ground before the Adrasi—the tribal people who harvest the vetivert that grows in Uttar Pradesh—begin their work. The Adrasi camp out for months in little huts which they build and thatch from *khus* grass. With handmade implements that look like Iron Age tools, they wrench up the roots and disentangle them from all the weeds that have grown among them. The roots are knocked against stones to remove the soil; then they are deftly tied into bundles.

After weeks of digging and bundling the roots, buyers arrive at the Adrasi encampments to buy the precious *khus*, which is loaded onto bullock carts and taken to Kannauj by road. There the roots are either treated in the traditional copper stills with bamboo pipes, or modern techniques are used—but most vetivert connoisseurs agree that the older method is better because it treats smaller quantities and the result is a much more refined oil. Vetivert connoisseurs can tell which area the *khus* they are buying has been harvested from and whether it has been harvested at the right time.

I knew by then that I definitely wanted wild vetivert in my bespoke scent because it is a fixative *par excellence*, which would unite every ingredient in my scent, from the ethereal top notes all the way down to the deep base notes.

Attar of henna is distilled from vetivert flowers, and in Lucknow, the city of attars, it is blended with agarwood, ambergris, musk, patchouli and saffron. Other lesser-known attars are *kewara*, which is produced over sandalwood oil; *davana*, a sweet, almost fruity herb; the sweetflag of *bach*, the long rhizomes of which contain oil that lends oriental notes to scents; and the musk-scented leaves of the butter tree are also used to make an attar. Spikenard, an Indian nard which grows in the Himalayas, is a holy fragrance often referred to in the Bible: it was used to anoint Christ's feet.

A few days later, I crossed the subcontinent back down south to Coimbatore to meet a producer and exporter of concretes and absolutes of zambac jasmine. On the way I scanned the countryside for jasmine plantations, but I was to learn later that most of the jasmine farms are north of the city, near Mettupalayam. Coimbatore is not on the tourist map; it is a stopping-off point en route to the distinctly British hill station of Ootocumund (Ooty for short), the center for eucalyptus oil. Lemon gum, or eucalyptus, is an Australian tree with a clean, silvery green trunk and strongly scented leaves. The plant is coppiced to yield more foliage and contains the aromatic oil. It is grown commercially in the Nilgiri hills and the leaves and tender branches are distilled in Ooty.

Next day I had a meeting with Mr. K. C. Sethuraman, the producer and exporter of concretes and absolutes. We drove out into the countryside to his farm and factory. It was a modest three-story house, with factory buildings behind the house, built around a courtyard. His mother-in-law greeted us on the threshold covered with the traditional delicate Hindu *scolams*—chalk markings which look like a hopscotch grid. I heard a very young baby crying above us.

In the fields the jasmine bushes, which were about a foot high and were planted about 3 feet apart, had just been pruned (in mid-February). Harvesting begins in June and goes on until December. Mr. Sethuraman told me that they farmed organically, that all the manure was green, made from sun hemp, a perennial grass, which they plowed into the soil. His was, obviously, a lovingly tended crop.

Thin, spindly neem trees, or *Azadirachta indica*, grew near the jasmine bushes, and Mr. Sethuraman explained that neem cake, an extraction from the neem seeds, was used as a biofertilizer. This native Indian tree is thought to ward off evil spirits and also provides a natural insecticide, which is applied to the soil around the jasmine plants. Neem oil is considered good for skin ailments and is used in soaps; it is also used as a natural "morning-after" contraceptive pill.

Musk
(and a little about Castoreum)

MUSK, AMBERGRIS, PATCHOULI AND VETIVERT ARE SCENTS MUCH loved by the Indians. The Himalayas and Tibet are still the haunt of the musk deer, and the Chinese have known about musk for thousands of years: they called it *shay heang*, *shay* meaning deer and *heang* meaning perfume.

The hunting and killing of musk deer—a small animal about the size of a goat—is now illegal, but there is a flourishing black market, and the musk deer is in danger of extinction. Musk is a reddish brown substance secreted from glands in the penile sheath of the male musk deer. Like civet (see Chapter 8), musk marks territory, and its scent can radiate for several miles to attract a mate. The glands, which are about the size of a walnut and known in the trade as musk pods, are cut off by the hunter. The sale of one musk pod (which is sealed with wax) used to keep a Buddhist monk financially for a whole year. The glands can be removed without hurting the animal, but, unfortunately, the deer are often killed unnecessarily, and since females and males are hard to tell apart, many females are also needlessly killed. The Chinese are conducting experiments to produce a synthetic musk, and I sincerely hope they succeed, because, when I discovered how real musk was obtained, I found the whole process abhorrent.

Musk was known and used in India, China and Persia for centuries before it was brought to Europe via Arabia. The word "musk" derives from the Arabic word *"mesk,"* and musk is mentioned in the list of presents sent to the emperor of Rome by Saladin, sultan of Egypt and Syria, in 1189. It was brought back on Arab ships from China and much prized by the caliphs of Baghdad, but, because of its high value and the many hands it passes through, musk has been adulterated for centuries.

The best musk is tonquin musk, which comes from Tibet and China, while the strongest is from Assam and Nepal. The poorest kind comes from Russia. Musk perfume is prepared in the form of a tincture by macerating the musk in alcohol for a month to extract the smell. It is then diluted and blended with other perfumes.

Musk imparts its odor to anything that is brought near it. The scent is fecal and clinging; chemically, it is very close to that of human testosterone. The only scents musk cannot overpower are camphor and bitter almonds, which completely destroy it. The smell of musk is so powerful, however, that for a while the East India Company would not allow it to be shipped in the same vessel with tea; and many other ships refused to carry it in case the scent escaped and impregnated the rest of the cargo. It is said that crews were fond of it for its aphrodisiac and narcotic properties.

The scent of musk is also very long-lasting; if it is placed on a handkerchief its scent will last for as long as forty years. In 1996 Coimbatore Flavors & Fragrances introduced an ambrettolide, a macrocyclic musk, which resembles natural musk. Ambrettolide is derived from aleuritic acid, a compound, which comes from insects that produce the lac resin in Bengal.

Artificial musk substitutes, prevalent in Yves Saint

Laurent's Opium, for example (a heady perfume which is synonymous with the 1980s), cannot compete with the real thing. Real musk gave women the vapors and was regarded in Victorian times as positively satanic. Eugène Rimmel, in his nineteenth-century *Book of Perfumes*, warns that "the nervous should use simple extracts of flowers rather than musk which is likely to affect the head." In Edmond de Goncourt's *Chérie* the heroine sniffs musk like a drug and brings herself to orgasm, and when Napoleon left Josephine she sprayed her civet and musk scent all around her boudoir at Malmaison so that he would never forget her.

I went to see Richard Taylor, a filmmaker, who had made a documentary about musk and "antler velvet." Both are used in the Far East as oriental versions of Viagra; they're also used in traditional Far Eastern medicines. Musk, for example, is used in four hundred medicinal preparations. But the footage of the musk deer farms in China was harrowing and haunted me for ages. The antlers of the musk deer, when they have reached full growth, are cruelly sawed off and ground down to make a sought-after aphrodisiac. The blood from the sawed-off antlers is collected and decanted into bottles, and sellers of this liquid promise that it guarantees priapic powers.

When this wild deer is captured it instantly loses weight and, in its almost permanent state of terror, it can no longer produce musk, which means that it has lost the important ability to mark its territory when—if—it is released. In Russia alone 80 percent of all musk deer that are killed are killed for their musk pods, and the musk deer population of Mongolia has been hugely

➤ depleted; it is now just one-fifth its former levels. And yet the tragedy is that musk pods can be removed without harming the animals.

I had no way of knowing whether the musk in my scent would be removed in a humane way—without the death of the animal—and so, short of going out and trapping the deer for myself to see how the musk pods were removed, I felt that it was distasteful to have any musk in my scent and decided against it.

Since the UN Convention on Trade in Endangered Species (CITES) voted to protect the musk deer and other endangered species, these animals—and the ingredients for perfume for which they are hunted—have been banned from international commercial trade. Despite this, in many countries enforcement is minimal and illegal trafficking is rife. The worst European perpetrator of the illegal musk trade is France, the country at the heart of the Western world's perfume-making industry.

Castoreum, a by-product of the Canadian and Siberian beaver fur trade, comes from the egg-shaped secretory glands in the abdominal pouch of the beaver. The scent is fetid when undiluted, but as a tincture it has a masculine, leathery note. Trade in castoreum, and in beaver fur, is also banned now.

Although Mr. Sethuraman had only 30 acres of jasmine, the bushes produce 350 to 450 kilograms of flowers, which in turn yield 1 kilogram of concrete—a sticky, viscous substance. The concrete is reduced by a further 50 percent into an absolute. We stood in the dry fields surrounded by great rocky outcrops which were so smoothly sculpted that I could imagine Constantin Brancusi or Henry Moore being inspired by their shapes.

But I was puzzled by the fact that I could not smell any jasmine. Mr. Sethuraman explained that although jasmine can live for two or three years without water, the plants will not flower without water. For three years now the monsoons had failed and the wells had run dry. Nonetheless, although there had been water shortages, they had still managed a harvest. He told me that at harvest time twenty harvesters arrive early, at four a.m., to pick the flowers before the volatile oils evaporate in the heat. Like roses, jasmine has to be picked while there is still dew on the plants, and Mr. Sethuraman said, ruefully, that persuading the pickers to arrive that early in the morning was becoming more difficult—the wages he pays have to compete with the delights of late-night satellite television.

We left the fields to go back to the factory, where we sat in Mr. Sethuraman's office under a fan. The room was crammed with cabinets full of bottles of attars and synthetics, and he told me that his father-in-law was an innovative man who was the first to sell zambac jasmine commercially, and that their company, Coimbatore Flavors & Fragrances, was the first to distill zambac jasmine in India. The *Jasmine grandifloram*, he said, when compared with zambac, is milder; the zambac has animal notes and is used in India at weddings and other functions, which pushes its price up.

I tested some jasmine concrete made from wax and oil on my skin. It was not a delicate smell and, like most Indian perfumes, it had a potent and cloying effect. Then one of Mr. Sethuraman's female relatives brought in a platter of jasmine flowers and buds and I buried my nose in them. It was like the scent that follows a fall of rain on warm earth. The absolute is extracted from the concrete with alcohol of distilled sugarcane and then the wax is removed to obtain the absolute oil. French companies usually buy the concrete to turn into an absolute themselves. The concrete can be stored for three or four years at room temperature.

To make 1 kilogram of concrete of *Jasmine grandifloram* requires 300 to 400 kilograms of flowers. It also takes 600 kilograms of zambac jasmine to produce 1 kilogram of concrete. Mr. Sethuraman said that his yield is 100 grams of concrete per plant and that each harvester can collect 2 to 3 kilograms of jasmine flowers in a couple of hours, depending on their dexterity and skill: some manage more, some less.

As soon as the jasmine flowers are picked they are placed in bamboo baskets and taken to the extraction units. The flowers must be extracted within hours of being picked, otherwise they wilt and lose their smell. Mr. Sethuraman took me out to the extraction units, where men were vigorously polishing and oiling the machinery. The stainless-steel vats; for the different flowers are kept scrupulously clean, and the flowers are never mixed in the vats; otherwise the stronger scents overpower the weaker ones. Hexane, an odorless by-product of petrol, is blended with the petals to extract the scent from the flowers.

When the flowers arrive at the extraction unit from the fields they are immediately put on trays that look like cylindrical sieves. The flower trays are put into the extractors in layers; each extractor has a 150-kilograms capacity. Once the flowers are loaded and the lid closed, the solvent and the flowers are passed through the vats at a high temperature for two hours, during which time the flowers absorb the oil. Four hundred liters of oil are condensed to 80 liters and then the hexane is removed. There is hardly any wastage of the spent flowers because the hexane is recovered and the spent flowers are used as manure. Then chilled water is passed through the condenser at the end of the whole process to cool it down.

When I asked Mr. Sethuraman if he cultivated any other flowers, he gave me a sample of tuberose concrete which smelled like sugared lilies dipped in clotted vanilla cream. I used it up within days; it smelled so delicious that it was impossible to save.

Coimbatore Flavors & Fragrances is a small company, but their products are 100 percent natural and pure. During the jasmine harvest aromatherapists from all over the world come to visit the company and buy their oils, and, Mr. Sethuraman told me in a disparaging tone, although the Americans think his company's oils inferior, they can't actually distinguish between them and the French ones.

Most female gods in the Hindu pantheon are offered jasmine at their shrines, so there will always be a market for Mr. Sethuraman's company's jasmine flowers and products. All they need is rain. As a parting gift he gave me several samples of jasmine absolute and oil in microscopic glass vials and, as I thanked him and looked around at the parched countryside, I told him that I hoped the monsoon rains would soon return.

Holy Basil

THE HINDUS REVERE *TULSI* (BASIL) AS A HOLY HERB AND THEY USE it in temples dedicated to Vishnu and to Krishna, one of Vishnu's ➤

incarnations. They also believe that *tulsi* will safeguard the family, and in every Hindu house you will find a basil tree. However, in India, basil is not used in cooking.

Dr. George Birdwood, a Victorian botanist, wrote, "The most sacred plant in the whole indigenous *Materia Medica* of India is the *tulsi* plant or holy basil . . . called after the nymph Tulsi, beloved of Krishna and turned by him into this graceful and most fragrant plant. She is indeed the Hindu Daphne. The plant is also sacred to Vishnu, whose followers wear necklaces and carry rosaries made of its stems and roots . . . It is . . . daily watered [in every Hindu house] and worshipped by all the members of the household. No doubt it was also on account of its virtues in disinfecting and vivifying malarial air that it first became inseparable from Hindu houses as the protecting spirit . . . of the family."

In India, holy basil is blended with tonquin musk (which can still be found on the black market), vanilla, geranium, tolu (a resinous, viscous balsam that is collected from the bark of a Peruvian tree with a sweet vanilla and woody, slightly cinnamony scent), orange flower, cassia, jasmine and tuberose to make the most sublime scent.

Modern perfumers use basil in light citrus scents. Examples are Jo Malone's Basil, Diptyque's Virgilio, which is a pastoral blend of basil, thyme and vetivert, and Maître Parfumeur et Gantier's Baume, which is a blend of basil with rose and black coffee.

I took a taxi to Mysore and on the way I saw women in vermilion, pink and saffron saris which stood out like beacons of color in the parched fields and bleached light of midday. No matter how poor they are, Hindus always wear freshly laundered clothes: Hindu custom dictates daily ablutions, and women washing their saris at water pumps is a common sight. The men's white dhotis dazzle against their brown skin, and they hitch them up into folds, making them look like the bottom half of a doublet. A shepherdess tending her goats was dressed exquisitely in an emerald green sari threaded with gold, and a young man cycled by with a goat tied to the handlebars of his bicycle. When we finally arrived on the plateau we saw colossal banyan trees with overhanging tendrils, and tamarind and jacaranda trees, paddy fields and village dwellings painted light blue.

After seven hours on the road, we arrived in the princely city of Mysore with its pink and white Indo-Saracenic palaces and pavilions. I had booked into the eco-friendly Green Hotel, which proved to be a real sanctuary. There were ponds filled with tilapia fish, which eat mosquito larvae; the hotel was run on solar energy and the laundry was done outside on the riverbank in traditional *dhobi-ghats* (which literally translates as "laundry hills"). At night in the garden the trees and flower beds were lit up with a forest of fairy lights, and candles were brought to the table. It was a charming, simple and peaceful place.

The following morning I took a rickshaw to Devaraja market, which is enclosed by mogul walls and shaded by sacking awnings so it is wonderfully cool. The air was laced with the sharp zest of oranges, lemons and limes, and filled with the balmy scents of sandalwood, dust and honey, almonds and musk, petrol and nutmeg, incense and bidi smoke, mint and coriander. On the stalls the vegetables and fruits were artfully arranged into neat piles, and huge bunches of bananas were shaped like swans' necks. Cupboard-sized apothecaries burst with mountains of crimson and viridian-green pigments, sandalwood soaps, henna and *puja* (worship) clay bowls for offerings.

I found a tiny stall of perfumes where I bought some sandalwood, a perfume of nine flowers and a green rose scent made from the leaves of roses. Unlike the ostentatious and often vulgar Western perfume bottles, packaging in India is simple. The scent is decanted from flagons into smaller bottles fitted with plastic stoppers, and little labels with the names of the scent are handwritten and pasted onto the bottle. The bottles are individually wrapped in neatly cut squares of newspaper and deftly tied with yards of colored thread.

I drank sweet *chai* (spiced milky tea), and while I signed his visitors' book the attar wallah continued to dab scents along my arm. The sandalwood was just as I remembered it from previous travels in India: woody and luxuriant, but the nine-flower fragrance was acidic and made my eyes water.

I went to a specific corner of the market which a helpful Englishwoman at the Green Hotel had told me about. She'd said I would be picked up by a young boy who would show me to the best perfume shop which sold real essential oils. Just as she'd said, a young boy appeared. He possessed a wisdom beyond his years and spoke several languages. He ushered me into a shop full of mirrored shelves of perfumes. A handsome young alchemist presided over the jars of oils and, in the afternoon heat, the oleaginous, liliaceous and spicy aromas of gardenia, patchouli, tropical watermelon, sandalwood and vetivert emanated from the jars as he took off their stoppers. En masse the scents wove a heavy, narcotic tapestry that caught at the back of my throat. I began to feel as if I were drowning in the overwhelming vapors. I left clutching potent bottles of watermelon and gardenia oils.

On my way back to the Green Hotel I walked past the flower market, where there were stalls as big as stables, piled high with meadowsweet and all kinds of freshly cut flowers, their scents euphoric and intoxicating. I inhaled deeply, reminded of the scent of bluebells in May in the woods in England.

Sandalwood

EIGHTY-FIVE PERCENT OF THE SANDALWOOD GROWN FOR PERFUME comes from the province of Mysore. Sandalwood trees are parasitic and scraggy. They absorb the roots of neighboring trees and plants, such as guava and bamboo, and suck the life out of them. But once sandalwood trees are mature they are felled, and it is the oldest trees, those between thirty and fifty years old, that yield the best-quality oil. Sandalwood is a heart note in perfume: it has both a cool and yet an aphrodisiac odor and it is also an excellent fixative.

The trunks and roots of sandalwood trees are pulverized and the dust is distilled. The best oil comes from the heartwood, and from the roots. In the first distillation process the oil is siphoned off in a funnel; then it is redistilled. The steam distillation method is used, without chemicals, and the whole process takes four days. After distillation the oil is boiled in great cylindrical

➤

---

drums, then separated from the water by siphoning and decanted into flasks. When sandalwood is being distilled there is a lovely, balmy, oily aroma from the steaming copper cauldrons, which has a wonderfully calming effect.

About 1,000 kilograms of sandalwood dust yield 55 liters of oil. In its purest form, sandalwood oil looks like liquid red gold. Sandalwood is usually associated with incense and soap, but a sublime, voluptuous perfume is also made from the warm, expansive essential oil.

Sandalwood has been highly prized for centuries. Its oil is mentioned in Indian texts from as early as 500 B.C.: the sandalwood trade was established between India and the Mediterranean in ancient times. Indian courtesans rubbed their breasts with sandalwood paste—it contains a steroid similar to testosterone—and sandalwood paste was also used for fumigation, religious purification and for embalming royal corpses. It was so lavishly used that Confucius recorded that the great sandalwood forests of the East were in danger of depletion. There is a shortage today, too. Supplies of sandalwood have dried up because the trees have been culled but not replanted. Sandalwood trees are now listed as a protected species to prevent excessive culling; each piece of Mysorian sandalwood is registered and stamped to ensure its authenticity, and there is now a five-year waiting list for sandalwood oil.

Sandalwood retains its sweet, penetrating scent for years, and Indian cabinetmakers and craftsmen still carve ornaments and chests from it because of its scent. In Kashmir a statue of Buddha was carved entirely from sandalwood, and after the Queen of

> Sheba visited Solomon and presented him with many scented gifts, he commissioned pillars for his temple, and harps and lyres to be carved from sandalwood.

In the late afternoon I went to find the *agarbathi* (incense makers), but, as I was trying to retrace my steps through the labyrinthine lanes to the attar wallahs, I succumbed to a doe-eyed boy, who must have been only eight or nine years old. He was clutching a bunch of incense sticks and said that his mother made a thousand incense sticks a day. He grabbed my arm, we left the market and, like the Pied Piper, I attracted a legion of barefooted children, some carrying their smaller siblings. I felt panic rise up in me because, suddenly, I knew that we weren't going to see the boy's mother but that I was being led into some kind of trap.

Swiftly I turned on my heels and said I'd changed my mind. The young boy pleaded with me to buy the incense sticks so that he could eat that day, so I bought them all and then had quite a time persuading the other children that I had no more money left. The incense boy disappeared into the crowd and, eventually, the other children dispersed and I found my way back to the main market, a little shaken and somewhat frustrated. India is such a volatile place; one minute it is noisy, tawdry, smelly and infuriating; then something happens to lift you out of the confusion and it is a magical, wonderful place once more.

Agarbathi

MYSORE IS A TREAT FOR THE SENSES: THE SMELLS OF SANDALWOOD, rose and jasmine linger in the air from the hundreds of thousands of incense sticks made there every day. Incense sticks are a quintessential part of Indian life. The ubiquitous agarbathi stick is used by both rich and poor in India, and Nehru often carried a short sandalwood stick in his hand.

The agarbathi industry is essentially a cottage one: women and children make the incense sticks at home, but the Indian government is responsible for more than half of the planting: 60 percent of sandalwood trees are planted by the government and, in Mysore, ten thousand incense sticks are churned out every day. To make incense sticks you need bamboo sticks, spent chips of sandalwood and sandalwood leaves, herbs like *tulsi* and spices like cumin, coriander and cardamom. The incense makers mix a paste of perfumes from these aromatic barks, roots and herbs, then hand-roll it in slivers of bamboo which act as molds until the incense sticks are dry, which takes a few days. The result is a fine blending of natural roots, herbs and resin oils—such as patchouli, roots of vetivert, ambrette seeds (which impart a musky smell), exudates of guggal (a kind of Indian myrrh), cinnamon and sandalwood bark—but more than one hundred different natural materials can be used.

The agarbathi industry combines traditional artisan skills with modern management. This rural cottage industry has developed into "a pavement industry," because the sticks are rolled on

> pavements and roads in front of dwellings in the cities. The in-
> dustry employs around five thousand people who earn about £1 a
> day, and this low-wage labor force—which is made up mostly of
> women and children—produces a staggering 147 billion incense
> sticks a year, valued at 700,000 rupees.
>
> At an essential-oils shop I watched sandalwood putty being
> rolled in slivers of bamboo. Then the slivers were dipped into
> powdered perfume and dried on a flat roof in the shade. It was
> all done deftly and swiftly, and the whole process reminded me of
> watching sushi chefs in Tokyo rolling up sushi on tatame mats.

While I was in the market, still thinking about the little
incense-selling boy, I literally bumped into a man who introduced himself as Tintin. We got talking and he told me he was a
photographer and had worked on the Merchant Ivory films *Heat
and Dust* and *Cotton Mary*. When I told him why I was in India
he said that he knew a perfumer and purveyor of aphrodisiacs
who was a friend of his father's. He said he'd introduce me.
And so, over the next few days, Tintin gave me several lifts into
Mysore on the back of his Enfield—a welcome relief from the
tut-tuts, which were invariably driven crazily, at least by British
standards, although the way Tintin drove his Enfield wasn't that
much safer.

Tintin introduced me to Naveen, who sold, among other
things, pearl dust which, he said, if you sprinkled on your
genitals would improve your performance. I quickly steered him
away from that subject and toward jasmine. Naveen said he'd

been a perfumer, or attar wallah, for forty years and, like me, he loved the idea of re-creating antique perfume formulas. I told him I was having my own signature scent made and seeking out the best ingredients I could find from around the world. I asked him what the best jasmine was.

Naveen said it was difficult to know exactly which was the perfect jasmine essence or oil because jasmine has three hundred different components, but he told me that he thought some of the best jasmine had a fruity aroma, and I agreed; I said I thought that sometimes it could smell like overripe pears. Naveen went on to describe the zambac variety—the kind that I was planning to use in my bespoke scent; he said he thought of it as positively animalic. He liked to mix a luminous layer of zambac jasmine with a backdrop of herbs and patchouli. I tried his blend and, as I breathed it in, I realized that it could have come from nowhere else in the world but India; the jasmine and the patchouli complemented each other perfectly.

Naveen also pointed out that in India no distinction is made between perfumes for men and perfumes for women. Both sexes wear essences of jasmine, sandalwood, vetivert and henna flower attars.

When I eventually arrived home from this leg of my scent trail, I discovered that my jasmine absolute had leaked in my suitcase. Its scent filled my bedroom for months and months; even now, whenever I open that suitcase, the jasmine scent comes flooding out and my Sri Lankan and Indian travels come rushing back to me, filling me with excitement and pangs of desire to return.

The scents of jasmine, sandalwood and patchouli always bring memories of India flooding back: a misty damp monsoon morning, the tabla playing an evening raga, the flash of a vermilion sari in a field of maize, a saffron-clad Brahmin traveling in a palanquin, a mauve fort with sky blue majolica along the parapets, the scream of the crows and the endless horizons.

I pulled out my notebook and turned to the page where the nutmeg sample was. I smelled the jasmine beside it and realized that the peculiar spicy nutmeg scent prevented the overtly floral jasmine from being too vulgar or pretty, and that it had the effect of making the jasmine more mysterious. I was really beginning to look forward to smelling my bespoke scent in its final form.

And I realized, as I contemplated my bottle of rare ruh, that emanating from its thick, rich brown syrup was a smell that plunged me deep into my olfactory memories of earth roots, damp forest floors and truffles beneath towering beech trees. Ruh would add an earthy, damp autumnal strain to my scent, harnessing the summery, flighty and outrageously sweet jasmine. It would give my scent a breath of fresh aromatic air and cool it down just as the air-conditioned vetivert roof matting cooled me down in the Ambassador taxi that took me to the airport for the next, and final, leg of my scent trail.

I was about to fly to Yemen in search of the earliest forms of scent: frankincense and myrrh.

CHAPTER EIGHT

FRANKINCENSE
AND MYRRH

Yemen, and Socotra:
the Island of Dragons' Blood

A bundle of myrrh is my well-beloved unto me; he shall lie all night betwixt my breasts.

Song of Solomon

IMAGINE A SAILOR COASTING DOWN THE RED SEA TWO thousand years ago. When he sailed past the land of frankincense and myrrh, the land that is now Yemen, he would have breathed in the scent from the blooms on the frankincense and myrrh trees, a scent which would have been carried down to the sea by the offshore winds. It is the kind of sensory experience that is almost impossible to encounter now.

In *Paradise Lost* John Milton wrote:

Off at sea north-east winds blow Sabean odors from the spicy shore
Of Araby the blest.

In the first century B.C., Diodorus Siculus wrote that the whole of Arabia exhaled an unearthly fragrance, and Agatharchides, a second-century B.C. Greek historian and geographer, wrote that "the quality of perfume . . . excites the senses in a manner which is quite divine."

Frankincense and myrrh—which used to be known as the "gold of the East"—are both gum resins that contain a small amount of volatile oil, and it is the oil that imparts the fragrance. There is considerably more oil in myrrh than there is in frankincense. In the first millennium B.C. a process was developed for extracting the oil from myrrh to produce the highly prized oil known as *stacte*. Frankincense is also known as olibanum, its

Latin name, and it was the preeminent material for creating fragrant smoke by burning. Olibanum is a very good base in a fragrance. It lasts for a long time because it is not volatile and it imparts a certain heaviness to an odor. The scent of olibanum is associated with worship: Muslims use it and Buddhists burn it, while Hindus use an incense containing myrrh.

Incense emits its fragrant fumes by volatilization (rapid evaporation caused by heat). It is made from gums, resins and spices, then sprinkled on lighted coals, or it can be applied to the body in the form of an unguent. Frankincense is an exudation from a kind of terebinth (turpentine) tree called *Boswellia thurifera*, which is principally found in southern Yemen and parts of Eritrea. Myrrh is also an exudation, from a tree called *Balsamodendron myrrha*, which is found across Arabia. Frankincense and myrrh are obtained from unimpressive-looking, scrubby, squat trees, which, in addition to those trees named above, also grow on the Yemeni island of Socotra; in Dhofar, the most important agricultural area in Oman; and in Somalia. Myrrh also comes from *Commiphora ornifolia* trees, which grow on the Nujad plain in Socotra. The incense that was made from frankincense and myrrh became the all-pervading scent of the ancient world, and their lucrative production and export contributed to the wealth of Arabia, just as oil wells have made the Gulf states fabulously rich now.

Southern Arabia, or "Arabia Felix" (happy Arabia), as the philosopher and historian Strabo (64 B.C.—24 A.D.) called it because of its fertility—the mountains and highlands catch the monsoon rains on their way to India—was the ancient kingdom of Saba, whose ruler was the Queen of Sheba. The Sabeans lived under the shadow of the great Marib dam, which, with its curtain walling and colossal sluice gates, was one of the great engineering feats of the first millennium B.C. Because of the dam, elaborate irrigation and a level of rainfall lacking in the rest of Arabia, Yemen, as it is now called, grew agriculturally rich: it was a land of incense forests and prosperous cities.

The Egyptians collected myrrh as early as 1500 B.C. They sailed down the Red Sea to the Land of Punt, the myrrh-growing region in southern Somalia, and brought myrrh saplings back to Egypt; but they did not thrive there, so the Egyptians continued to collect supplies of myrrh from Punt. They used myrrh as an embalming agent for mummification, and from Karnak to Nineveh incense smoldered in the temples: in 1200 B.C., 189 jars and 304 bushels of incense were brought to the temple of Amon at Thebes alone.

The Greeks used huge amounts of incense at public festivals. Thessalian virgins carrying baskets of incense and spices led processions to honor Artemis at Ephesus and at ceremonies to honor the oracle at Delphi. In Alexandria, in 278 B.C., women dressed as Victory (complete with golden wings) carried 9-foot-high censers in a parade organized by Ptolemy II. Behind the winged Victories, boys in purple tunics walked bearing frankincense and myrrh on golden dishes and gilded incense burners. They were followed by chariots drawn by elephants and zebras, carrying 364 kilograms (800 pounds) of frankincense, myrrh, saffron, cassia, iris and cinnamon. And in Italy the Etruscans burned incense on long-stemmed incense stands that looked like staffs.

By Roman times, transport costs and the high demand for incense far exceeded the supply of frankincense and myrrh. These precious commodities were so expensive by then that their value equaled the value of gold—hence the gifts of the Magi: gold, frankincense (which also symbolized divinity) and myrrh (which represented the healing powers of the child). In the New Testament, Mary Magdalene anoints Christ's feet with spikenard; the repentant prostitute became the patron saint of perfumers. Myrrh was also widely used in cosmetics and in poultices to heal wounds, and the Romans used frankincense lavishly, to the point of excess.

Rome became the greatest consumer of perfumes and spices, and imports of frankincense were an enormous drain on the empire's financial resources. More than 3,000 tons of frankincense were imported by the Romans and the Greeks each year, and, by the Roman Imperial period, the original sacred use of Arabian spices—to honor the gods—had transmuted into extravagant, luxurious use for mortals. It was burned, for instance, at the funerals of the rich. When Nero's wife, Poppea, died after he'd kicked her in the stomach while she was pregnant, Nero, no doubt racked with guilt, ordered so much frankincense to be burned on her funeral pyre that it is said to have exhausted Arabia's supply for an entire year. The air in Imperial Rome must have been heavy with frankincense fumes on that day. Eventually, Caesar issued a decree forbidding the sale of perfume in an attempt to restrain the extravagance of the citizens.

Perfumes in the first millennium B.C. were more pungent and powerful than they are today because of the abundant use of spices like cinnamon and pepper. Today we tend to differentiate between spices and incense, but then there was considerable overlap and no sharp distinction between the two. Fragrant wine was also added to strong perfumes to make them sweeter.

The incense and spice trade routes covered vast distances across India, Arabia, east Africa and Asia. The "incense road" began at Shabwa in southern Arabia, from where it trailed through the vast desert wastes to Petra in Jordan and on to Palmyra, in Syria. From there it continued to the Levant and then on to Europe. Caravan cities like Petra and Palmyra grew rich on the proceeds from ointments and scents, but the merchants' journeys across the desert wastes were arduous and dangerous. The caravans were sometimes attacked by Bedouin bandits, and cargoes were seized by pirates at sea. The journeys lasted for months, and sometimes for years, as the merchants waited for the right season to travel overland, or the right winds to sail.

After the collapse of the Roman empire, trade in frankincense and myrrh declined, but the basilicas of Byzantium continued to be filled with clouds of incense, and in the tenth century consumption of frankincense and myrrh was so great that priests in Syria planted 10 square miles of frankincense trees for their own personal consumption. The Yemeni ports of Hodeidah and Aden still trade in frankincense and myrrh from Somalia and Socotra today.

The foreign office had issued a warning that we should on no account travel to Yemen unless our journey was absolutely necessary. Nonetheless, Stephen and I flew into Sana, the capital. (I had asked Stephen to come with me on this leg of my scent trail because it is still difficult for a woman to travel through parts of Yemen on her own.) Sana is a city of Arabic baroque tower houses which was once proclaimed an earthly paradise by the prophet Mohammed; it is now a world heritage site. Feeling jittery about the foreign office's warning, we queued up at immigration, but the airport was empty, save for a few crows perching on the carousel. I covered my head with a black, scented scarf lined with shavings of oudh—which I'd bought at Dubai airport, knowing that I would need a head covering in Yemen—and we got into a taxi. The driver thrust his dagger into his silver, rhino-horned scabbard before he switched on the ignition. The taxi was held together with wire and gaffer tape and decorated with sheep fleece, red velvet curtains, and trinkets and tinsel, which hung from the rearview mirror.

I first came to Yemen in 1982 with my mother, and I know that my memories of our thwarted attempts to find frankincense and myrrh trees partly fueled the idea for this book. This journey to Yemen was also, partly, a journey of remembrance for me, because it was on one of my mother's many subsequent visits to Yemen that, on an archaeological dig, she picked up a mysterious virus that slowly killed her.

As our cranky chariot hurtled into the medieval walled city I was reminded how the Yemeni architecture, customs, cars and dress all bear witness to their eccentricity and originality. They settle tribal disputes with poetry competitions, and many of them have aquiline features which give them a noble, fierce appearance. They carry the *jambiya*, a dagger with a curved blade, and their turbans and belts are embroidered. But they also carry mobile phones and wear well-tailored Western jackets—often with an AK rifle nonchalantly slung over their shoulders. The women wear the hijab, or the sitara, as it is called in Yemen.

The streets we drove through that afternoon were deserted

because, every afternoon, the whole nation comes to a standstill for the "big chew," when Yemenis rest and chew qat leaves, which are a mild narcotic. When we checked into a sixteenth-century inn—with its own well and a satellite dish—I noticed that the innkeeper's cheeks were distended with qat. We climbed the stairs, which were almost one foot deep and so steep that it felt like a Norman keep, and once in the bedroom we watched sunlight filter through the fan-shaped stained-glass windows, covering the walls with lines of colored light: it was like being at the end of a rainbow. I sank into a deep sleep and didn't wake until the calls of the muezzin—whose voices sounded more like cries from underworld spirits—infiltrated my dreams.

We wandered along the narrow streets between soaring towered mansions painted with white gypsum. The façades were decorated with calligraphic *istisqa* (prayers) and, as a full moon rose, the gypsum glowed on the lofty Sanani houses as if spiders had woven phosphorescent friezes of stars, lozenges and crescent moons. It was surreal—but then in Yemen the boundaries between reality and fantasy are pretty thin, or at least they seem so to me.

The Prophet Mohammed decreed that the Yemenis had the kindest and gentlest of hearts, and it is still true today: one Sanani offered to share his breakfast with us the next morning. A medieval traveler once observed that no gaze is more penetrating than that of the Yemenis. I did feel, on occasion, that they could see right through me.

Sadly, I discovered that Yemen's ancient incense terraces had been given over to qat cultivation, so Stephen and I flew to the Yemeni island of Socotra, where I knew frankincense and myrrh trees still grew. Socotra was known to the ancients as Dioscorida, which derives from the Sanskrit words *Drippa Sakhadra*, meaning "Island of Bliss"; the Arabic for Socotra is more literal: *suq* means market and *qatra* means a single drop of liquid. Socotra is about the size of Corsica and lies off the coast of Somalia, level with the Horn of Africa. The Indian Ocean, the Red Sea and the Arabian Sea lap at its shores, and spinner dolphins, giant nesting turtles and pink flamingos are all found there. There is nothing but sea between Socotra's southern coast—which is girdled with pink coral beds—and the frozen Antarctic. It felt a little like arriving at the edge of the world.

Before Socotra's aerodrome was built, in 2001, the island was cut off from the rest of the world for six months of the year because of the monsoon winds. While they are blowing the sea is too rough to navigate and our plane swayed under the force of the wind. From the air the island looked barren and yellow, with the granite Haggier mountain range rising up like a gigantic gray cathedral, piercing the tempestuous sky with its jagged spires.

I had been warned about the monsoon winds and, as I stepped off the plane into the howling gale, my black linen and chiffon sitara—which I had bought so that I wouldn't offend the Yemenis and which actually made me feel strangely protected from their curious gazes—blew out like a funereal ship's sail. The wind tore my handkerchief away, and sudden gusts raced through the aerodrome as I watched a strange combination of apples, satellite dishes and lavatories being unloaded onto the rotating carousel.

Some barefooted Socotrans shepherded us to Hadibu—a small shanty town, indeed the only town on Socotra—where there wasn't a woman in sight, and only one *funduq* (an Arabian inn, or bed-and-breakfast) with a restaurant called the Ritz. There were no Bellinis or waiters here, just goats wandering down the passageway and sheltering from the wind while we lunched on kingklip fish and nonalcoholic beer.

I knew I had to find a dragoman—a driver and guide—because the forty thousand islanders speak Socotran, which is an ancient unwritten language quite different from modern Arabic. So we set off for the tourist board, staggering along and leaning into the wind as it tore up the scrub; even oil drums became airborne. In the tourist office we found an English volunteer who looked baffled when I asked him if he knew where I might find frankincense and myrrh plantations, but, eventually, we came across a driver called Mohammed outside the *funduq*. We hired him, climbed into his jeep and drove out of Hadibu.

The dust dispersed, the air was crystalline and the light had a hallucinatory intensity. Every rock face showed extraordinary geological strata, and there were seashells on the plateau from the pre-Cambrian period—when it would have been beneath the sea. Meanwhile the highest peaks of the mountains—which at 5,000 feet formed the spine of the island and would never have been submerged—must have been, I thought, one of the oldest surfaces in the world.

There are nine hundred plant species on Socotra, three hundred of which are indigenous. No rain had fallen for almost a year, yet bulbous hyacinths, violent red foul-smelling *Carallumas*, violets, begonias, feathery acacia, phallic *Euphorbia* and pomegranates all thrived. The poisonous desert roses and cucumber trees, with their pendulous tendrils and swag-bellied trunks, also thrived, but most bizarre of all were the dragons' blood trees, looking like static atomic mushroom clouds, silhouetted along the skyline or clinging to the crags of gorges. On closer inspection I saw that their branches spread out in all directions with the symmetry of Gothic fan vaulting.

We arrived on a plateau full of dragons' blood trees and desert roses. Mohammed told us that Socotrans call the desert roses "bottle trees" and I realized that their swollen trunks, which store water during the dry season, were very much like Jeroboams or Nebuchadnezzars of champagne. A young goatherd persuaded me to buy some dragons' blood. It was a bundle of brick red glassy globules—not unlike red gobstoppers—wrapped in a torn shirtsleeve.

Only a few months before I had seen some dragons' blood in the window of a Florentine apothecary. It comes from droplets that ooze out of slits in the tree trunks which then harden in the sun into red beads. When water is added to them their red resin makes a deep red dye. *Dracaena cinnabari* or, in Arabic, *Dam-a-akhawayn* means the "blood of two brothers," and it is used as a varnish for violins. Chinese cabinetmakers use cinnabar lacquer which has dragons' blood in it. It is an ingredient in lipsticks; once it was even used as the dye in British £10 notes. Medieval scribes used it for ink, and Roman soldiers carried it to heal their wounds. Today, in Aden, it is used as an antirust agent and, in Socotra, for painting decorative motifs on pots and censers.

We drove on into a valley framed by an amphitheather of ancient terracing which rose steeply in steps that looked as if they'd been carved from the glittering granite and limestone escarpments. Lichen-covered dry-stone walls, which had once formed the boundaries of the incense groves, reminded me of the walls I can see from the window of my cottage in the Pennines.

There are twenty-five species of frankincense in the world, nine of which are indigenous to Socotra, and, in this valley, we saw hundreds of frankincense trees. The most ancient of them were probably three hundred years old, and they were bent double; they looked like black-clad, lumbago-ridden dowagers, while the sinuous branches of the younger trees resembled sexy limbs as they moved gently in the breeze. The purplish trunks were shot through with silver and the bark was flaky, like dried beeswax. Beneath the flakes a green resinous sap oozed and, when I rubbed some on my hand, it smelled like eucalyptus oil or the scent of a warm wind blowing through a pine forest. Incisions or "wounds in the bark" had been made and a milky-white liquid had hardened in the sun into "teardrops." Farther up the grove harvesters were tapping the trunks with little axes, which is done for about three months at fifteen-day intervals, to get the resin to flow. The tapping involves small areas of the bark being removed, and the timing of the tapping depends on the onset of the monsoon rains.

The harvesters were chanting with an intense, driving rhythm as they tapped away at the tree trunks with their small chisel-like *mangafs*. A few strokes revealed the pistachio-green gum; then slowly the globules began to drop down into the bowls and baskets laid out on the ground to catch the resin. It looked to me like green clotted cream. The harvesters, Mohammed told me, called the operation *tawqi*, a word that translates as "to gall a camel's back."

Care has to be taken not to cut the actual bole of the tree, but the more you keep tapping in the same spot, the more resin the tree produces. The precious resin, which was once worth its weight in gold, is harvested twice a year, in spring and then in the autumn, the latter producing a higher grade of frankincense. Once the season's resin has been collected, it is sorted on the floors of caves and left to dry there for three months before being sold.

Pliny describes in great detail how frankincense was collected in southern Arabia:

It used to be the custom, when there were fewer opportunities of selling frankincense, to gather it only once a year, but at the present day trade introduces a second harvesting. The earlier and natural gathering takes place at about the rising of the dog-star, when the summer is at its most intense. The frankincense from the summer crop is collected in the autumn; this is the purest kind, bright white in color. The second crop is harvested in the spring, cuts having been made in the bark during the winter. The forest is divided up into definite portions and, owing to the mutual honesty of the owners, is free from trespassing, and though nobody keeps guard over the trees after an incision has been made, nobody steals from his neighbor.

At Alexandria, on the other hand, where the frankincense is worked up for sale, good heavens! No vigilance is sufficient to guard the factories. A seal is put upon the workmen's aprons, they have to wear a mask or a net with a close mesh on their heads, and before they are allowed to leave they have to take off all their clothes; so much less honesty is displayed with regard to the produce with them than as to the forests with the growers.

These days, by unspoken agreement, each frankincense tree is still owned by a family who lives near that tree, and guardianship of each family's tree is passed down from generation to generation. This custom of custodianship remains exactly the same today as it was when Pliny was writing, in the first century A.D.

The balsamic aroma of the resin cleared my mind as we sat under an old tamarind tree, its branches drooping to the ground and propping the tree up like walking sticks. At the foot of the mountains the air was cooler and the wind had dropped. Egyptian vultures swooped down and foraged for food. They are the dustmen of Socotra; they eat all the rubbish on this strange island.

We drove back along the dried-up wadi beds, which, in October after the rains, are rushing torrents, transforming the island. Clouds were already gathering around the Haggier mountaintops, bringing some moisture to the plants; however, back in Hadibu, it was a dustbowl of monsoon madness. The winds blowing off the African coast were extraordinarily hot; it felt as if someone had left a furnace door open by mistake. The wind howled through the *funduq*, blowing dust everywhere, and the lino mats became airborne magic carpets, while the innkeeper and his staff sat listlessly under mosquito nets chewing qat. The fans spun around in vain, and the only way to attempt sleep was to douse our beds with water and wrap ourselves in soaking wet towels for a few fitful hours. At dawn the shutters banged in the wind, and sweat trickled down my chest in rivulets.

We found Mohammed waiting for us in the morning and set off again along the coast road. Ten-foot waves crashed against the cliffs, which towered above us and were honeycombed with caves. Fishermen squatted in the caves having their morning tea; it was far too rough to put out to sea.

Beyond Hadibu we saw no traces of modern living at all and, except for modest gardening, agriculture is unknown. Apart from the fishermen, the Socotrans are seminomadic pastoralists, and some of the mountain dwellers live in caves. Like their plants, the Socotrans are an indigenous population. No one knows where they came from, nor when. What is known is that in A.D. 600, when the Sabeans ruled the island, there was an influx of Nestorians from Ethiopia, but by the ninth century their religion had lapsed and they had turned to piracy. In 1204 Marco Polo observed the Socotrans as having only "scanty covering before and behind," and in 1507 Padre Vincenzo, a Carmelite, noted that the island's people observed a mixture of Christian and Islamic rites, but that they also worshipped the moon.

We found a young translator, Jamil, who spoke good English and had a broad smile and an engaging, intelligent manner. Jamil was diplomatic, too. He told me not to worry if the men didn't shake hands with me; they observed the Muslim tradition which prohibits women from shaking hands with men.

In Socotra man and nature have a fierce alliance: every drop of water, every dropping, every bird, insect or plant has a role to play. Many of the plants and trees are sticky with saps, juices, resins and gums, making Socotra one big open-air apothecary. The white latex of jatropha trees is used to stop bleeding from cuts; dragons' blood is a remedy for eye diseases and hemorrhages, including postnatal bleeding; the succulent bitter aloes cure sores, sunburns and eczema, and are also used for cleansing; while the juice of *Euphorbia* gets rid of unwanted hair.

At the *tafrita*—a gathering of women to celebrate the birth and the naming of a baby—frankincense is lit. Oil of frankincense is also rubbed onto the stomach to ease the pain of childbirth, and after the child is born the air is cleared and cleansed with frankincense smoke which is lit "to keep the child safe," as Jamil told me, and to ward off illness and keep vermin at bay, just as it once was in ancient Rome. And now, as then, foul smells from the inevitable putrefaction in warm climates are disguised with incense and with perfume; flies and other pests are also kept at bay by the smoke from incense. The most effective incense for all these tasks is that made from frankincense or myrrh. Incense also disguises the smell of burning flesh on funeral pyres. The Romans incinerated their dead with fragrant incense, while the Egyptians infused mummies' bandages.

Medicinally, frankincense was used for all kinds of maladies: for headaches and other aches and pains, for nosebleeds, palsy, gout, spasms and coughing. It was also thought of as a spiritual cleanser and a dispeller of dark moods and forgetfulness. It is known as the Queen of Sheba's incense, and there is a saying in Sana that if you light her incense in the morning it will chase away the devil and usher in the angels.

Today, in Yemen, they pound frankincense in a drink for various ailments; they sweeten and purify drinking water with it and they treat guests to a censer so that they can fumigate their clothes. It is also used as a deodorant, in shampoo, for chewing gum, as a tooth filler and to seal cracks in pots and pans; and one of the Socotran species of frankincense is chewed to boost concentration. Frankincense and myrrh are added to sesame, olive and almond oils to make unguents and scented ointments, and the myriad uses of frankincense even stretch to cleaning icons, because its smoke gently dissolves dirt on the delicate gesso. Myrrh, which was once the gift of kings, now finds itself used—among other things—as an additive to toothpaste.

The following day Jamil took us on a field trip. The jeep kept slipping down the track, so we walked until we reached a plain of shrubland where herds of goats, sheep and even a few scrawny cows were grazing. Most of the cattle and African wild donkeys are feral: they wander at will and answer only the calls of their owners, the lone shepherds and herders. We saw a wild-cat bounding away which Jamil said was a civet cat. He told me that civets have been imported from Ethiopia.

Civet

CIVET WAS DISCOVERED BY ARABS IN THE TENTH CENTURY AND was much prized in Shakespearean England. Civet paste has the same sewerlike smell as musk; it is an excretion from the anal glands of Ethiopian cats. At one time these were caught and kept in cages by Ethiopian women, who prodded them with sticks to enrage them: more of the excretion is produced when a civet cat is angry. The buttery excretion was scraped from the cat's anus—

once their legs had been tied to the top of the cage—with a spatula dipped in fat. The process was repeated every ten days until, eventually, the cats were released. Before the civet hardened and darkened it was mixed with babies' excrement, then packed into zebu horns, sealed with leather and exported.

Civet farms used to exist in Yemen, Ethiopia, various other parts of Africa and in India. However, since the UN Convention on Trade in Endangered Species (CITES) voted to protect the civet cat and other endangered species, civet and civet cats have been banned from international commercial trade, and civet is no longer collected in this cruel way.

Once civet was diluted and mixed with other smells—so that it formed a minuscule proportion of the mixture—it imparted a mysterious animal odor which gave resonance to scents, making them less innocent and more carnal, more mysterious and erotic. Civet lends a visceral note to scents, but in its raw, undiluted form it smells foul and fecal.

Civet was so widely used in seventeenth-century Europe that the civet cat became the trade sign for perfumers, and Daniel Defoe, before he wrote his classic novels, was a breeder of civet cats.

These days, however, civet has generally fallen out of use in the West, but in the Islamic world it is still used in heavy perfumes. The Omani perfumer Amouage uses synthetic civet in its scent of the same name—it smells like washing-up liquid, I think. I have never come across civet in any other modern scent, but where real civet is used it is often as a base note; it forms an accommodating platform for other aromas in a perfume. It is also a fixative and so prolongs the life of an aroma.

I had heard that civet milk has similar properties to those of calamine lotion: Socotrans spread it on their children's skin if they catch measles to alleviate the itching. The mountain women also put a mixture of civet milk and cream behind their ears as a perfume.

I soon discovered that crossing tribal territory in Socotra is a very social business. Village elders received us, and there was a chorus of *"Salam Alaikum"* as Socotran clan elders greeted one another by rubbing their noses together and flourishing their left hands. From stone houses—hewn from the rocky terrain and surrounded by gardens of cucumber trees and date palms fenced in with driftwood where camels were tethered—beautiful children with matted hair swarmed out like bees to stare at us, while the younger ones ran away crying.

We were invited into the largest house in one village, where we took off our shoes and walked on a floor covered with rush matting. Inside there were goatskin rugs and big cushions but hardly any possessions. The house was kept meticulously clean, and air-conditioning was provided by ventilation holes at ground level. The roof was made of wishbone-shaped boughs skillfully fitted together. I discovered that the villagers who didn't live in houses like this one lived in caves.

A thermos of sweet, fatty ghee tea was poured into eggcup-shaped glasses and constantly replenished, while the hut began to fill with children and younger men; the women peered in through the door. The Socotrans soon lapsed into their native language and I listened, fascinated, as their tongues corkscrewed; some of the noises they made sounded like gurgling, as if they were bringing the sounds from the pits of their stomachs.

A large bowl of sour goat's milk and another of rice soon appeared and were put on a circular straw mat for us all to share. I copied the Socotrans by rolling the rice into balls and dipping them into the milk. When dusk fell, kerosene lamps were lit and the leftover milk was passed around. It tasted like those yogurt health drinks which cost a fortune in health-food shops in Britain, but this bacterial yogurt came wrapped in a goat's skin which the Socotrans inflate by blowing into it.

The Socotrans are very hospitable and kind, and they expressed no surprise that strange Europeans should be billeted on them for the night; our offers of money in return were refused despite their extreme poverty. But instead of bedding down for the night Mohammed said he wanted to drive us all to the next village for a wedding, where, Jamil interpreted for me, I would be shown samples of frankincense and myrrh the following morning. So we bundled our rugs and mattresses back into the jeep. Excited by the prospect of a wedding, Mohammed drove recklessly. Sometimes the track simply disappeared and gave way to sheer rock, and then there was a loud thump and we discovered we had a puncture. Mohammed changed the tire by the light of my torch.

We heard the beating of drums long before we saw the village. By the time we arrived kerosene lamps were glowing like fireflies around a canvas tent which turned out to be the wedding marquee. I was taken to the women's quarters, where the only visible parts of the bride were her hennaed ankles and feet. A raw egg was thrown at the lintel of the door for a blessing, and inside the women's quarters the haunting scent of frankincense pervaded everything. It seemed to effervesce and sparkle with pine and lemon notes at first—it was very fresh—and then the plumes of smoke gave off a more mysterious, heavy and sweetly meditative strain; the aroma induced a trancelike state. I sat with the bride and the rest of the womenfolk while she waited for her betrothed.

When the groom arrived I thought he looked absurdly young—perhaps he was only fourteen. He was flanked by his brothers and his father and they were all dressed in tartan sarongs, which I thought made them look a little like a lost tribe from the Scottish Highlands. The ceremony was not exactly ceremonious, but consisted of a series of calls in the strange Socotran tongue as the men circled the bride. Eventually the groom sat down next to her and, although they were still strangers, he at last had the chance to catch a glimpse of her face.

The drums and high-pitched songs carried on for some hours, but when I woke up in the middle of the night lying on a mattress next to a goat's pen which Jamil had arranged for me, all was quiet and I saw the moon racing through the mist. Stephen stayed up long into the night celebrating in a tent with the men.

Sixteen children were staring at me intently when I awoke in the morning and, transfixed by my every move, they watched me brush my teeth. I don't think they had ever seen a toothbrush or a hairbrush. Then we were ushered into the sheik's hut to sample frankincense smoke. As it billowed from a clay pot on a bed of embers of cinnabar wood, it had both a euphoric and a soporific effect and I experienced an aromatic "rush": I was transported back to the cold, damp aisles of the Renaissance churches full of quattrocento frescoes that I'd so often visited with my parents, while Stephen was reminded of his days as an altar boy.

Our hosts also brought out crystals of topaz yellow frankincense, ruby red globules of dragons' blood and rubbery gems of white myrrh. Sitting in such bucolic surroundings in a nebula of frankincense smoke, I thought about the fact that frankincense was once an expensive, highly esteemed luxury and how tastes in scent have changed. After the fall of the Roman Empire the demand for frankincense dwindled; now it is not so revered as a scent, although it is still expensive, and it is thought of as sacred—which, perhaps, explains its secular unpopularity. I also thought about the way that trade in frankincense and myrrh has accompanied the spread and movement of faiths and culture over the millennia, but how today's Socotrans, who subsist on a diet of dates and sour goat's milk, don't make a good living from the aromatic gums that exist in such profusion on their island.

Jamil told me that a Pakistani had been sniffing around Socotra and that he wanted to buy frankincense in bulk, as well as pearls. I had also heard that the Somalis, just across the water, had a monopoly on Socotran frankincense and cultivated it on the island in bushes that they cut down annually, literally pouring the resin from the trunks. But, sadly, the riches of frankincense, myrrh and dragons' blood are no longer the stuff of international trade, because the modern Socotran export of these rare ingredients has simply not been developed—mostly because the island is so remote.

There is, obviously, potential for the development of trade in these resins, but there is no up-to-date information on the scale of production in Somalia, Ethiopia, Yemen or Oman, nor on what the market for resins might be. However, records do exist from British colonial rule in Aden, which was, then, the entrepôt for gums and resins. Socotran aloes and gums were traded in Aden, and the trade was a complex and skilled one because there are many different varieties of gum, and hundreds of different grades of myrrh and frankincense, which all had to be sorted before being shipped to far-flung parts of the world such as Italy and Britain.

Records from 1875 show that 600 tons of resins, including 300 tons of frankincense and 70 tons of myrrh, passed through the hands of Aden merchants that year. In 1913 exports of myrrh from Aden exceeded 1,000 tons, but since then these exports have dwindled. The demand today for frankincense and myrrh is difficult to quantify, but there is a lot of unofficial trading between the producing countries. China is the largest market for frankincense because they still use it in their traditional medicines; both frankincense and myrrh are used to treat many ailments, although the main resin used is Eritrean frankincense.

In 1987 the Catholic and Orthodox churches in Latin America and in Europe imported 500 tons of frankincense and myrrh, and a similar amount was imported to Africa—where it is chewed! The Middle East, and in particular Saudi Arabia, imports a high grade of frankincense from Somalia for domestic incense use, although sandalwood and other aromatics are becoming more popular than frankincense. Also in 1987, approximately 50 tons of frankincense and myrrh were imported by Europeans for essential oils and perfume; the major customer was France.

Somalia and Ethiopia are by far the biggest growers and producers of these resins; Somalia supplies most of the world's myrrh and exports some 900 tons of frankincense each year. They export the high-quality Maidi, or *Boswellia frereana*, grade of frankincense, which is found predominantly in northern Somalia. Ethiopia and Sudan produce the most widely traded frankincense, an Eritrean species, and exported some 2,000 tons per year in the late 1990s. More recent records have not been kept, or are not available to Westerners, and climate change has played its part: severe drought means that the trees have not produced as much resin.

It is very rare to find pure myrrh or frankincense. The Omani perfumer Amouage does make attars from these resins, although they are not sold in the West. There are a few other scents which use these ancient aromas as top and middle notes. Diptyque's L'Eau Trois and Ormonde Jayne's Champaca both have delicious myrrh notes, and Rose des Hommes, available from Les Senteurs (a scent shop in London's Elizabeth Street) has notes of myrrh and cedarwood. Frankincense is even harder to find in contemporary scents: so far I have come across it only a few times: in Ormonde Jayne's Tolu and in Apogee from Les Senteurs, which has notes of frankincense and patchouli. Meanwhile, there is one Western scent made from frankincense and myrrh: Abahna, which is made in the Lake District.

Most perfumers do not trek out to the groves of myrrh and frankincense in Yemen, Oman or Eritrea, although a few adventurous aromatherapists might travel to find the best resins—but even they tend to get their oils from French suppliers. Even Amouage, in Oman, has to send its crystals and resins to France to be extracted or distilled before they are returned to Muscat to be blended and bottled in lavish cut-glass flagons.

We left the village where the wedding had been, and Mohammed drove us to the southern region of the island, to the Nujad plain, where 5 square miles of myrrh trees, or *Commiphora ornifolia*, grow. There are four species of *Commiphora* that grow only on Socotra, and it was an awesome sight to see rows of stately myrrh trees stage-lit by the shafts of sunlight that pierced the clouds. Myrrh trees look like low cedars; their foliage spreads horizontally and they have a lot more foliage than frankincense trees. Jamil told me that the Nujad tribes don't bother to gather myrrh, but that they eat the clusters of succulent berries. I tried one but was disappointed to find it similar to an unripe apple, and bitter. Obviously my taste buds have been educated differently from those of the Nujad tribes.

Sap with the consistency, smell and color of milky white glue oozed from the bark of the myrrh trees and, farther up the trunk, I noticed that the sap had crystallized into honey-colored globules that looked like burned sugar; they even smelled like burned sugar when we put a match to one of them.

Incense Stories

THE ANCIENT KINGDOM OF SABA CAST A SPELL OVER THE GREEKS and Romans. Cut off by the sun-scorched deserts of central Arabia, these remote southern regions with their exotic exports of incense and spices were considered mysterious and fantastic by the early classical writers. And the Sabeans played up the mystery. They guarded their myrrh and frankincense groves fiercely, deliberately spreading rumors that the groves were watched over not only by them, but also by winged quadrupeds and serpents. Fabulous tales and mythologies sprang up about Arabian perfumes and Indian spices: cinnamon was said to be gathered from the nests of phoenixes, and bats were rumored to snatch out the eyes of anyone who went cassia picking. Stories ➤

like these kept the prices high and the trespassers away, which was exactly what was intended.

As early as 2000 B.C. incense was considered essential for eternal life; it was thought to be the gateway to the spirit world and, by 450 B.C., Herodotus was recording that Arabia "was the only place producing frankincense, myrrh . . . and cinnamon." The privilege of tending the trees and gathering the incense was the preserve of three thousand families who cloaked the whole process in religion and mystery, which also helped maintain its high price. Herodotus wrote that "The [men] . . . of these families are called sacred and are not allowed to . . . [meet] a woman or [to attend] funeral processions when they are engaged in making incisions in the trees in order to obtain the frankincense."

Incense was used not only as a spiritual cleanser but also as an early form of hygiene. Strabo mentions the Assyrian postcoital custom of burning incense for purification, while in other parts of the classical world incense was burned to arouse passions before sex. Writers such as Sappho and Ovid emphasize the erotic properties of incense, and it is said that Egyptian women used to fumigate their vaginas with myrrh smoke. Yemeni women today still stand with their skirts over incense burners.

The Scythians, the transasiatic nomads of the Steppes, were addicted to perfume. Herodotus wrote that "The Scythian women bruise under a stone wood of the cypress and cedar, with frank-incense; upon this they pour water until it becomes of a certain consistency. This imparts an agreeable odor and gives the skin a soft and beautiful appearance." They invented a novel vapor bath too by throwing this paste and some hemp seed onto hot stones beside the bath. It is said that the Scythians enjoyed these scents so much that they squealed with pleasure.

The Greeks attributed a fabulous origin to the resin of myrrh, telling that it came from the tears of Myrrha, daughter of the King of Cyprus, who had been metamorphosed into a shrub after she fell in love with her father and tricked him into sleeping with her for twelve nights.

Myrrh was also believed to have magical effects; its elusive fragrance was thought to have supernatural powers and the ability to banish bad luck, and incense burners filled with juniper and myrrh were placed on thresholds to protect the household from evil spirits.

Pliny described myrrh as "being tapped twice a year at the same season as frankincense, but the incisions are made all the way up [the trunk] from the root to the branches. Before the tree is tapped, the root exudes of its own accord a juice called stacte which is the most highly valued of all myrrh [resins]."

The Latin word *myrrha* derives from the Hebrew *murr*, meaning bitter. Like frankincense, myrrh was used in most incense compounds, and specifically in perfume. In his treatise *Concerning Odours*, Theophrastus noted that the scent of myrrh could last for as long as ten years; in fact *stacte* oil had the longest life of any known perfume and was steeped in wine to make the perfume itself even more fragrant. A Greek perfumer by the name of Megallus created a wine-and-myrrh mixture, and his perfume came to be known as Megaleion: Megallus was

obviously the Guerlain of the classical world. Another rare perfume made with myrrh was the Balm of Gilead, a scent from
biblical times thought to be comforting and to possess healing
qualities. It was probably an aromatic gum or spice, but it has
never been precisely identified with any plant in Gilead. Some
references suggest that it is mastiche or *Pistacia lentiscus*—an
oleoresin—which came from Palestine. Myrrh is still highly
esteemed in perfume making and also in the making of incense
sticks; it has stood the test of time.

We stopped at one of the Nujad villages for the night. I was
shown to the women's quarters, where they removed their veils
to reveal beautiful brown faces and inquisitive flashing eyes.
They prodded me and flourished their hands and we managed—
in sign language—to establish how many children we each had
(they had lots and I had only one) and how old Tarquin was—I
held up three fingers. They studied the gold nail varnish on
my toes while I admired their *tawqs*—the clasps on their gold
necklaces.

The women's toddlers had pouches of myrrh pinned to their
bibs to ward off illness and evil spirits, and *mizabs*—portable
cradles—dangled from the driftwood roof. These *mizabs* were
made from sarongs bound with rope, and looked just like the
bundles storks are supposed to deliver, according to Western
mythology. The babies slept soundly in their *mizabs*, and if one
of them woke, usually because of the flies, a woman would light
a censer and waft the frankincense fumes over the child so that
the flies dispersed and the child stopped crying.

I asked them if they would give me some myrrh, by showing
them the rubbery gems of white myrrh that I had already been

given and kept in an empty cigarette packet. I had discovered by then that myrrh is considered feminine while frankincense is regarded as masculine, partly because its globules resemble testes. They kept their myrrh wrapped in plastic (from food wrappings bought in Hadibu, which they conserved carefully) because it is oily, whereas the delicate crystals of frankincense were put into old plastic food tubs. In the old days, caravans of camels used to carry frankincense and myrrh in cagelike baskets which stopped the frankincense crystals from getting crushed, while myrrh was tightly enclosed in goatskins.

The women lit some myrrh and, as the bittersweet fumes billowed around the cramped hut, it was difficult to isolate the scent because there were so many other smells: the kid goat, the rank ghee tea, the mustiness of the rushes on the floor and the sweat of all our bodies. But, as the smoldering plumes of myrrh smoke filled the hut, it truly did seem less powerful and more feminine than the masculine frankincense. It was redolent of the forest floor, honeyed and oleaginous, with hints of lemon and rosemary. Myrrh is considered to be less holy than frankincense and more pastoral.

Socotra is the last home of true incense. The smell of Somalian commercial frankincense, adulterated with chemicals, which I bought in the souk in Sana, bears no relation to the real thing when it is harvested from Socotran incense trees. And when I smell incense now I no longer think of the dank, stone smell of churches but of warm zephyrs carrying the billowing, spiraling smoke of resins gathered from the valleys of frankincense and the virgin forests of myrrh.

Grade one Somali frankincense retails at about $6 per kilogram and is the quality used to make perfume. Usually about 1 to 3 kilogram of resin per tree is collected, but in times of drought looking after livestock becomes more important than tree tapping, so the resin is not collected. Unlike most essential oils, there has been no systematic study of myrrh and frankincense, partly because there are so many different varieties.

Strictly speaking, an absolute should be prepared by alcohol extraction of the resinoid—the dry resin which has been extracted to form a pastelike substance—but in the case of frankincense and myrrh the absolutes are directly extracted from the crude resins with alcohol without making the resinoids first. They can be extracted by a hot or a cold process; each gives different olfactory results. Different essential oils of frankincense are prepared in different ways, as CO_2 extracts, phytonic extracts and solvent/alcohol extracts. The oils that result from these processes are either essential oils, absolutes, attars or concretes. Some frankincense is distilled in the Indian city of Cochin, but it is rarely distilled in the countries where it grows, primarily because those countries are underdeveloped.

Frankincense gum resin is composed of 5 to 9 percent volatile oils and 50 to 70 percent alcohol-soluble resins. The essential oil component of frankincense contains more than two hundred different chemicals, hence its complex bouquet. These components vary, depending upon the microclimate in which the tree grows, the soil type and the season in which the frankincense is harvested. Harvesters and traders are able to discern all these subtle differences simply by smelling the raw material. Myrrh also has many different varieties, the poetically named "cave-dweller" variety being the most sweet-smelling, according to Pliny.

Before we came to Socotra I went to the souks in Sana. I retraced my steps along the narrow streets, following paths I'd taken with my mother all those years before. Going deep into the souk to find the incense sellers, I really only needed to follow my nose, and I found them squeezed among their wares, which spilled out onto the pavement. There were baskets and wooden boxes overflowing with petrified rivers of crystals of frankincense and myrrh. The shops were lined with rickety shelves of incense burners, vials of oils and jars of ingredients waiting to be pounded.

I stopped by the one who looked the least fierce (all Yemenis tend to look a bit intimidating) and whose cheek was not distended with qat. I asked for the best grade of frankincense he had, and he held up a fistful of Hasik crystals which come from Oman. When I asked him if he had any Socotran frankincense or myrrh, he shook his head as I'd thought he might. I asked if he had any oils of frankincense or myrrh, but he shook his head again, and when I wanted to know why, he said that the resins were distilled only in Oman. He threw his hands up and said that in Yemen they were too poor to make scents.

I inquired what was in the little bottles I could see on the shelves behind him and he told me that, although the labels stated that they were made in Hodeidah, the Yemeni port, they actually came from Switzerland. There was a scent called Sword which was divine, but too strong to wear—although, as I discovered later, it was perfect for the bath. The best vial of all was an exquisite tuberose; it was as delectable as the one I found in India. Tuberose is so erotically charged and deliciously velvety that it stands on its own and needs no other scent to back it up.

So, I could not buy any attars of frankincense or myrrh, but I did have a suitcase filled to the brim with crystals and globules of myrrh and frankincense, which smelled dusty and fragrant. I had enough for a few seasons of fires, and they were the very best grades. I realized that I would simply have to get them extracted in a laboratory when I got back to England.

When I finally did arrive back in England I think the customs officers must have thought I'd just raided several churches, but I was delighted to have "exported" so much incense, because even now, two years later, I throw the crystals on my fire as the nights draw in and place the globules of myrrh on wax church candles, and I instantly find myself back on the magical island of Socotra.

Even though the fabulous riches of frankincense and myrrh are no longer the stuff of the once-great incense trade, these Sabean scents still exist on Socotra, and it is these Sabean scents—these ancient aromas from distant lands—that I have grown to love and that I knew I had to have in my own bespoke perfume. To my mind, nothing evokes the sense of antiquity and what I imagine to be the scent of ancient unguents more than these two resins of frankincense and myrrh. The spiraling plumes of smoke and piney zephyrs are ethereal, seeming to me to harbor otherworldly spirits: the very qualities I would like to haunt my scent as they once haunted the temples and basilicas of the ancient world.

But before I left Socotra for England, I embarked on the last leg of my scent trail. It was the shortest journey in all my travels but, in a way, it was the strangest. Stephen, Jamil and I remained on Socotra and went in search of that most extraordinary of perfume ingredients: ambergris.

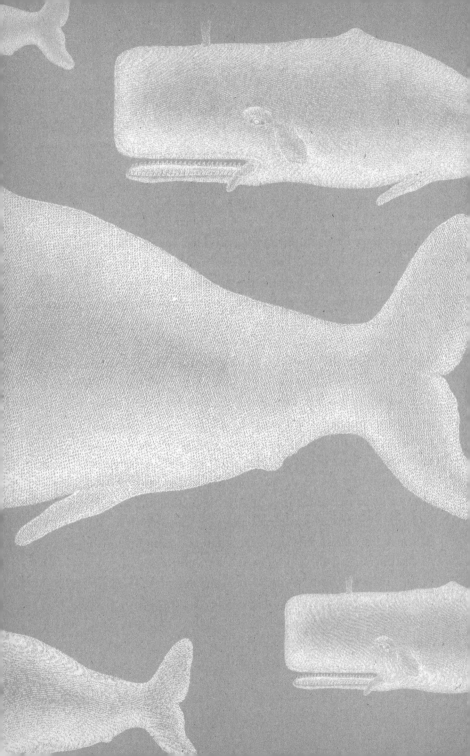

CHAPTER NINE

AMBERGRIS

Socotra, Part Two

Have you seen the zeal of my she-camel
In any she-camel moving
a smooth-paced hand and a hardened sole?

It left the smoke of the dwarf tamarisk
in its native land,
seeking a people who kindle ambergris
AL MUTANABBI

I FIRST HEARD ABOUT THE MYSTERIOUS ISLAND OF SOCOTRA when a Yemeni told me that Socotran women were "broad about the pants" and scented with the ambergris that is washed up on Socotra's shores. He told me that the aphrodisiac qualities of ambergris, and the chewing of qat, gave these women enduring sexual appetites that exceeded those of their men, and so, ever since hearing all this, I developed a strong desire to find Socotra's ambergris. I got my opportunity when the idea for this book became a reality.

Marco Polo, in 1294, was the first Western chronicler to realize that ambergris came from the sperm whale, *Physeter macrocephalus*, which he saw hunted on Socotra.

> *They have a great deal of ambergris. [it] . . . comes from the stomach of the whale and it is a great object of trade. The people contrive to take the whales with barbed iron darts which, once they are fixed on the [whale's] body, cannot come out again. A long cord is attached . . . to [a] buoy, which floats on the surface, so that when the whale dies they know where to find it.*

Ingenious.

Ambergris is a very strange substance indeed. It *is* found in the bellies of sickly whales, or washed up on the beach, but it is extremely difficult to track down. Its natural rarity has rendered it almost mythical, and it still remains the most mysterious substance in perfumery. It is not often used by itself, as a solid perfume, but it is the finest fixative because it binds together the numerous raw materials that perfumes contain; it even works in the cheaper synthetic perfumes. But because it is so rare, and therefore so expensive, only a few private perfumers still use it. Some say it smells like a mixture of truffles, BO and good cigars, and certainly ambergris's unique smell does not always appeal on its own. When its aroma is blended with other more fleeting scents, however, its particular properties fix those fugitive odors and makes them last far longer than they would without it.

At first ambergris has a pungent smell, but the weathering of months, even years, at sea matures it. When it reaches the perfumer's laboratory, it is macerated in alcohol for several months and gradually develops a velvety, complex and powerful odor with remarkable tenacity. It can retain its scent for as long as three hundred years. It clings to materials even after they have been washed several times, and the longer it lingers the sweeter the odor becomes. One single drop of ambergris tincture applied to paper and placed in a book will stay fragrant for forty years.

Trade in ambergris has been banned for years by treaty and by various national maritime protection acts, but, except since 1973 in the United States, it is not illegal to gather ambergris that is washed up on beaches. Ambergris, or *Physeter catodon*, is derived from the sperm whale's favorite diet of squid and the common cuttlefish and consists of 80 percent ambrein, a cholesterol derivative. Jacques Cousteau discovered that sperm whales swallow squid in one gulp because the squid have soft flesh that does not require mastication. There is only one hard part to a squid: the beak. Ambrein may be either an indigestible component of the squid, or a secretion from the whale's gut in response to the constant irritation caused by the squid's sharp beak. Chemists believe that ambergris also contains benzoic ester, which is a compound of alcohol and acid radicals. (Aspirin is an ester.)

In addition to ambergris, sperm whales offer another treasure from their bodies: spermaceti—a milky white substance found in the head of the whale and originally mistaken for sperm. Spermaceti forms—among other things—an exceptionally pure wax from which in 1748 Jacob Rodriguez Rivera invented the smokeless candle.

In the gut of the whale ambergris is a black, semiviscous and foul-smelling liquid. However, on exposure to sunlight and air it quickly oxidizes and hardens into an aromatic, marbled, waxy pellucid substance in which the squid beaks are still imbedded. It is a grayish color, hence its name, amber *gris*—French for gray—which distinguishes ambergris from amber, a resin that comes from the common rockrose and from bee balm. (Amber, also known as labdanum, is often substituted for ambergris. Compounds made from clary sage, oak moss and various fungi can be converted into ambergris-like odorants, and ambreic smells can also be synthesized from chemicals, although with great difficulty because of the complex odor of ambergris.)

While the waxy quality of ambergris has given rise to the belief that it originated from gelatinous honeycombs that floated on the surface of the sea, ambergris is, literally, the vomit of the sperm whale. Once the ambergris, a pastelike secretion, has been re-gurgitated, or released during decomposition after the whale's natural death, it refines itself naturally as it floats on the ocean currents until it is washed up on the beaches.

Sometimes, however, ambergris is taken straight from the whale when it has been harpooned. This is vividly described in Herman Melville's *Moby Dick*:

> *He thrust both hands in, and drew out handfuls of something that looked like ripe Windsor soup or rich mottled old cheese; very unctuous and savoury withal. You might easily dent it with your thumb; it is of a hue between yellow and ash color . . . the motion of a sperm whale's flukes above water dispenses a perfume as when a musk-scented lady rustles her skirt in a warm parlour.*

Ambergris was unknown in the Western world until one of Alexander the Great's admirals collected it from the coasts of Oman (the conqueror was particularly fond of perfumes). The ancient Greeks believed that ambergris came from springs in or near the sea. They discovered that it enhanced the effects of alcohol if smelled while drinking wine, and no doubt many a bacchanal was enlivened by a pinch of ambergris. Pliny wrote that the Romans used pounded mollusks and cuttlefish in per-fumery: these products of the sea are, of course, part of the sperm whale's diet.

The ancient Chinese referred to ambergris as *Lung sien hiang*, which means dragons' spittle perfume, because it was said to come from the drooling dormant dragons that lolled on the rocks by the sea. To the Chinese mandarins it was an elixir for the libido, and in the Orient it is still widely used as an aphrodisiac. The Japanese are equally keen on what they call *Kunsurano fuu*, or whale droppings, as an aphrodisiac.

The Arabs call ambergris *anbar*, or amber, and they used it medicinally for the heart and brain. It is still administered to growing children in the way that the British used to give cod liver oil to make children healthy and strong. The Arabs, like the Greeks, also believed that raw ambergris emanated from springs near the sea and they trained camels to sniff it out.

Ali Ibn al-Mas'udi, a tenth-century historian and traveler, maintained that the best ambergris came from the Sea of Zing off the coast of eastern Africa; that it was pale blue; and that a lump was as big as an ostrich egg. He wrote that "When the sea is much agitated it casts up fragments of amber almost like lumps of rock and the fish swallowing these are choked thereby, and [it] floats on the surface. The men of Zing then come in their canoes and fall on the creature with harpoons, draw it ashore, cut it up and extract the ambergris."

To the earliest Western chroniclers, ambergris was variously thought to come from the sperm of fishes or whales, from the droppings of mythical birds (probably because of the confusion over the squids' beaks that were still buried in the stuff) or, due to its waxy appearance and mellifluous smell, from a hive of bees living by the sea. For centuries there was great confusion over the origins of ambergris.

In Pomet's *Compleat History of Drugs*, written in the seventeenth century, ambergris is classified as "the dearest and most valuable commodity in France." Pomet poetically writes, "It is brought to us from Lisbon and is nothing else but a mass of honeycombs that fall from the rocks into the sea. These honeycombs being in the sea, whether by a property of the sea water or by the virtue of sunbeams, are rendered liquid and floating upon the water."

It is mentioned in *The Howard Household Books* (1481–3), as "Imber-gres," for its medicinal properties. Some authors have referred to it as "ambergrease" and considered it to be a vegetable of some kind, or a deep-sea mushroom torn up by tempestuous seas, because of its mushroom aroma. Dr. Johnson, in his 1755 *Dictionary of the English Language*, like Pomet, considered ambergris to be one of the noblest substances in perfume, describing it as, "A fragrant drug that melts almost like wax." But he too struggled to define its origins.

In 1783 the botanist Joseph Banks gave a paper at the Royal Society by Dr. Franz Xavier Schwediawer, a German physician living in London, which ended the confusion and showed that this mysterious waxlike substance the color of ash was in fact a secretion found in the intestines of the sperm whale. In 1820 two French chemists, Pierre-Joseph Pelletier and Joseph-Bienaimé Caventou, isolated, characterized and named ambrein as the principal active fragrant ingredient of ambergris.

Casanova liked to add small amounts of ambergris to chocolate mousses to aid his amorous adventures. Queen Elizabeth I was enamored of ambergris and other scents from the East, especially scented gauntlets. She was reputed to have had the wood paneling in a dining room at Hampton Court doused with ambergris, where, apparently, the smell still lingers. Ibn Battuta, the great fourteenth-century Islamic traveler and writer, was astonished to find men gobbling down hashish cakes laced with ambergris in Baghdad. Today it is sold in the souks of the Middle East, where men still eat it to stimulate their libido. In Morocco they drink an ambergris tisane, and there was a time when ambergris was burned as incense.

Ambergris is particularly deceptive because it looks like a gray pumice stone, or a pebble, and is weightless; it is very difficult to spot, but Jamil—who continued to be our guide and translator in Socotra—told me that his father, a fisherman, once found some *anbar*. And he said that the sea surrounding Socotra teems with whales and dolphins, particularly sperm whales and short-finned pilot whales. The majority of the Socotran working male population are fishermen, and their main catch consists of shark, king fish and tuna, which they preserve in salt or dry; reef fish and lobster are also caught. The fishermen were not working when I was there because it was the monsoon season. However, that meant that it was a good time for me to talk to them.

We walked along the beach beyond Hadibu to find a fisherman friend of Jamil's father. The jagged shoreline was covered with razor-sharp reefs; nets and low, flat fishing boats, designed for shallow waters, lay idle. We found Abdulla, the fisherman, sitting on an anchor, his face weathered and leathery. He crossed his legs and surveyed us suspiciously through his glasses. He was wily and guarded. He said he had some ambergris, but that it was not for sale.

But Jamil was an excellent interpreter, not only from Arabic but also from Socotran, and when Abdulla tried to steer the conversation away from ambergris, suggesting an alternative aphrodisiac—he seemed to think us merely sex-hungry

Westerners—Jamil persisted with his questions about the sperm whales. And eventually Abdulla, realizing that we were serious, told us that there were different kinds of ambergris whales and that, on Socotra, it was the Hihadra whale that provided their ambergris. He also told us that not all sperm whales contain the substance, but if a whale is sickly, it will probably be full of ambergris—that is, if they have eaten too much they vomit, and it is the vomit, that makes the ambergris. He said that a few years before he had found a large piece of ambergris caught up in his net and had taken it straight to the Hadramawt, a fertile, quite prosperous wadi on the mainland, where he knew he could get a good price for it. Because ambergris commanded high prices it was usually sold to the Omanis and the Saudis.

Abdulla told us that ambergris used to be preserved in oil and kept in large and beautiful shells. He also said that before the unification of North and South Yemen ambergris was traded for 300,000 shillings for a lump the size of an ashtray. Jamil calculated that that amount equaled about $21,000—a fabulous sum.

Sperm Whales and Ambergris: the Costs

THE SPERM WHALE, OR *PHYSETER MACROCEPHALUS*, IS THE LARGEST of the toothed whales; in fact, it is believed to be the largest toothed animal ever to inhabit the planet. It is named after the spermaceti that comes from its head. The sperm whale has also always been known as the Common Cachalot; the word *"cachalot"* is a Portuguese colloquial term for "head."

The first sperm whale was harpooned in the eighteenth century by a Nantucket whaler called Christopher Hussey, and until 1750 whales were towed to shore stations for processing. Then, with the subsequent development of the Try-Works—so called because boiling the whales' blubber to extract the oil is called "trying-out" the blubber—the crew could process the whales at sea and so continue whaling until their holds were filled. American sperm-whale fishing flourished between 1750 and 1850, a whaling era immortalized in *Moby Dick*.

Between 1761 and 1920 records show that almost forty thousand sperm whales were killed. From 1918 on, catches increased to a record thirty thousand a year. By 1916 as much as $60,000 worth of ambergris could be extracted from the intestines of a single whale. The largest lump ever recorded, weighing 442 kilograms (983 pounds), was taken from a sperm whale caught in the Antarctic by the whaling ship *Southern Harvester* in 1953. In 1962, ambergris sold at an average of $100 per kilogram, but with the development of synthetic substitutes the price fell considerably, although it regained its value when it was realized that the substitutes did not have the subtle longevity of real ambergris.

Because of its rarity, and the uncertainty of supply, ambergris has always been very expensive; it is sometimes known as "Neptune's treasure." In 1691 a 52-ounce lump found in Ireland on the shores of County Sligo was bought on the spot for £20 and went on to fetch £100 in London. Two years later, the Dutch East India company bought 182 pounds of ambergris from the King of

> Tidore (in the Moluccas, or Spice Islands) for 1,000 talers. The Duke of Tuscany then offered 50,000 crowns for it. (A taler was a German silver dollar worth 3 shillings in 1864 and a crown, when last minted, was worth 5 shillings.)

Whalers dreamed of making their fortunes by finding lumps of ambergris washed up ashore or buried in the belly of a captured whale. The old whalers knew the places where the species could be found in greatest numbers: the west coast of South America; the north Atlantic; the west coast of Africa; the Arabian Sea; the coast of Japan; the west coast of Australia; and the Tasman Sea between Australia and New Zealand. In a study of the movement of sperm whales, marine biologists have discovered that the whales form herds at full moon and seem to disperse at other times. This could coincide with the movements of squid, the whales' principal source of food, but the movements of the squid are even less well known than those of the whales.

The following morning we walked along the coast watching the white light bounce off the titanium-white sand dunes, reminding me of beaches in the Greek islands. But the desolate villages, half-buried in the sand, soon dispelled this Hellenic idyll. Eventually we came to a village with freshwater and an oasis of date palms and papayas. Jamil said we should stop there for a thirst-quenching papaya. We saw cattle and camels penned in by bamboo and driftwood fences which were so artfully put together that they reminded me of Andy Goldsworthy's environmental sculptures; and there were clusters of dwellings built with mortar and fossilized coral gleaned from the reefs, and encrusted with mollusks and sea anemones.

These primitive houses looked like the kinds of shell grottoes you might stumble across beside a lake in an arcadian park landscaped by Capability Brown. I almost expected to find an inscription by Alexander Pope in the coral gesso of these cottages ornée and resident hermits spouting Virgil. But the inhabitants were what appeared to be a band of shipwrecked punk rockers.

They gathered around us, smiling shyly. They had bright orange hair which was so matted that it stuck up on end. Jamil explained that they hennaed their hair and that the sun and salt water bleached it this color. We sat down with the orange-haired tribe and breakfasted on their delicious papayas. After the tea was poured Jamil waited for the right psychological moment to ask about *anbar*. Although Socotra is rich in natural resources, ambergris is the most precious of them all, so, I thought, why should these poor islanders reveal the secrets of this mysterious and valuable product of the sea to me? But, eventually, the oldest man of the village, the sheikh, came and squatted in the middle of the circle and began to speak. He had an authoritative manner, and his face was so weathered and deeply lined that it looked like a relief map of the Himalayas.

He told us that his great-great-grandfather used to harpoon whales off Socotra, and that one of his cousins had found so much ambergris in a dead whale that he went to Oman and became a wealthy merchant. But he said that, usually, it was extremely difficult to find ambergris, although crabs and birds gathering in a frenzy on the beach are a sure sign that ambergris is nearby.

Then he told us that anyone who finds ambergris must give

away one-third of it to the first person he sees after finding it; otherwise he will die or go crazy. He also explained that Satan guards a red tree that grows deep in the ocean and allows only the sperm whale to eat from it. When the whale vomits after eating from the tree, the vomit is black, but as it slowly floats to the surface of the sea it loses its color . . . and becomes ambergris. So, I thought, just as those who guard the groves of frankincense and myrrh spread stories that winged quadrupeds and serpents watched over the groves, so the peculiar conditions in which ambergris is found have given rise to fabulous stories.

In *Moby Dick* Ishmael makes several more literal and less poetic observations on ambergris. He says:

> *Now this ambergris is a very curious substance. [it] . . . is soft, waxy, and so highly fragrant and spicy that it is largely used in perfumery, in pastilles, precious candles, hair powders and pomatum. The Turks use it in cooking, and also carry it to Mecca for the same purpose that frankincense is carried to Saint Peter's in Rome. Some wine merchants drop a few grains into claret, to flavor it. Who would think that such fine ladies and gentlemen should regale themselves with an essence found in the inglorious bowels of a sick whale!*

One of the orange-headed girls in the village offered us a lump of ambergris she said she'd found on the beach. I was suspicious and thought it could be tar, or flotsam, but Stephen said we should buy it as a gesture of goodwill, because the islanders were so poor. I rolled the piece of ambergris in my palm and studied it closely. I looked for all the qualities—concentric layers of various colors: gray, brown, yellow and white streaks; and I smelled it to see whether it had the peculiar aroma I'd heard about, redolent of sea kelp, seawater and ozone. I tested it to see whether it softened in the warmth of my hand—it didn't—but I knew one sure way to test ambergris—you put it in water, in which it is insoluble. (It does dissolve in hot alcohol, but there wasn't a drop of booze on the island.)

We bought the "ambergris" and, when we got back to the jeep Jamil smiled mischievously and brought out a plastic bottle of what could only be described as very stale scrumpy that even someone desperate for alcohol would balk at. We put the lump of "ambergris" into it and simmered it on a little primus stove, but it refused to dissolve. We decided we would have to wait until we could immerse it in hot hard liquor.

We left the marmalade-haired tribe and, the following day, went on an expedition to the southwest of the island, where whales have often been sighted. In the late afternoon we came to the last village on the southwest tip of Socotra, where the cliffs plunge 300 feet down into the sea. We were at the end of the road, the end of the island, and it seemed to me as if we were at the ends of the earth.

The tribe who live in the southwest of Socotra have olive skin and straight hair. They look as if they might have Latin blood in their veins—perhaps from the Portuguese who had settled on the island 500 years before. I wondered if some of them could even have been descended from the Greek colonists whom Aristotle sent to Socotra. This tribe were sophisticated and worldly; their houses were big by Socotran standards, there was an abundant supply of freshwater rushing down from the escarpment and there was a village jeep, affectionately called "Monica Lewinsky." Jamil told me that jeeps were usually named after corpulent Egyptian actresses, and I was impressed that these islanders were so well-informed about Bill Clinton's sex life, because they had only battery-powered wirelesses to tune in to the outside world; I hadn't seen a television, even in Hadibu. One of the villagers assured us that Socotra was the safest place in the world, and I have to say that, despite having asked Stephen to travel with me to Yemen because it still isn't easy for a woman to travel alone in this part of the world, on Socotra I never felt in any danger.

The villagers told us that whales were usually seen in March and April, and that ten years before a whale had been beached on the Nujad plain and lumps of ambergris had been found in its belly. More recently, *anbar* was found on Abdul Kuri, a desolate island in the archipelago which makes Socotra seem positively cosmopolitan. Its few inhabitants live in driftwood shelters and eke out an existence from fishing. I thought that there might be a better chance of finding ambergris there, but the monsoon winds were too strong for us to sail.

The village sheik told us stories about islanders who had mistaken ambergris for tar and used it as waterproofing, or for mortar and used it to build houses. And how, when they realized that it was ambergris, the waterproofing was undone and the house razed to the ground. The islanders took the ambergris to Oman and were never heard of again. The sheik's stories showed the power that the possibility of finding ambergris has over the lives of the islanders.

He also told us that when the villagers had found small

quantities of *anbar* they'd had to keep their discoveries secret in case other people came to find some. The sheik explained that there was both a black and a white ambergris, and that the white was of a better quality: they call the black ambergris "mutton" and the white "beef." Ambergris is indispensable to the Socotrans as a medicine. It is administered for stomachaches, fevers and even for polio and paralysis before it sets in. For children they put it in ghee tea or hot milk, but they don't expose children to the fumes or let them smell it at all, because *anbar* can have a narcotic effect.

As darkness fell we gathered around kerosene lamps, which threw dramatic shadows on the walls of the village compound and reminded me of a Chinese shadow-puppet theater. The villagers lapsed into their secretive native tongue and recited Socotran poetry. Many Socotran men are forced to leave the island to search for work in the Gulf States; but Socotra is always on their minds and the Socotran migrants' verses are usually about returning to their beloved island. Jamil translated a verse for us:

> *I loved you and I loved myself*
> *And I had no pain from woes.*
> *My pain is from Socotra*
> *From Asoqan I'm lonely.*

After a supper of rice mopped up with a dish of sour goat's milk, the village sheik beckoned me to a cluster of trees behind the village. It turned out to be the shower room. There were duckboards and buckets of freshwater hanging from the branches. I showered the dust and sand off, watching the water trickle away into their garden; not a drop was wasted. It was the best shower I have ever had—the water was sweet and soft, and for soap they had a ball of frankincense which I rubbed all over my skin.

We lay down on a woolen goatskin rug for the night and listened to the sound of moths' wings beating against the kerosene lamp. Above the roar of the ocean I was sure I could hear sirens singing. I had fallen under the spell of Socotra, an island that seemed quite magical to me.

Socotra: the Real and the Magical

SOCOTRA HAS BEEN ISOLATED FOR SO LONG, CUT OFF BY THE ROUGH seas and without a harbor, that it is one of the world's most remote and inaccessible places. The island is also one of the few places that has escaped cement mixers and the avaricious gaze of developers, but strategically it has always been important. Over the centuries nations have tried to settle and colonize the island. The most recent to leave were the British, in 1963, who left their tanks behind to rust; they are still on the island.

In A.D. 600 the Socotrans were converted to Christianity by Saint Thomas, who was shipwrecked on the island, but by the tenth century the Socotrans' Christianity lapsed. They turned to piracy, which continued well into the twentieth century, when navigational charts still warned sailors to avoid the waters off Socotra at all costs. Socotra gained even greater notoriety when Southern Yemen became the only Marxist state in the Arab world ➤

and, in 1977, it ceded Socotra to the Soviet Union as a military base. Rumors spread that in its vast limestone cave systems were sophisticated underground facilities and weaponry, and all ships were forbidden to venture near the island. It was finally returned to Yemen in 1990 after reunification.

Socotra has exercised the imaginations of men for millennia: it was a vehicle for their fantasies and an island full of natural resources. Even Aristotle tried to persuade Alexander the Great to conquer Socotra because of its apparently unlimited supply of frankincense and aloes. Socotra has excited the imagination and romantic daydreams of travelers in pursuit of the exotic; of merchants in search of valuable commodities; and of those groping for explanations for the origin of man and the site of the original Garden of Eden.

Socotra was probably better known in medieval Europe than it is now. Then it was known for its aloes, its dragons' blood and its ambergris, not to mention its frankincense and myrrh. Medieval writers did their best to shroud the island in a mist of magic. They wrote that invading ships would vanish without trace; in reality, the ships were probably wrecked by the monsoon winds.

The island's tribes were said to practice witchcraft. Marco Polo called the Socotrans the best enchanters in the world; he said that they could summon the winds at will, and Ibn al Mujawir, a thirteenth-century geographer and traveler, observed that "Dhofari women are sorceresses on account of their proximity to the island of Socotra. They go from Dhofar to Java [a distance of 500 miles] in a single night."

When we got back to Hadibu the following day we went to the United Nations development project headquarters to meet Abdulla Issa, a botanist.

It was cool in the air-conditioned laboratories, while the temperature outside was rising to 43°C. Abdulla showed us into his office, where there were jars of preserved insects, chameleons and snakes, and sheets of pressed plants, all neatly labeled on his desk. We asked him about the story of the tree in the sea. He told us that the Socotrans believe that *anbar* does not come from the sperm whale and squid, but from a marine plant called Elyesor. He also said that when he was a child he was given ambergris to drink and told that it would make him grow. He told us that there were many different kinds of *anbar*, but that he thought the best was the one treated by the acids in the whale's stomach.

Socotrans, he said, are superstitious: when his father collected *anbar* he sacrificed three goats. And he reiterated the custom of giving away a third of any *anbar* you find to the first person you see, to a stranger. Good fortune must be shared; otherwise the punishment of Satan will be upon you.

Abdulla Issa looked through the window at the sea, which was being whipped up into mountainous waves by the monsoon wind. He smiled and told us that the monsoon was a good thing, that it actually saves Socotra because the winds cleanse everything and blow away the rubbish. When the Socotrans retreat to the mountains during the monsoon everything is purged. The air becomes crystal clear after the monsoon so that it is like breathing freshwater. He said that the wind also keeps people away from the island. Socotra hasn't lost a single species for 150 years, while in other parts of the world species are becoming extinct every day. But he told us also that there has been more change in the years since the aerodrome was built, in 2001, than in the last hundred years together. There was a tinge of sadness in his voice.

Abdulla Issa gave us directions to a village where we might find the strange marine tree that the whales eat. We walked westward along the beach, coral and shells crunching under our feet, and found the village nestling in a cove that was strangely unaffected by the wind. I saw a brand-new blue mosque glittering in the sunlight.

In the windless village we were shown into the main hut, where there was a solidified, brittle seaweed plant that resembled a small tree with tendrils for its branches. I thought it looked like a piece of stage scenery propped up against the wall, but the villagers told us that for a year after they had fished it out of their nets it smelled like incense. They said we could have it as a souvenir, and I thought it would make a decorative clotheshorse, but Stephen pointed out, pragmatically, that we'd never get it through customs. Defiantly, I said I would try—and anyway, I didn't want to offend the kind Socotrans who wanted to give me this gift. So I set about wrapping it up in a sarong.

The tribe of the Elyesor tree had crisp black hair and finely chiseled features, and were of Abyssinian descent, from the Ethiopian Nestorians who settled on the island in the sixth century. A smartly dressed fisherman, wearing a tartan sarong—or *futa* as they are called on Socotra—wrapped tightly, a T-shirt bearing the inscription "No 12" and a pair of silver-lensed shades, told us, with an air of finality, that they didn't know where the *anbar* was anymore.

This set the other villagers talking, and Jamil told us that the Socotrans had lost their knowledge of *anbar* because more intense fishing methods meant that their boats have been fitted with outboard engines. They no longer row their boats, with their oars gently dipping into the sea at a slow pace, allowing them more time to spot the honeycombs of *anbar*, or "Neptune's gold." The pace of Socotran life has speeded up: Jamil said that before they had had engines fitted onto their boats they had had time to notice everything. But now the roar of engines probably frightens the whales and other fish away anyway, and the wake from the boats would send any lumps of ambergris floating away from the island. He also said that, because of their new fishing methods, they don't need to go so far out to sea. So, because a way of life has ceased, the Socotrans have lost the small amount of ambergris that they once used to find.

I asked one of the fishermen what ambergris smells like. He said that, at first, it smells like shit, but that when you burn it—he made an appreciative humming sound—it smells like incense. I pulled out my sample of ambergris, which they smelled, and then, they laughed. They told me that it was tar. I wasn't really surprised and I tossed it onto the sand. Then an old fisherman, who looked like a merman, with his long gray hair hanging in strands around his bare chest and his harpoon shaped like a trident, whispered in Jamil's ear.

I shot an inquiring look at Jamil, who translated. He told us that the village had a secret. He said that they had a little ambergris left: it was thirty-five years old and they wanted $75 for it. We were hesitant after our last—dud—purchase, but the merman went to fetch it. When he came back he took a grayish lump from a bottle, scraped some grains from it and sprinkled them onto a bed of embers of cinnabar wood in a clay pot.

We all sat around the censer; it was just like sitting in a circle smoking a joint. As the grains dissolved and bubbled like toasting cheese, the fumes rose, spooling slowly upward in a cobwebbed skein to the rafters, where some young fishermen lay supine in the hammocks that were strung between the boughs, and I knew that, at last, we'd found the real thing.

At first the smell was overpowering, but as it evaporated—the scent is as elusive as the ambergris itself—I smelled a velvety, sea-briny effervescent aroma that reminded me of oysters on a bed of rose petals doused with vintage champagne. Ambergris has an invigorating effect because of its oceanic, ozonic, sea-kelp aroma. It smelled like my own suntanned skin, yet the aroma was more mysterious than that; it was evocative of dried sea-weed infused with mint and lilies, of truffles and mushrooms, of ferns and moss. It was like damp, rich lichen and it was slightly moldy, redolent of a misty autumn morning.

I was sure the stuff was having an aphrodisiac effect on me: they say ambergris stirs the loins. And, as the last spools of smoke drifted away in the saline air, I had a euphoric recall. I suddenly understood why ambergris has been compared to cigars and mushrooms. I remembered the smoke of my grandfather's cigars hanging in the air in his library, while the mushroom odor from the ambergris took me back to the time when I ate some hallucinogenic mushrooms and the elation I felt.

Everyone agreed that, although what we were smelling was a good smell, if the ambergris has been taken straight from the whale's belly its odor would be distinctly fecal. They said that many people throw it away thinking it is shit, but Jamil told us that, because ambergris is so difficult to find, nobody tells anybody else where they find it, if they find it. He also told us that if you mix ambergris with hot milk it will smell good for days, and he echoed the earlier information we'd gleaned: that floating *anbar* looks curiously like a palm-tree trunk, but he said that fish usually eat it before it is washed up onshore.

I wanted to buy some of their ambergris, but the merman—in a change of mind caused, perhaps, by my initial mistrust—said that it was impossible to know the true value of this miracle from the sea and that they had decided to keep it for their village. He said that they could not part with it because it cured all kinds of illnesses.

That evening we went to see the pearl fishers, who are also the custodians of the giant turtles. Darkness came quickly as the sun set on a violet ocean. Pearl oyster shells were strewn across the beach, and clustered around the huts were piles of salted fish. A smoky wick illuminated the fishing huts, and sacks were laid out on the sand for us to sit on. We gazed out into the darkening ocean while stars like gems streamed down toward the horizon. It was absolutely silent.

Then the pearl fishers struck out across the shore in search of turtles. They keep a nightly vigil when the turtles are nesting and, after twenty minutes, they flashed their torches; Jamil said that meant they'd found some turtles. He leaped up and we followed him along the beach. Giant tracks appeared in the sand and, suddenly in the torchlight, I saw a colossal turtle waddling along. The pearl fishers held it by its shell and measured it; it was almost 100 centimeter long. Then the turtle dug furiously into the sand, making a deep nest for her eggs. We counted sixty eggs in all as they plopped out; they were the size of Ping-Pong balls, and they were white, slimy and shiny.

Marine turtles can swim huge distances. Because the turtles are tagged, the pearl fishers knew that one turtle had swum all the way to Oman, which is a day's sailing, or roughly 60 miles away. So far, they said, they had counted 173 giant turtles. When the turtle had finished laying her eggs the pearl fishers began the delicate operation of tagging her. They flipped her upside down, revealing a huge white belly. As she floundered her flippers flapped so powerfully that she knocked one of the pearl fishers over. They tagged her with what looked like a huge staple gun and put her back on her course. In the tearing wind they made notes and a diagram of where the eggs had been laid and buried. The turtle would return in six days and find the eggs, by which time they'd be ready to hatch.

We staggered back to the fishermen's huts to drink tea and, as the kettle sizzled on the rusty old stove, the pearl fishers told us rags-to-riches stories about the lucky few who'd found ambergris on the waves. Then we stumbled back through the gales, humming the duet from Bizet's *The Pearl Fishers*. I hummed through a lump in my throat because I was so moved by the pearl fishers' love of the turtles and their care for them.

Something quite uncanny happened on our last night on Socotra. On the desk of the *funduq* I noticed a pile of dusty leaflets from the Socotra Conservation Fund. Intrigued, I picked one up and discovered, to my astonishment, that the headquarters of the SCF were in my local town, but I'd never known it was there. I loved the idea that the magic of this enchanted island had spread as far as the Pennines.

We left Socotra without any ambergris—we had to leave before gale-force winds kept us there for another six months, until September. Not that I would have minded: I had fallen in love with the island and its noble and kind inhabitants.

In Sana, en route for northern climes, we went to the souk on one last quest for ambergris. In the attar souk a merchant held out a bottle of syrupy amber, but we shook our heads. Then, as the pungent, honeyed, spicy air swirled with incense smoke, the merchant sent his nephew deeper into the souk. The merchant smiled at us from behind his mounds of henna and cones of incense, his crystallized fruits of frankincense and vials of unguents, and his oudh from Mecca. When his nephew reappeared he was holding a little bottle with a thumbnail-sized lump of ambergris inside it. We bought it with our last dollars, all one hundred of them.

Ambergris is infused in alcohol for at least ten years, but the longer the better. Its ozonic, sea-briny odors become much, much stronger the longer it is macerated—so strong that it can make you dizzy when you breathe it in. The ambergris in my bottle was grey and the alcohol it floated in was cloudy.

Several perfumers still use real ambergris in their scents, including Diptyque in their Tam Dao, which smells woody and reminiscent of the jungle, but it is rare and therefore very expensive. There is a substitute, synthetic ambergris called ambrox, which is made from extracts of clary sage, cis-abienol and thujone (a colorless chemical compound), and it seems to me that synthetic ambergris will be used more and more because of the great difficulty of finding real ambergris, although it is still commercially collected in the Bahamas.

I took my small piece of ambergris or "floating gold," as it is sometimes known, back to England and then sent it to the laboratory; some was decanted into my bespoke perfume and I knew that its aroma of the sea would anchor my scent—just as the ancient Arabs who first discovered the fixative properties of ambergris knew that it would.

Since I got back to my cottage after my travels, I sniff the ambergris occasionally. It is like a drug: it seems to me to strengthen the heart and lift the spirits, and it will always remind me of Socotra. The little grain in my bottle will mature for the rest of my life. And as for the Elyesor, the so-called amber tree, it survived the trip back to the Pennines despite British customs officials' attempts to take it from me, and now it sits beside the bath and, in the damp English climate, it still gives out a whiff of the sea and the distant Socotran shore.

So, sitting in my cottage in the Pennines surrounded by the odors of the various ingredients I had brought back from my scent trail, there was only one thing left to do.

I took all the ingredients to Anastasia and asked her to send them on to the lab to make up my bespoke scent.

EPILOGUE

My Bespoke Scent: the End of the Scent Trail

Reader, have you with greedy pleasure never
Slowly inhaled blue incense in the dark
Of churches filled with it, or breathed sweet musk,
That makes a sachet odorous forever?

BAUDELAIRE
"The Perfume," from Les Fleurs du Mal

AT LAST THE TIME HAD COME FOR THE FRUITS OF ALL my journeys to be brought together in a final sublime synthesis: an encapsulation of the scents of the ingredients I had discovered and collected.

The ingredients were sent off to the laboratory to be blended into my bespoke scent. There were granules of frankincense and myrrh from Socotra; Indian vetivert and jasmine; the finest attars of roses from Turkey; a mimosa absolute from Grasse; Moroccan vials of neroli and petitgrain; Tuscan orris butter; Sri Lankan nutmeg oil; and, rarest of all, ambergris from the Arabian Sea.

Some time later, I arranged to meet Anastasia Brozler for tea at the Connaught Hotel in London. She had just had a baby and I was about to have my second; but despite these exciting events our attention, and our noses, soon turned to the large black bag full of essences that she had brought with her. Other guests in the hotel turned their heads in an attempt to discover the origin of the cloud of aromas that began to envelop us.

Anastasia pulled out a bottle of Himalayan jasmine; then she rummaged around for my frankincense and myrrh, which had been extracted. In their oil forms on Anastasia's blotter they smelled quite different from the fragrant smoke that I remembered billowing around the huts on Socotra; they were almost medicinal yet camphorous. Anastasia said that purple—the color associated with frankincense—also represents the place where frankincense is most often found: the church. The color of the whorled frankincense trees grounded in the earth is red, but the color of the plumes of resinous smoke that rise to the sky from the incense is blue, symbolizing heaven. When you put blue and red together you get purple: papal purple. I had partly chosen these resins for their spiritual associations and, slowly, as the frankincense began to develop on my skin, it made my mind more lucid. Anastasia said that my ancient and unrefined frankincense and myrrh were the finest she had yet smelled. I told her that the resins came from trees indigenous to Socotra which grew nowhere else in the world.

Before we met, Anastasia had suggested that ambergris would make a daring top note in my bespoke scent—instead of a base note, as we had originally planned. I agreed, but when she pulled out a bottle of grayish liquid in which little grains floated I didn't think it looked very pretty; it looked more like a medicine. I knew it was ambergris, although it was not the ambergris I had bought in the Sana souk. Anastasia explained that she was decanting a ten-year-old ambergris into my scent because the older the ambergris the better it is—just like a vintage wine. Over the years ambergris becomes a tincture; then it becomes what is known as the "caviar" of ambergris: it actually turns into a paste as the alcohol slowly evaporates and the ambergris absorbs it.

Anastasia put twenty drops of ambergris into a crystal flacon which was wrapped in violet gauze and tied with gold thread. Then, with a pair of tweezers, she fished out a grain of ambergris and dropped that in too. It was an extreme dosage, but then to my mind all the best scents have an overdose of one ingredient. I knew that it would float in my scent for the rest of my life and that I could refill the flacon with my scent (because once my formula is made up it can be repeated at any time) and the grain of ambergris would continually evolve and mature, releasing its mysterious odor over the decades.

Anastasia then suggested that we should think about the middle notes of my perfume: the mimosa, orris and rose. She said that they were all "friends of musk" and she took a silver tin of synthetic musk from her black bag and held it under my nose. It smelled erogenous and wicked; it was very enticing and tempting, but in the end I resisted. I knew I couldn't have an ingredient in my scent—even if it was only a copy—that was the result of such harm to an animal. Anastasia agreed and said that ambergris collection did not harm the whales and that anyway it was a much more unusual ingredient for a scent than synthetic musk. Traditionally, she told me, ambergris was only found, given or exchanged, never sold, usually passing only through royal hands and among the very privileged. Ambergris, which comes from a mammal, would give my scent a visceral, primal aura and it would bring out the natural scent of my own skin because we are also mammals.

Then the moment came to open the flacon of my own bespoke scent.

It was almost too much to bear. I could hardly contain my excitement, but when I finally smelled it I was amazed. It was not at all how I'd imagined it would be. An overwhelming smell of orris swept over me, and I could barely discern the top notes of citrus, although I could detect the nutmeg. Anastasia explained that she had made the nutmeg a contralto top note too, so that its spicy nuance set off the citrus smells. She dabbed a little on her wrist and commented that the chemist and nose Norbert Bijaolii had toned down the top notes. Then I noticed that the scent was oily, which is the height of extravagance in a scent because it means that there is no alcohol in it at all. Anastasia said that the base notes in my scent would reverberate later; she told me to be patient and wait. So I did.

The Sabean incenses did begin to seep through—the aura of a high priestess at her fragrant altar during an Eleusinian mystery began to pervade the atmosphere of my scent, but, as it lingered, the iris was still the dominant note in the symphony; the soprano, the orris diva. Anastasia pointed out that I had not only chosen a "high Church" scent but what she called "high flowers" or holy plants: rose is symbolic of the rosary, while jasmine is associated with Hindu marriage ceremonies.

At first I wondered why Norbert had chosen iris as the predominant feature in my scent, but then I realized that he had selected, with Proustian olfactory accuracy, the scent of my childhood: the fields of violet irises and their harvested peeled roots floating in buckets of water below my bedroom balcony every May. There was certainly something mellow, calming and serene about my scent; it had a powdery mellifluence. I recognized that the honeyed tone was the mimosa making its presence felt. But I still could not smell the jasmine or the vetivert.

Anastasia explained that the scent had many layers and it would be hours before the heavier notes would develop. It would take me some time to get to know my scent in its entirety: in fact, getting to know my scent was going to be a journey in itself. And then, as a pale, shrill yellow whiff of petitgrain sent out its aroma of lemons and a slightly richer neroli made itself known,

I was suddenly transported to Morocco; then I was heading down toward Italy and Calabria, and on to the Turkish borders and the damask rose.

Now that 10 percent of my scent was made up of ambergris it had become quite addictive, and we opened the bottle again and put a drop more on our wrists. Then Anastasia brought out some agarwood which she'd been contemplating adding, but in the end, even though I liked it, I thought it too heavy and oriental. Also, there are hardly any *Aquilaria* trees left, and I didn't want to contribute to their extinction, even though I knew that the attar wallahs cunningly made attars that replicated the smell of this priceless rotten-wood fungus. As with the musk, however, I didn't want even a copy of an aroma whose original extraction caused harm to the environment. Anastasia also observed that, whereas ambergris in a scent "whispers," agarwood "screams."

Continuing on the theme of the "high flowers" in my scent, she said that almost all the ingredients I had chosen were "high" ingredients—ancient, mystical, mythical and full of symbolism. For instance, the iris survives floods and droughts. She also said that the indolic jasmine counteracts the austere, cold iris and represents the middle C note on the piano of perfume. But I still had not smelled the vetivert, with its stunning stoic smell which would impart "greenness" to my scent.

Later that evening I went to a poetry reading and people clustered around me. It seemed that my scent had pulling power! The base notes were developing, just as Anastasia had said they would, and at last I could smell the vetivert. People said that they had never smelled anything quite like it before; but commercial fragrances don't often use the magnificent ambergris tincture or the beautiful *Iris fiorentina*. Today, people are not familiar with these smells, and when I explained that one of the ingredients they could smell came from rancid whale's puke and another was a dried-up root, they laughed, until I elaborated.

Despite other accords that floated up and emerged, the silvery iris and the aquatic ambergris remained the "soul" of my scent. Even at that stage the scent was still developing on my skin. And since the seashore and Florence are my two favorite places, I thought that the chemist had successfully hunted me down, aromatically speaking; like an alchemist, he had sensed which smells were the closest to my heart and would evoke my earliest memories. It was as if he'd imagined me as my perfume.

When I asked if I could meet Norbert Bijaolii, Anastasia said that he was too shy to talk to me, which was a pity. But then I thought that, perhaps, meeting him might break the spell.

This is the final pyramid formula he used for my bespoke scent:

MY BESPOKE SCENT
The Final Pyramid Formula

THE TOP NOTES

Neroli citrus: *heavy but fresh*
Citron petitgrain: *aromatic, zingy and slightly bitter*
Nutmeg: *spicy, musky and masculine*
Ambergris: *breezy, euphoric, sea-briny, ozonic and redolent
of warm suntanned skin*

MIDDLE (HEART) NOTES
Mimosa: *earthy, powdery and spicily floral*
Damask rose: *musky and floral*
Iris: *warm and richly rooty—as the air smells after a summer shower—with aromatic fennel-like overtones*
Zambac jasmine: *erotic, exotic, warm, fruity and rich*

BASE NOTES
Vetivert aromatic: *earthy, damp and cooling*
Frankincense: *pine and lemon notes at first, then heady, spicy and sweet*
Myrrh: *redolent of the forest floor; honeyed with hints of lemon and rosemary*

For reference, I have included a list of scents made from single notes of each of the ingredients in my bespoke scent at the end of this book (page 287).

After a day of wearing my scent I found that it was quite hypnotic, reminding me of the way dreams move quite naturally between one apparently unconnected event and another. Sometimes the scent was spicy, as if I were walking through the souk in Aleppo; and then it was quite earthy, as if I were planting bulbs in the earth of a rain-soaked English garden. I tried to think of my scent as a painting and realized it was definitely more of a Piero della Francesca—mysterious, spiritual and pure—rather than, say, a voluptuous courtesan in a Boucher or a Watteau.

I couldn't quite decide whether it was a scent I would go to great lengths to find—as Marie Antoinette had done. She even stopped off to have her scent bottles refilled before fleeing Paris and the Revolution. (Later, it is said, when she was caught disguised as an ordinary citizen, it was her heavenly Houbigant scent that gave her away.) I wondered whether my scent was too powdery or too dry, or whether it was making enough of a statement. But you can "overthink" a perfume, and the first impression is often the right one. My first impression, of amazement—in the sense of "overwhelmed with wonder"—was, I realized, holding true.

I thought about my two years of traveling and the thousands of miles that I'd covered; now those miles were compressed into one little flacon. I thought of the vast distances the incense caravans used to travel across the sun-scorched deserts to convey precious and rare perfumes to pharaohs, priests, Chaldean princes, Roman senators and Chinese concubines. I thought about how the frankincense trail was 2,000 miles long and that the route ended in Petra, the "rose red city half as old as time."

And I thought how lucky I was to have my very own bespoke scent. Most people want a scent they can call their own, a signature scent. They want their perfume to be holistic and made from tangible fragrances that they can identify with, especially, often, the rare woody, spiritual notes like sandalwood. Buddha is in and boudoir is out. Both perfumers and customers are moving toward more mystical, spiritual aromas in scents and away from the synthetic; and people are looking into aromachology—the study of the physiological and psychological effects of different scents on the wearers.

My own scent is infused with the spirit of place or, more to the point, places. It allows me to revisit all the countries I have loved and still love, without moving. I can relive all those old emotions and rekindle old loves without leaving my cottage in the Pennines, just as Des Esseintes in Huysmans's *À Rebours* re-created the scents and smells of places so that he would not have to travel to them.

When I smell the jasmine I can feel and smell the heat of the temples and the burning wicks in the *puja* oil in Ranakpur in Rajasthan. When the damask rose lingers I can see the storm clouds rolling across the Anatolian plateau and remember the Chimera in a Lycian pine-scented forest. The fanfare of Hesperides notes takes me to the Atlas Mountains and down into the steep valleys of orange orchards, where blossoms were deftly plucked by women and children who stood on ladders and dropped the flowers onto sacking spread out below them. Then the heart notes of my scent creep up on me. First the mimosa, and I see myself drinking a Sauternes and eating a crème brûlée while I look out at Mont Saint-Victoire from my restaurant table. I am practically *in* a Cézanne painting. Then comes the iris, which delves right down deep into the earliest of my olfactory memories, and I am a child again, walking through the villa across the cold, polished terra-cotta tiles, watching the shafts of sunlight that stream through the green shutters.

Then the baritone notes, the base notes, begin to play to me. The frankincense and the myrrh take me to scenes of swirling clouds in high Yemen, where towered hamilliliterets cling to the mountain crags like eagles' nests and I can hear the plangent calls to prayer echoing across the terraces of incense trees. The vetivert transports me to a monsoon-soaked rest house in southern India as a damp breeze blows the vetivert scent through a mosquito net. The fragrantly musky nutmeg takes me to the steaming valleys of Sri Lanka and I see a gleaming Buddha sitting in the lotus position. And then the ambergris, "Neptune's treasure" or the ocean's "floating gold," calls me—like the Sirens—to Socotra's coral-girdled shores and I can almost taste the sea salt.

My scent has become part of me and I know that no one will ever be able to copy it, because the exact amounts of each ingredient remain a secret. I decided to call it Reminiscent.

As Adam James, the color analyst with whom I chose the pastel colors (the sapphires and aquamarines of my favorite gems that characterize my scent), accurately predicted, my journey in quest of scents had been cathartic, and since then there have been changes and new beginnings. Before I left I was stagnating, but travel is a great palliative to stagnation, and as I traveled I thought about the way I was living. Adam said, correctly, that I had suffered a lot, but, on my travels, I learned how to rise above that suffering, how to embrace life and adopt a more philosophical approach, instead of simply escaping.

I learned to nurture the inner joy that Adam detected in me, and I managed to transform myself from an urban sybarite into a rustic stoic. All this, I am sure, was born of those long Indian journeys and from sitting in the moonlight watching the turtle custodians by the Arabian Sea; from seeing the eternal flames of the Chimaera and from experiencing the endless horizons and silence of the Sahara; from listening to the unearthly calls of the muezzin echoing from minaret to minaret, like spirits from the underworld, and from hearing the carillon of church bells at Mass in Florence.

My scent is an archive of that journey, dissolving time and igniting recall. My scent encapsulates distant lands, and its aromatic composition is filled with stories.

My travels have found an afterlife in my scent.

SINGLE-NOTE SCENTS

made from the ingredients in

*Celia Lyttelton's
Bespoke Perfume*

NEROLI AND PETITGRAIN

Bergamot Citrus by Fresh Index
Pomegranate Anise by Fresh Index
Tangerine Lychee by Fresh Index
Fleurs de Citronnier by Serge Lutens

JASMINE

Pure jasmine grandifloram essential oil by Aveda
Pink Blossom by Fresh Index
À la Nuit by Serge Lutens

NUTMEG

L'Autre by Diptyque
Ginger and Nutmeg by Jo Malone

AMBERGRIS

Femme by Rochas
Narcisse Noir by Caron
Nerol Sauvage by Creed
Royal Delight by Creed
Royal Scotch Lavender by Creed
Tam Dao by Diptyque
Poison by Christian Dior
Miss Dior by Christian Dior

MIMOSA

Mimosa pour Moi by L'Artisan Parfumeur

ROSE

Rose Absolue by Annick Goutal
Sa Majesté la Rose by Serge Lutens
Rose de Nuit by Serge Lutens

IRIS

Iris by Santa Maria Novella Profumeria

Bois d'Iris by the Different Company
Iris Poudre by Frédéric Malle
Giaggiolo Dottore Bizzari by Dottore Bizzari, Florence

VETIVERT

Vetiver Extraordinaire by Frédéric Malle
Vetiver Oriental by Serge Lutens
Vetiver by Guerlain
Vetiver by Lorenzo Villoresi

FRANKINCENSE AND MYRRH

Apogée by Les Senteurs (a scent shop in Elizabeth Street, London)
Rose des Hommes by Rosine
Endymion by Penhaligon's
Taif by Ormonde Jayne
L'Eau Trois by Diptyque

Glossary

SOME OF THE TERMINOLOGY USED BY PERFUMERS IS similar to the terminology used by musicians; some terms are hundreds of years old.

Absolute
Once a **concrete** or a **resinoid** has been obtained by solvent **extraction** from the raw ingredient, it is refined into a very pure absolute by rinsing in alcohol. The resulting substance is then filtered and distilled to remove the wax. Absolutes smell exactly like the plant from which they are extracted, whereas steam-distilled **essential oils** differ somewhat in aroma from the original plant.

Accord
A composition of harmonious **notes** that **blend** to form a perfume.

Alcohol
In perfumery, it is usually 90 proof and added to perfume **concentrates**.

Aldehydes
Molecules of carbon atoms that lift perfumes and make them fizz like champagne. Chanel No. 5 evolved, famously, by lucky mistake. The **nose** Ernest Beaux threw in ten times more aldehyde than he'd intended but did not dare to admit his mistake to Coco. Chanel No. 5 went on to become the world's most famous perfume.

Amber
See **labdanum**.

Ambergris
A by-product of the sperm whale and a highly valued ingredient which has a pungent, sea-briny smell. Used sparingly, ambergris makes an ephemeral floral scent tenacious and long-lasting.

Ambrette seed
From the plant *Hibiscus able-moschus*; sometimes known as musk seed because it smells like musk, although, in perfume, musk seed is a poor substitute for musk. The most prized ambrette seeds come from Martinique.

Attar
Another term for **otto** or **essential oil**. The most famous attar is attar of roses. The oil from the **distillation** of rosewater was, traditionally, skimmed off with the blade of a sword lily.

Balanos oil
An Egyptian blending oil, used also by the Greeks and recommended by Theophrastus as good for absorbing aromatic material and for its low viscosity.

Balsam
Another word for resin. Comes from trees. Examples are **galbanum** and **labdanum**.

Base notes
Fixatives, or the foundation of a scent. Base notes are the least **volatile** of the notes and they "fix" scents—i.e., they make a scent last. Base notes are also the most persistent elements in a scent; their scent lingers on the nose long after the **top** and **middle notes** have evaporated. Examples are orris and oak moss.

Benzene
A synthetic musk.

Benzoin
Also called Benjamin, this is a hard gum resin found in Borneo, Java and Sumatra, although the best kind comes from Thailand and Myanmar.

Bergamot
From the peel of the *Citrus bergamia*, a greenish orange which is too bitter to eat but yields one of the rarest and most valuable essential oils, which imparts a richness to other floral essential oils and a sweetness to spicy oils. It is still grown exclusively in Calabria.

Blends
A harmonious mixture of ingredients that form a balance of fragrant intensity.

Bouquet
Describes **blends** of floral compositions, just like a bouquet of flowers.

Cassia
The essential oil of cassia comes from distilling the bark of the *Laurus cassia*. It is pale yellow and smells like cinnamon. It is used to perfume old-fashioned "military" soap with an aromatic spiciness. Not to be confused with **cassie**.

Cassie
Another name for mimosa, or *Acacia farnesiana*.

Castoreum
A pungent, spongy substance secreted from the glands of a beaver and used in minuscule quantities to create **leather notes**. But trade in castoreum and in beaver fur is now banned.

Chassis en verre
Glass trays used for *enfleurage*. Fat is spread on them and the flowers or petals are immersed in the fat.

Chypre
A heady and heavenly perfume from Cuprus which Françoise Coty reinvented, in 1917, from **labdanum, patchouli**, oak moss and **bergamot**. Smells mossy and green.

Cistus
See **labdanum**.

Citrus
A fragrance **family** whose essential oils are usually obtained by **expression** from the zest of citrus fruits. Otherwise known as Hesperides **notes** and featured in most eau de colognes.

Civet
A secretion from the anal glands of Ethiopian civet cats, which, like all animal **notes**, has a vile odor, but when diluted lends a tenacious and carnal note to scents. Trade in civet and the Ethiopian civet cat is now banned.

Concentrate
Term used to describe a perfume composition once it has been blended, but before it is diluted with alcohol.

Concrete
A waxlike substance which results from a process of **extraction** of flowers. If the concrete is further refined—by rinsing with alcohol in machines called *batteuses*—the result is the **absolute** essence.

Coumarin
Synthetic derived from the tonka bean, which smells like vanilla.

Diffusion
The way a scent develops when it is exposed to air.

Distillation
Odoriferous elements of a plant are coaxed out by a process using steam, which releases the lighter aromatic molecules; distillation is based on the

principle of evaporation. Subsequent condensation carries the **essential oil**.

Enfleurage
The most delicate of all processes in perfumery. Petals from volatile and fragile flowers, such as tuberose and jasmine, are individually laid out on trays of cold fat called *chassis en verre*. The aromas from the flowers—which would spoil if the flowers were heated—are absorbed by the fat, and the resultant product is called a **pomade**. The aromatic oil is retrieved from the fat by dissolving it in alcohol, but because this process is so time-consuming it is not often used these days.

Essential oils (or Essences)
Volatile aromatic essences procured from plants by **distillation** or **expression** and prized for their scents and for their healing properties. About 300 species of plants produce essential oils.

Expression
Cold-pressing: squeezing in iron presses. Used for plants that have **volatile** and prolific amounts of **essential oil**, such as citrus fruits.

Extract
The most potent product of perfume, diluted in very pure **alcohol** and containing up to 30 percent **concentrate**.

Extraction
Treatment of plants with volatile solvents, such as **hexane** or **benzene**, in large 3,000-liter vats, in which plants are laid on tiers. Once the solvent is saturated with fragrance and then vacuumed, it leaves a pastelike mixture called a **concrete**. Plants which yield only a little **essential oil** are better treated by extraction. One such is mimosa.

Family
There are seven families of smells in perfumery: **fougère (fern), floral, citrus, chypre, woody, leather** and **oriental.**

Fern (or **fougère**)
This family of aromas does not smell like fern, but denotes a family of **notes** of lavender, wood, oak moss, **coumarin** and **bergamot.**

Fixative
Prolongs scents and anchors otherwise quite ephemeral ingredients, especially floral ones. Fixatives nail the **bouquet.**

Floral
This is the largest of the fragrance families. The principal **blends** are flowers, but within this classification there are variations: single **notes,** green florals, **woody** and fruity.

Formula
A detailed instruction or recipe of ingredients and quantities—which are often in milligrams—for a perfume. A formula resembles a musical score and is kept a closely guarded secret by its creator, or **nose.**

Galbanum
A gum resin.

Heart notes
See **middle notes.**

Hexane
A scentless by-product of petrol used to extract odors.

Incense
A combination of resins, odorous woods and gums used for sacred fumigations to create a "heavenly staircase of ambrosial clouds" to invoke the gods of many religions, including Catholicism, Judaism and Greek Orthodoxy, Taoism and Buddhism.

Indole
One of the strongest odors around. Fecal matter is full of indoles.

Infuse
Absorption of the soluble elements of a solid such as **ambergris**, or **musk**, by infusion in a liquid for a long time, sometimes several years.

Kyphi
A magnificent Egyptian perfume. Dioscorides said that it was "A welcome to the gods." A luxurious, heady brew of sweet flag, aromatic tree grasses, peppermint, juniper, acacia, honey, myrrh, saffron and cardamom which is steeped in wine for several days.

Labdanum
A gum resin from the cistus or rockrose. It is sticky and viscous and is known as amber when it hardens. Hence the phrase "like a fly in amber."

Leather
Dry masculine **notes** in a perfume which seek to evoke the smell of leather, wood and cigar smoke.

Linalool
A synthetic substance found in many essential oils, such as **bergamot**, coriander, gardenia, lavender and **neroli**.

Maceration
Infusion of flowers and plants in hot liquid fat which draws out the fragrance. The fat is strained from the spent flowers and fresh ones are added. The fat itself becomes highly perfumed and the process is repeated until the required strength of pomatum or **pomade** is achieved. Then the **pomade** is rinsed with pure **alcohol** so that just the pure scented extract is left. These days the extracts are put into vats with alcohol and left to stand for weeks, even months,

before they are finally filtered. Maceration is one of the oldest techniques.

Middle notes
Often called heart notes, they form the heart and soul of the perfume. Examples are mimosa and jasmine.

Musk
Musk is a secretion from the glands of male musk deer and is a powerful olfactory aphrodisiac; the word "musk" is widely known and yet has rarely actually been smelled these days.

Nard
See **spikenard**.

Neroli
Oil extracted from orange flowers by **distillation** with water. Not the same as **extract** of orange flower, which is produced by **extraction** with chemicals and **alcohol**.

Nose
An expert creator of perfumes.

Note
The characteristic scent of an ingredient, raw material or a **blend** of two or three raw materials which are then made into a harmonious composition, or an "octave of odors." A layer or nuance of smell in a perfume.

Oleoresin
A by-product of **essential oils** used for flavorings.

Olivaceous
Olive-oily. Some old French **pomades** were made with olive oil.

Oriental
The ingredients of this **family** of scents often come from the Far East and include **benzoin** and agarwood, for instance. The smell of this family of scents is musky and spicy.

Orris
The dried rhizome of *Iris fiorentina*, which has a faint aroma, but has the power to strengthen other aromas.

Otto
Another word for **attar** or **essential oil**.

Patchouli
Used sparingly it is herblike and "sandalwoody." Made from distilled leaves and flowers but has a somewhat negative image because of its associations with the hippie era; can overpower if used too abundantly.

Petitgrain
A Hesperides **note** distilled from leaves and orangettes (unripe oranges). A sweetly cloying scent.

Pomade
The result of **maceration** after the fat is strained from the spent flowers.

Pulverulence
Very fine powder. For instance **orris** roots are pulverized before they are treated.

Qat
A mildly narcotic "speedy" plant chewed every afternoon after prayers in Yemen. The leaves have to be chewed and ingested fresh. Sadly, qat cultivation has replaced many frankincense groves.

Rectification
Method of clarifying perfumes: **terpenes** are removed by molecular **distillation**.

Resinoids
Dry plants, such as the roots of irises, cumin and coriander seeds, mosses, **balsams** like **tolu** and **storax**, gums such as **labdanum** and **galbanum**, and resins like myrrh and **benzoin** which have been extracted to form a pastelike substance. Many resinoids are

little known outside the perfume trade, but they are of great value to the perfumer.

Séage
See **trail**.

Senteur
A French **nose** or perfumer.

Spikenard
An esteemed Asiatic perfume from the Valerian genus. Europeans tend to turn their noses up at its strong scent. Also known as nard.

Storax
An odoriferous gum resin from the wounded bark of shrubby trees common in Asia. An ancient ingredient once used by priests for altar incense.

Sweet rush
Acorus calamus, used by the ancient Egyptians and Greeks. Sometimes called the cinnamon iris and used in a

Greek perfume called Metopium, which was a mélange of almond essences, sweet rush, honey, wine, resins and myrrh.

Terpenes
A group of hydrocarbons. **Volatile** and aromatic, occurring naturally in **essential oils**.

Tolu
A resinous, viscous Peruvian **balsam** which has a sweet vanilla, woody and slightly cinnamony scent.

Top notes
Known, in French, as *tête* or *départ*. **Volatile** odors which don't necessarily endure but kick off the scent. Airy, like colognes, usually **citrus**, and they make themselves known to the nose first.

Trail
Or, in French, *séage*. A term

used in the perfume trade to describe the fragrant scent impression that the wearer leaves in his or her wake.

Unguents
Antique name for perfume oils. *Unguentarii* were perfumers and, in Roman times, the center for *unguentarii* was Capua.

Vegetals
In the perfume trade the leaves, seeds and roots of plants are known as vegetals. French vegetals include moss, blackcurrant, mimosa and violet leaves.

Vetivert
Grass roots, or rhizomes, used in perfumery for damp, earthy, mossy **notes**. A distinctive, uncompromising scent.

Volatile
The term applied to a scent or a smell that evaporates very quickly, like citrus **notes**.

Wax
See **concrete**.

Woody
A **family** of **notes** such as sandalwood, cedar, **vetivert** and **patchouli**.

Zambac
The heaviest, strongest variety of jasmine. As an **absolute** its color is deep red.

Bibliography

Ackermann, Diane, *A Natural History of the Senses* (New York, Random House, 1990).

Alphandery, Benedetta, *The Iris* (Milano, Idea Books, 1998).

Bean, Professor George, *Turkey's Southern Shore* (London, John Murray, 1968).

Burr, Chandler, *The Emperor of Scent* (New York, Random House, 2003).

Corbin, Alain, *The Foul and the Fragrant* (Cambridge, Mass, Harvard University Press, 1986).

Dufour Nannelli, Inna, *Roses* (Milano, Idea Books, 2003).

Edwards, Michael, *Perfume Legends: French Feminine Fragrances* (Sydney, Michael Edwards and Company, 1996).

Irvine, Susan A., *Perfume: The Creation and Allure of Classic Fragrances* (London, Aurum Press, 1996).

Kaufman, William, *Perfume* (New York, E. P. Dutton & Co., Inc., 1974).

Kennet, Frances, *History of Perfume* (London, Harrap, 1975).

Pavia, Fabienne, *The World of Perfume* (USA, Knickerbocker Press, 1975).

Piesse, Septimus, *The Art of Perfumery* (London, Piesse and Lubin, 1891).

Pillivuyt, Ghislaine, *Histoire du Parfum* (Denoël, Julia Kristeva, 1988).

Rimmel, Eugène, *Le Livre des Parfums* (Le Lavandou, Editions du Layet, 1870).

Theophrastus, *Concerning Odours* (Loeb Classical Library, 1916).

Thompson, C. J. S., *The Mystery and Lure of Perfume* (London, Bodley Head, 1922).

Turner, Jack, *Spices, The History of a Temptation* (London, HarperCollins, 2004).

Villoresi, Lorenzo, *L'Arte del Bagno* (Firenze, Ponte alle Grazie, 1996).

Villoresi, Lorenzo, *Il Profumo* (Firenze, Ponte alle Grazie, 1996).

Watson, Lyall, *Jacobson's Organ* (New York, W. W. Norton & Company, 2000).

Worwood, Valerie Ann, *The Fragrant Mind* (London, Doubleday, 1995).

Index